# Hazardous Waste Sites

# Hazardous Waste Sites

## The Credibility Gap

### Michael R. Greenberg
### and
### Richard F. Anderson

CENTER
FOR URBAN
POLICY RESEARCH

Published in the United States of America
by The Center for Urban Policy Research
Building 4051 - Kilmer Campus
New Brunswick, New Jersey 08903

**Library of Congress Cataloging in Publication Data**

Greenberg, Michael R.
  Hazardous waste sites.

  1. Hazardous waste sites—United States.
I. Anderson, Richard F., 1950–    . II. Rutgers
University. Center for Urban Policy Research.
III. Title.
TD811.5.G74      1984           363.7′28                84–12115
ISBN 0–88285–102–0

*To our friends Susan, John, and Katie Caruana*

# Contents

# List of Tables

# List of Figures

# Acknowledgments

The authors would like to thank Carole Baker, George Carey, Janet Crane, and Frank Popper for helpful comments. We owe the following government employees a debt of thanks for providing information: William Torrey, U.S. EPA, Region I; Curtis Haymore, U.S. EPA, Office of Solid Waste, Washington; Dan Derkics, U.S. EPA, State Programs Branch, Washington; Karen Gale, U.S. EPA RCRA/Superfund Hotline, Washington; and Steven Dreeszen and Larry Giarrizzo, Massachusetts Hazardous Waste Regulatory Task Force. We would like to thank Rutgers University for providing a FASP leave for Michael Greenberg, much of which was used to write portions of this book. We also thank the George A. Miller Committee, the Department of Geography, and the Institute of Environmental Studies of the University of Illinois for providing a home away from home at Urbana-Champaign. To our former students William Byrd, Nancy Haydu, Kevin Ivey, Karen Kaduscwiz, Sanford Kaplan, Kevin Keenan, William Kerr, Sandra Lautenberg, Neil Newton, and Pat Terziani, we owe a debt of thanks for helping analyze the date used in Chapter 5. We thank Kirk Rosenberger for the analysis of Minnesota sites presented in Chapter 7.

# Preface

Mutual distrust is probably a charitable way of characterizing the relationship between those who are the sources of hazardous wastes and those who oversee their activities. Furthermore, it appears that a large segment of the public trusts neither party to protect them. A lack of credibility is a formidable, if not the biggest, obstacle to properly managing hazardous waste in the United States. Nowhere is the credibility gap wider than where there are hazardous waste management facilities or where sites have been proposed.

Exaggeration is one cause of the credibility gap. Some abandoned sites are revolting; they severely impact their neighborhoods. Others are less troublesome than a variety of existing environmental hazards found in many neighborhoods. Every time a reporter, writer, or commentator overzealously portrays a newly discovered abandoned waste lagoon as the worst since the one which bred the creature from the black lagoon, we should collectively wince. While the threats from abandoned waste sites are sometimes substantial, they are, almost as a rule, exaggerated well out of proportion. These exaggerations have bred some creatures of their own — most notably frightened and very angry people who systematically brand public and private employees as incompetent and uncaring at best, or insidious and untrustworthy at worst. The psychology of fear is further fueled by a deep-seated American phobia that the unsightly appearance of the worst sites is directly related to cancer, birth defects, miscarriages, and a host of other illnesses. Such relationships may exist at certain abandonded waste sites. But they may not apply to the vast majority of abandoned waste sites. What has become obvious is that the indiscriminate public objections to existing and new hazardous waste sites and to the development and testing of new technologies at these sites have acted to retard the implementation of some of the most promising mitigative measures. The psychology of fear and confusion has been crystallized into a single-minded public response: people do not want hazardous waste sites near them.

Some of the credibility gap is due to ignorance. We are all victims of the great complexity of the hazardous waste issue. We really do not know the public health or ecological effects of existing and proposed sites. We are uncertain about who should be responsible and how many resources should be allocated to dealing with hazardous waste problems and planning solutions. In fact, we do not even have a consensual definition of hazardous waste. The public need not have advanced degrees in engineering and environmental science to recognize a high level of uncertainty. More than any other public health and environmental problem to date, the management of hazardous waste sites is research dependent.

Much of the credibility gap has roots in the way American business, the government, and the American people ignored the consequences of generating and disposing of hazardous substances. Industry opted for the cheapest, short-run solutions. Government opted to ignore the problem and because of strong air and water protection laws exacerbated the solid waste problem. The public followed the out-of-sight, out-of-mind principle. In light of media hype, the lack of information, and the past record of hazardous waste management, it is not hypocritical for people to support new initiatives in hazardous waste management at new sites while at the same time to fight to keep the new initiatives from being implemented in their neighborhoods.

Given the plethora of questions and dearth of answers about hazardous waste management in the United States, it is difficult to deal with all types of hazardous waste sites in one book. However, it is unrealistic to view new management initiatives, technologies, and the search for sites as untouched by the stigma of their primitive ancestors. The public lumps existing and proposed management methods into the same, if you will, garbage heap. The purpose of this book is to try to trace the origin of the credibility gap in hazardous waste management in the United States objectively and to suggest ways of closing the gap. Six questions provide the framework for the book:

1. Do we know what hazardous waste is, where it is generated, and in what quantities? (Chapter 1)
2. What legal and technical controls have been exercised by private interests and governments over its disposal? (Chapter 2)
3. How and where has hazardous waste injured the public and damaged the environment and property? (Chapters 3, 4, and 5)
4. What are the legal, economic, and political realities of searching for new sites in the United States? (Chapter 6)
5. How can constraint mapping and location standards be used to increase the credibility of the siting process at the local scale? (Chapter 7)
6. What private actions and changes in public policy are needed to close the credibility gap? (Chapter 8)

The book is primarily intended for planners, environmental scientists and public health officials whose responsibility is at the state and local levels. However, we hope that people who may have read one of the popular books about abandoned sites and are looking for a more dispassionate treatment will benefit from reading this book along with people who may have already read one of the new facility-siting books which lack a historical perspective about the origins of the siting problem. In order to assure that the absence of background in math and science will not act as a barrier to reading the book, explanations of mathematical methods and technology have been kept to a minimum in the text.

Lastly, we have written a book about hazardous waste management sites because sites are at the intersection of all the sources of the credibility gap. But we firmly believe that too much attention has been paid to sites, especially to siting. We want to caution planners against the tendency to equate hazardous waste management with finding new sites. Industry can and will find alternatives that do not require new sites. These include changing processes and expanding waste storage, treatment, and disposal on existing sites. We must not become so engrossed in the issue of new sites that changes are allowed at existing sites without appropriate consideration of their impact.

Michael Greenberg
Richard Anderson

# 1

# Hazardous Waste Sources and Volumes: The First Dimension of a Credibility Gap

This chapter summarizes existing knowledge concerning the types, amounts, and sources of hazardous wastes in the nation, selected regions and states. First, hazardous wastes are defined. Then, the sources of hazardous waste generation and how they are keyed to the American economy and the processes of urbanization and industrialization are presented. The chapter shows that one of the reasons that it is so difficult to control hazardous chemical by-products on any but an ad hoc basis is because we do not yet know how much waste has been and is being created. These shortcomings are explained by the long-standing absence of concern with discarded chemical substances, the absence of a clear definition of what constitutes hazardous substances, and wide variations in how the states and federal governments have gone about estimating the size of the waste stream.

## WHAT ARE HAZARDOUS WASTES?

Hazardous wastes are a subset of by-products emanating from manu-facturing processes, scientific and medical research, discarded consumer products, diverse processes used in the delivery of services, and a variety of other activities in the public and private sectors. Hazardous substances are defined and regulated by a plethora of laws designed to control their pro-duction, distribution, and application. A hazardous substance becomes a waste only when it has outlived its useful economic life. Not all hazardous by-products are hazardous wastes.

In contrast to the multitude of definitions which exist for hazardous sub-stances (see Chapter 2), the Resource Conservation and Recovery Act of

1976 (RCRA) deals directly with hazardous wastes. RCRA defines hazardous waste in Section 1004 (5) as:

> a solid waste, or combination of solid wastes, which because of its quantity, concentration, or physical, chemical or infectious characteristics may
>
> (a) cause or significantly contribute to an increase in serious irreversible, or incapacitating reversible illness; or
>
> (b) pose a substantial present or potential hazard to human health or the environment when improperly treated, stored, transported, or disposed of, or otherwise managed.

The definition was worded such that a broad array of wastes could fall under control of the Act, and it allowed the administering agency leeway to define the specific characteristics of hazardous wastes.

The U.S. Environmental Protection Agency (EPA) was mandated by Congress to administer RCRA. The administration of RCRA involved a regulatory overhaul of the hazardous waste management industry by imposing a "cradle-to-grave" manifest system designed to track wastes from generator to final site of treatment, storage, or disposal. The centerpiece of this regulatory approach, which is found in subtitle C, Section 3001—Identification and Listing of Hazardous Wastes, was the system for entering wastes into the hazardous waste tracking network. Congress intended that wastes whose characteristics suggest potential hazardous qualities, as well as wastes falling under the 1004(5) definition, be included in the waste tracking network.

In May of 1980 EPA promulated criteria to implement the identification and listing of hazardous wastes in the Federal Register. Essentially, the initial and later adjusted realm of regulated hazardous wastes is comprised of substances with recognized pathogenic qualities and wastes having characteristics which may render them toxic to public health and natural resources. Subpart C lists four criteria for identifying characteristics of hazardous wastes: ignitable, corrosive, reactive, and toxic (Table 1-1). Substances with these characteristics could cause damage to human health and the environment. The EPA selected available test protocols which it determined sufficiently accurate for the characteristics listed above; but because of a lack of confidence in testing protocols, the EPA rejected testing for the following characteristics: carcinogenicity, mutagenicity, teratogenicity, bioaccumulation potential, and phytotoxicity. Since much of the media presentation on hazardous wastes has dwelled on cancer and birth defects, it is noteworthy that these characteristics are not directly included in the EPA definition.

Subpart D of the regulations uses the characteristics outlined in subpart C to add these characteristics to listed waste substances to comprise the regu-

**TABLE 1-1**

## EPA Listed Wastes Based on Hazardous Characteristics

| Characteristic | Subpart | Considerations | Hazard Code |
|---|---|---|---|
| Ignitable | 261.21 | 1. liquids with flashpoint of less than 140°F (60°C)<br>2. non-liquids liable to cause fires through friction, spontaneous chemical change, etc.<br>3. ignitable compressed air<br>4. oxidizers | (I) |
| Corrosivity | 261.22 | 1. aqueous wastes exhibiting a pH of LE 3 or GE 12.<br>2. liquid wastes capable of corroding steel at a rate greater than 0.250 inches/year. | (C) |
| Reactivity | 261.23 | 1. readily undergo violent chemical change<br>2. react violently or form potentially explosive mixtures with water<br>3. generate toxic fumes when mixed with water, or mild acidic or basic conditions.<br>4. explode when subject to a strong initiating force.<br>5. explode at normal temperatures and pressures.<br>6. DOT forbidden explosives, and Class A and B explosives. | (R) |
| Toxicity (Extraction Procedure) | 261.24 | 1. a representative sample of the waste contains concentrations equal to or greater than the 8 metals listed: arsenic, barium, cadmium, chromium, lead, mercury, selenium, silver; or the 6 organic compounds: endrin, lindane, methoxychlor, toxaphene, 2, 4-D, 2, 4, 5-TP Silvex.<br>2. a solid waste that exhibits the characteristic of EP toxicity | (E) |

Source: Adapted from 40 CFR Part 261, May 19, 1980, Subpart C, pp. 33107–33112.

lated waste stream. In addition to the four characteristics listed in Table 1-1 the EPA also uses acute hazardous waste and toxic waste classifications to list wastes. Each waste listed is assigned an EPA hazardous waste number and the appropriate hazard code (e.g., I = ignitable, etc.). The wastes are identified as originating from specific sources or nonspecific sources. For example, wastes generated from a specific source are often identifiable based on industrial process. EPA hazardous waste number K073 includes chlorinated hydrocarbon wastes which result from the purification process necessary for the production of chlorine. The K designation represents the category of specific source wastes. The nonspecific source wastes, designated by EPA with the F prefix, sometimes include combinations of hazardous wastes. An example is F009—spent stripping and cleaning bath solutions from electroplating operations.

Roughly 1200 substances have been listed in a series of Federal Register publications.[1] Some waste streams which may contain hazardous wastes are exempted from regulatory controls because of the nature and purpose of the waste stream, or because of preexisting regulatory control such as in the case of certain radioactive wastes. Major exempted waste streams include the following: domestic sewage, point source discharge of industrial wastewater regulated under Section 402 of the Clean Water Act, irrigation return flows, radioactive wastes, in-situ mining process residuals, household wastes, and wastes which are returned to the soil as fertilizers in specific processes. Many of these wastes contain substances which would be hazardous according to the EPA definition. A change in exempt status among these categories would have the effect of increasing total volume of regulated wastes. This will likely occur with the implementation of waste water pre-treatment regulations.

## WHO GENERATES HAZARDOUS WASTES
## AND IN WHAT AMOUNTS?

Hazardous wastes, as defined by EPA, are generated by a wide variety of sources. The sources range from the technically complex petroleum refinery and chemical production plants which employ thousands of workers to produce petrochemical feedstocks and inorganic and synthetic organic chemicals to the private homeowner who applies chemical cleaning fluids to septic systems, pesticides on lawns and in gardens, and chemicals to unclog drains. The average American household is the end-user of a wide variety of commercial hazardous substances that become hazardous wastes when used as directed. This is the case for products like toilet bowl cleaners, fabric softeners, spot removers, bleach, disinfectants, metal and furniture polishes, paint removers and thinners, etc. Since these products are discarded by households, they will likely enter sewage systems and municipal sanitary landfills rather than licensed hazardous waste facilities (see Chapter 2) (Pierson 1979).

The diffusion of hazardous wastes into the ambient environment is related to human activity. Once these dangerous wastes enter the air, soil or water they follow complex migration routes that are poorly understood by the scientific community (see Chapter 3). Many wastes enter or are helped along these migration paths by natural forces (e.g., precipitation, flooding, seismic activity, or bioaccumulation in plant life). The difficulty in understanding the fate of these contaminants in the environment suggests an urgent need to identify who generates the wastes and in what volume, and how to control their impact on public health and natural resources.

### Hazardous Waste Volume: Some Rough and Uncertain Estimates

According to the journal *Waste Age*, in 1977 hazardous wastes comprised roughly one percent of total wastes generated in the United States on an annual basis (Table 1-2). The categories shown in the table are broad and there are hazardous wastes included in each of the waste categories. For example, hospitals and university research institutions have traditionally disposed of hazardous substances—many of which are now defined as hazardous wastes—in municipal landfills where other municipal trash is dumped. The main point made by the data in Table 1-2 is that the legally defined hazardous waste system is relatively modest compared to industrial and extractive activity wastes.

Only recently has there been any concentrated effort to determine the quantities, types, and spatial distribution of the hazardous waste stream. National estimates of annual nonradioactive hazardous wastes were developed for EPA and reported (Council on Environmental Quality 1970) as roughly 9 million metric tons (or about 10 percent of all industrial wastes). EPA estimated in 1974 that by weight, 90 percent of these wastes were in liquid waste streams—of which 60 percent were organics in aqueous solution and 40 percent were inorganics in aqueous solution. The remaining 10 percent of wastes were comprised mostly of organics and a mixture of sludges, slurries and miscellaneous solids (Figure 1-1). These waste streams include toxic metals, synthetic organic compounds, flammable and explosive wastes, pathological hospital wastes, and biological and chemical warfare agents.

Less than a decade later the estimate of the total volume of hazardous waste was raised to more than three times the initial estimate, to about 29 million metric tons (EPA 1977). This estimate was derived from a series of 14 industry studies commissioned by the EPA which began in 1974 and were

## TABLE 1-2

## Major Categories of Wastes, 1977

| Waste Category | Estimated Annual Tonnage, in Millions | Percent of Total |
|---|---|---|
| Agricultural Wastes | 2,300.0 | 51 |
| Mining Wastes | 1,700.0 | 38 |
| Industrial Wastes | 340.0 | 8 |
| Municipal Trash | 145.0 | 3 |
| Hazardous Wastes | 35.0 20–50.0 (range) | 0.8 |
| Total | 4,520.0 | 100.8[1] |

Note: [1]Total exceeds 100 percent due to rounding.
Source: Adapted from *Waste Age*, 26, January, 1977.

completed in 1977 (Table 1-3). The 14 industry studies relied on a sample procedure supplemented by telephone interviews and plant visits. The 14 industries selected for analysis were considered to be the largest hazardous waste generating activities, and/or were the industries which generated some of the most toxic waste streams.

The 14-industry study series is interesting for three reasons. First, more than 80 percent of the 1974 estimate of the total volume of hazardous wastes originated from industries manufacturing primary metals; organic chemicals, pesticides and explosives; electroplating; and inorganic chemicals (see Table 1-3). Second, the study showed that 14 percent of the waste stream of these industries is considered hazardous, a figure higher than the commonly reported 10 percent. And third, the 14-industry study showed that hazardous wastes as a proportion of the waste stream vary by industry. For example, hazardous wastes range from roughly five percent of total inorganic chemicals to about 98 percent of organic chemicals, pesticides and explosives.

The national estimates of hazardous wastes generated by different industries discussed above are the result of intensive efforts to develop a foundation of information for planning and policy purposes. Because this type of information is essential for establishing an efficacious hazardous waste

## FIGURE 1-1

**Proportional Hazardous Wastes by
Major Category, 1974**

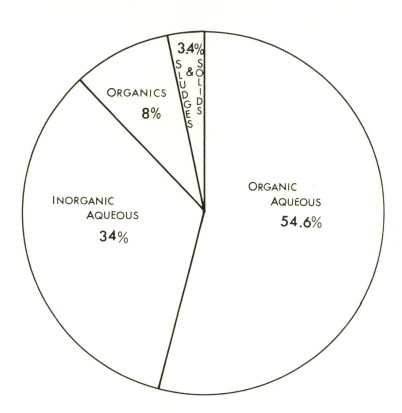

management strategy, and because knowledge of the volume of the hazardous waste stream is uneven at best, the national estimates reported by EPA
are, at the least, expeditious. However, the procedures utilized to derive the
estimates are worth reviewing here because they indicate how uncertain is
the present state of knowledge.

The major challenges for the estimation procedures are accuracy and
comprehensiveness. The Standard Industrial Classification (SIC) codes
used by the federal government to classify industrial production by the
private sector were used to derive the hazardous waste estimate, but do not
include household wastes and specialized waste streams emanating from
governmental activities (such as weapons and warfare agents generated by

**TABLE 1-3**

**Major National Industrial Waste Generators
Estimated Hazardous Waste Quantities, 1974
(Million Metric Tons Annually)**

| Industry | Dry Basis | Wet Basis | Percentage (Wet Basis) |
|---|---|---|---|
| 1. Batteries | 0.005 | 0.010 | 0.035 |
| 2. Inorganic Chemicals | 2.000 | 3.400 | 11.820 |
| 3. Organic Chemicals, pesticides, explosives | 2.150 | 6.860 | 23.857 |
| 4. Electroplating | 0.909 | 5.276 | 18.348 |
| 5. Paints | 0.075 | 0.096 | 0.334 |
| 6. Petroleum refining | 0.625 | 1.757 | 6.110 |
| 7. Pharmaceuticals | 0.062 | 0.065 | 0.226 |
| 8. Primary metals | 4.454 | 8.335 | 28.986 |
| 9. Leather tanning and finishing | 0.045 | 0.146 | 0.508 |
| 10. Textile dyeing and finishing | 0.048 | 1.770 | 6.155 |
| 11. Rubber and plastics | 0.205 | 0.785 | 2.730 |
| 12. Special machinery | 0.102 | 0.162 | 0.563 |
| 13. Electronic components | 0.026 | 0.036 | 0.125 |
| 14. Waste oil re-refining | 0.057 | 0.057 | 0.198 |
| Totals | 10.763 | 28.755 | 99.995[1] |

Note: [1]Total does not equal 100 percent due to rounding.
Source: Adapted from EPA—1977.

the Department of Defense). The SIC codes included in the waste inventory estimates are dubious for a number of reasons. For example, using the number of workers employed (total employed or production workers) or value-added as a multiplier to estimate the volume of waste generated may be misleading when applied to different facilities within a single industry. Another example may be seen in the large number of "captive shops" in the electroplating industry, where EPA (1974) points out that around two-thirds of the electroplating activity in the United States is conducted in plants which are not listed under the SIC code for electroplating. The estimates rely in large part on the SIC-grouped data in the *Census of Manufactures* as a source of information for employment or value-added. Other sources, such as *County Business Patterns* (which at least uses the same SIC codes as the *Census of Manufactures)* or the various state industrial directories, may not be complete or up to date. These problems suggest that these estimates were probably acceptable for purposes of general indication; but they were not appropriate as an accurate, detailed inventory of hazardous wastes.

Aside from hazardous wastes generated by federal and other governmental facilities, there are a variety of additional sources which are routinely excluded from many national volume estimates. These sources include off-specification products, bad batches, and discarded containers from the manufacturing industry. Some sources result from governmental regulatory controls such as the ban on PCB usage, the effect of which was to render raw material inventories as hazardous wastes. Sources also result from individual state designations of listed wastes beyond EPA designation. Other sources include accidental spills, abandoned sites, and small volume generators. The volumes of these sources are difficult to estimate at the national level since they are primarily affected by local conditions. Waste disposal facilities' estimates based on SIC code multipliers usually do not include these sources.

More recent estimates of national hazardous waste volume show a wide range from 27 to over 60 million metric wet tons. A study prepared for EPA by Booz-Allen & Hamilton, Inc. and Putnam, Hayes, and Bartlett, Inc. (1981) reports, with some acknowledged uncertainty, that the true volume was somewhere between 27.7 to 53.8 million metric wet tons in 1980. JRB Associates (1981) reported industrial hazardous waste volume at roughly 41.2 million metric wet tons in 1980. Yet another estimate by EPA suggests that national hazardous waste is in the vicinity of 60 million metric wet tons per year and that this volume is generated by some 760,000 large and small generators — five percent of which contribute 97.7 percent of total volume and 91 percent of which produce about one percent of the total volume.[2]

Overall, we have estimates of hazardous waste volume; but they certainly come with noteworthy limitations. Moreover, estimates would probably be more imprecise at the regional, state, and local levels, where more accurate estimates are essential to sound planning. Before discussing attempts to estimate volumes at these subnational scales, it is interesting and appropriate to review briefly the patterns of geographic distribution of hazardous waste generation in the nation in the quantities implied by the national estimate.

## THE GEOGRAPHIC DISTRIBUTION OF ESTIMATED
## NATIONAL HAZARDOUS WASTE VOLUME—1970–1980

A national hazardous waste stream of 28 to 54 million metric wet tons, generated by some 760,000 separate sources, is necessarily spatially dispersed by virtue of its sheer volume and the constraints placed on human activity in terms of both complex social organization and the physical form of human settlements. The activities of the primary sector extractive industries such as agriculture, silviculture, and mining, are obviously dependent upon the site-specific attributes of natural resources (e.g., fertile soil, deciduous forests, mineral fields). Hence, we expect that the resulting waste streams which may contain some fraction of hazardous wastes to be in a sense "indigenous" to the areas developed for resource and materials extraction. Manufacturing industries in the secondary sector have largely become footloose, partially as a function of such factors as land use zoning, labor supply and costs, taxation, and community amenities, so that the waste streams from manufacturing activities are widely dispersed. Sources of hazardous waste have become widely integrated among human settlement patterns including contributions from the service sector, households, and most importantly, the industrial waste stream studied by EPA. The volume estimates vary by category of waste, by the units of measurement (dry or wet metric tons), and by the scale of data collection (regions). Metric wet tons have been selected for presentation here because this measurement is reported with some consistency in the literature.[3]

Estimated national industrial hazardous waste volume for 1970 is shown in Table 1-4. This table adapts EPA (1974) estimates reported by nine aggregate, administrative regions. The largest volumes are generated in the East-North Central, Mid-Atlantic, and West-South Central regions. These are areas of high to moderate industrialization. The South-Atlantic and West regions produce medium amounts of hazardous wastes, ranging from 700,000 to 900,000 metric wet tons annually. The remaining regions generate relatively low quantities of 500,000 metric tons and below. The component hazardous waste categories exhibit diverse geographical distributions.

Volume estimates for 1980 are shown in Table 1-5 for the 10 U.S. EPA regions. The estimated 41 million metric wet tons represent hazardous wastes generated by 17 manufacturing and 10 nonmanufacturing SIC categories. EPA administrative regions IV, V, and VI account for 25.1, 15.6 and 25.5 percent, respectively, of total volume. The EPA administrative regions are not strictly commensurable with the Bureau of the Census regions since the former contains 10 and the latter contains nine regions.

## TABLE 1-4
## EPA Estimated Industrial Hazardous Waste Generation by Region in Metric Tons, 1970

| Region | Aqueous Inorganics (metric tons)[1] | Aqueous Organics (metric tons) | Organics (metric tons) | Sludges, Etc. (metric tons) | Total (metric tons) | States in Regions |
|---|---|---|---|---|---|---|
| New England | 86.0 | 154.0 | 30.0 | 5.4 | 275.4 | CT, ME, MA, NH, RI, VT |
| Mid-Atlantic | 907.2 | 1,000.0 | 90.6 | 50.0 | 2,047.8 | NJ, NY, PA |
| East-North Central | 1,180.0 | 770.0 | 132.0 | 81.6 | 2,163.6 | IL, IN, MI, OH, WI |
| West-North Central | 59.0 | 236.0 | 45.0 | 16.8 | 350.8 | IA, KS, MN, MO, NE, ND, SD |
| South Atlantic | 208.5 | 545.0 | 68.0 | 72.6 | 894.1 | DE, DC, FL, GA, MD, NC, SC, VA, WV |
| East-South Central | 81.7 | 350.0 | 40.0 | 8.6 | 480.3 | AL, KY, MS, TN |
| West-South Central | 290.0 | 1,315.0 | 163.0 | 35.4 | 1,803.4 | AR, LA, OK, TX, OR, WA |
| West (Pacific) | 109.0 | 500.0 | 103.0 | 27.7 | 739.7 | AK, CA, HI |
| Mountain | 113.5 | 4.5 | 45.4 | 10.4 | 173.8 | AZ, CO, ID, MT, NV, NM, UT, WY |
| TOTAL | 3,034.9 | 4,874.5 | 717.0 | 308.6 | 8,929.1 | |

Note: [1]In thousands of metric tons.
Source: Adapted from EPA, *Report to Congress: Disposal of Hazardous Wastes*, SW-115, 1974, p.4.

However, regions V and VI are roughly equivalent to the East-North Central and West-South Central regions, and both of these regions generate the highest total quantities of hazardous wastes. In 1970 the Mid-Atlantic region was among the highest waste-generating areas. But in 1980 when this area was divided into EPA regions II and III, neither was among the highest volume generators for total volume. Also in 1980, EPA region IV was a high-volume area, which was quite different from the low- and medium-volume categories exhibited by the East-South Central and the South-Atlantic counterpart regions in 1970 estimates (see Table 1-4).

These changes may be the result of rising or falling production rates and their subsequent effects on the hazardous waste stream. Another explanation might be a greater or lesser degree of accuracy in volume estimation

**TABLE 1-5**

**Industrial Hazardous Waste Generation by Region, 1980**

| EPA Region Headquarters | Quantity (Wet kkg) | Percent | States |
|---|---|---|---|
| I Boston | 1,104,000 | 2.7 | CT, ME, MA NH, RI, VT |
| II New York City | 3,113,000 | 7.5 | NJ, NY |
| III Philadelphia | 4,354,000 | 10.6 | DC, DE, MD, PA, VA, WV |
| IV Atlanta | 10,353,000 | 25.1 | AL, FL, GA, KY, MS, NC, SC, TN |
| V Chicago | 6,428,000 | 15.6 | IL, IN, MI, MN, OH, WI |
| VI Dallas | 10,536,000 | 25.5 | AR, LA, NM, OK, TX |
| VII Kansas City | 1,201,000 | 2.9 | IA, KS, MO, NE |
| VIII Denver | 318,000 | 0.8 | CO, MT, ND, SD, UT, WY |
| IX San Francisco | 2,838,000 | 6.9 | AZ, CA, HI, NV |
| X Seattle | 995,000 | 2.4 | AK, ID, OR, WA |
| TOTAL | 41,240,000[1] | 100.0 | |

Note: [1]The range in waste production reported was 27,765,000–53,864,000 wet kkg.
Source: JRB Associates Inc., 1981.

for the years 1970 and 1980. Still another explanation might be the change in delineation of reporting units (i.e., nine Census Bureau regions versus 10 EPA administrative regions). Breakdowns by category of hazardous waste —inorganic, organic, sludges were unavailable for 1980—and thus, comparisons for these categories were not appropriate.

Perhaps the volume estimate most rigorously arrived at, 41.235 million metric wet tons, was reported by Booz-Allen & Hamilton, Inc. and Putnam, Hayes and Bartlett, Inc. (1980). This report relied upon in-depth investigation of hazardous waste practices among 14 major waste generating industries (see Appendix R in that report). Appendix A of the Booz-Allen et al. report outlines the volume estimation method utilized. It also presents a detailed breakdown of estimated total, and the off-site fraction, of wastes by SIC code for manufacturing and nonmanufacturing activities for each EPA region. Nevertheless, three cautions are advised when considering the Booz-Allen volume estimates. First, the industry studies relied on for deriving estimates preceded the published list of reportable hazardous wastes in the May, 1980, Federal Register. Thus the wastes investigated in the studies are not identical to the wastes listed for regulation. Second, either a model plant or model process, or data from state surveys were also used to derive the volume estimates. There are inherent difficulties with extrapolating a model plant or process to an entire industry. State surveys may utilize broad industry categories, such as the 2-digit SIC code level, and they are insensitive to process differences within an industry. Third, there was an inconsistency in reporting the solid content of the generated hazardous wastes.

An effort was made to disaggregate national hazardous waste generation to the state level (EPA 1982) as part of determining hazardous waste grant allotments made by EPA to the various states. To make the actual allocations, the volume estimate for each state is combined with population, land area and number of generators. We are interested here only in the volume estimate factor and the method to derive it.

This investigation relied on the 41.2 million metric wet tons reported by Booz-Allen et al. (1980). The method interpolated the national volume down to the state level. With the benefit of the knowledge obtained about hazardous waste generation by industry, EPA staff used number of work hours for manufacturing, and total sales/receipts for nonmanufacturing industries to estimate volumes by state (see Table 1-6). These estimates are imperfect. On the one hand, they relied on promulgated wastes, defined before the fall of 1980 when the list was pared down. On the other hand, the estimates do not include wastes from governmental sources, spills and abandoned sites, discarded and off-specification products, and state designated wastes, among others that are missing.

A graphical representation (Figure 1-2) of the volume estimates by state

## TABLE 1-6

### Estimated State Hazardous Waste Volume, Demographic and Economic Factors

| State | 1982[1] Hazardous Waste Volume (million metric tons) | Rank | 1977[2] Rank Mfg. Production Workers | Rank Mfg. Value Added | 1980[2] Rank Population | Rank Population Density | Rank Urbanization |
|---|---|---|---|---|---|---|---|
| New Jersey | 3.12 | 1 | 10 | 8 | 9 | 1 | 2 |
| Texas | 3.01 | 2 | 8 | 7 | 3 | 30 | 14 |
| California | 2.63 | 3 | 1 | 1 | 1 | 14 | 1 |
| Ohio | 2.57 | 4 | 4 | 3 | 6 | 9 | 17 |
| Pennsylvania | 2.55 | 5 | 3 | 6 | 4 | 8 | 21 |
| Illinois | 2.53 | 6 | 5 | 4 | 5 | 10 | 11 |
| New York | 2.32 | 7 | 2 | 2 | 2 | 6 | 6 |
| Michigan | 1.99 | 8 | 6 | 5 | 8 | 12 | 19 |
| Tennessee | 1.82 | 9 | 13 | 14 | 17 | 18 | 35 |
| North Carolina | 1.33 | 10 | 7 | 10 | 10 | 17 | 45 |
| Indiana | 1.28 | 11 | 9 | 9 | 12 | 13 | 30 |
| Louisiana | 1.25 | 12 | 29 | 20 | 19 | 2 | 22 |
| Virginia | 1.22 | 13 | 15 | 17 | 14 | 16 | 28 |
| South Carolina | 1.14 | 14 | 16 | 25 | 24 | 19 | 38 |
| Florida | 0.96 | 15 | 20 | 21 | 7 | 11 | 8 |
| Missouri | 0.91 | 16 | 17 | 13 | 15 | 27 | 23 |
| Massachusetts | 0.82 | 17 | 11 | 12 | 11 | 3 | 9 |
| West Virginia | 0.79 | 18 | 33 | 32 | 34 | 25 | 49 |
| Alabama | 0.73 | 19 | 18 | 24 | 22 | 26 | 36 |
| Georgia | 0.70 | 20 | 14 | 15 | 13 | 22 | 34 |
| Kentucky | 0.70 | 21 | 22 | 19 | 23 | 23 | 43 |
| Wisconsin | 0.63 | 22 | 12 | 11 | 16 | 34 | 31 |
| Connecticut | 0.61 | 23 | 19 | 16 | 25 | 4 | 15 |
| Maryland | 0.59 | 24 | 26 | 26 | 18 | 5 | 13 |
| Washington | 0.38 | 25 | 23 | 22 | 20 | 28 | 16 |

**TABLE 1-6 (Continued)**

**Estimated State Hazardous Waste Volume,
Demographic and Economic Factors**

| State | *1982[1]* Hazardous Waste Volume (million metric tons) | *Rank* | *1977[2]* Rank Mfg. Pro-duc-tion Work-ers | *Rank Mfg. Value Added* | *1980[2]* Rank Pop-ula-tion | *Rank Pop-ula-tion Den-sity* | *Rank Urban-ization* |
|---|---|---|---|---|---|---|---|
| Arkansas | 0.37 | 26 | 27 | 29 | 33 | 35 | 42 |
| Minnesota | 0.36 | 27 | 21 | 18 | 21 | 33 | 26 |
| Kansas | 0.35 | 28 | 44 | 45 | 32 | 37 | 27 |
| Mississippi | 0.34 | 29 | 24 | 28 | 31 | 31 | 47 |
| Delaware | 0.30 | 30 | 40 | 39 | 47 | 7 | 20 |
| Iowa | 0.30 | 31 | 25 | 23 | 27 | 32 | 37 |
| Oklahoma | 0.23 | 32 | 30 | 30 | 26 | 34 | 25 |
| Oregon | 0.20 | 33 | 28 | 27 | 30 | 39 | 24 |
| Rhode Island | 0.19 | 34 | 32 | 35 | 40 | 2 | 3 |
| Colorado | 0.18 | 35 | 31 | 31 | 28 | 38 | 12 |
| Arizona | 0.16 | 36 | 36 | 33 | 29 | 40 | 10 |
| Alaska | 0.13 | 37 | 48 | 47 | 50 | 50 | 29 |
| Maine | 0.13 | 38 | 34 | 36 | 38 | 36 | 46 |
| Nebraska | 0.12 | 39 | 37 | 34 | 35 | 41 | 33 |
| Utah | 0.11 | 40 | 38 | 38 | 36 | 42 | 7 |
| New Hampshire | 0.10 | 41 | 35 | 37 | 42 | 20 | 41 |
| Idaho | 0.07 | 42 | 39 | 40 | 41 | 43 | 39 |
| New Mexico | 0.06 | 43 | 42 | 44 | 37 | 44 | 18 |
| Nevada | 0.05 | 44 | 47 | 48 | 43 | 47 | 5 |
| Montana | 0.05 | 45 | 43 | 43 | 44 | 48 | 40 |
| Wyoming | 0.04 | 46 | 50 | 50 | 49 | 49 | 32 |
| Hawaii | 0.03 | 47 | 45 | 42 | 39 | 15 | 4 |
| Vermont | 0.03 | 48 | 41 | 41 | 48 | 29 | 50 |
| North Dakota | 0.03 | 49 | 49 | 49 | 46 | 45 | 44 |
| South Dakota | 0.01 | 50 | 46 | 46 | 45 | 46 | 48 |
| Total | 41.2 | | | | | | |

Source: [1]EPA, 1982.
Source: [2]U.S. Bureau of the Census, 1981.

## FIGURE 1-2

### Estimated Hazardous Waste Generation
### by State, 1982 (48 contiguous states)

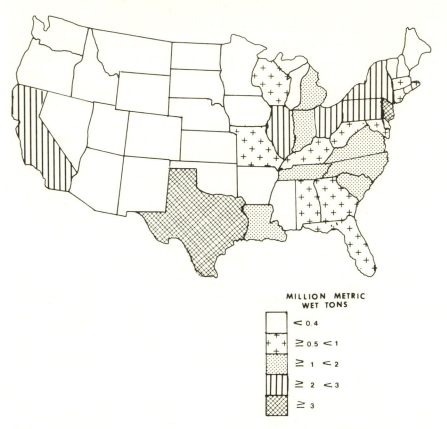

MILLION METRIC
WET TONS

< 0.4

≥ 0.5 < 1

≥ 1 < 2

≥ 2 < 3

≥ 3

as shown in Table 1-6 reveals a preponderance of high volume generators in the older, industrialized eastern and midwestern United States, once known as the "American Manufacturing Belt." The only exceptions are Texas, Louisiana, and California.

The hazardous waste generation rankings shown in Table 1-6 were compared with rankings for total population in 1980, and production workers and value added in manufacturing for 1977 in order to provide an initial perspective on the correlates of hazardous waste production. It was expected that there would be a high correlation between these variables since they are often used (in a variety of forms and by an array of investigators) to estimate volume generation. A Spearman Rho correlation between volume generation rank and two ranked economic factors (manufacturing production workers and value added) were both above 0.90 (p < .001). There is little doubt about the strong relationship between waste generation as measured by EPA and industrialization at the state scale.

The volume rank was also correlated with demographic factors such as: population, population density (persons per square mile), and percent urbanization. It was expected (and found) that a high, significant correlation existed between waste volume rank, population rank, and population density rank for 1980. The Spearman Rho (Rs) were 0.91 and 0.70, respectively (p < .001). A very weak positive Spearman Rho correlation of 0.28 (p < .05) was found between waste volume rank and urbanization rank.

In order to determine which states are responsible for this weak association, a bivariate linear regression was used to examine the relationship between urbanization and volume generation for each state. The residuals of this regression, a standardized measure of the difference between observed waste volume and predicted waste volume based on the regression equation, show which states exemplify the relationship and which states do not.

The residuals indicate three patterns of relationships. First, some of the first nine states listed in Table 1-6 as the highest volume generators were substantially underpredicted. Texas and Tennessee are not among the most urbanized states, but do produce substantial amounts of hazardous waste. This is also applicable to other southern states such as: North Carolina, Louisiana, Virginia, South Carolina, and West Virginia. The more urbanized, high-volume generators like New Jersey, California, Ohio, Pennsylvania, Illinois, New York, and Michigan, exhibited observed hazardous waste volumes substantially in excess of what may be explained by urbanization.

The second pattern is manifested by a group of states ranging between 80 and 87 percent urbanized and generating less than 200,000 tons of hazardous waste per year. The states are Rhode Island, Arizona, Utah, Nevada, and Hawaii. Using urbanization to explain waste generation for these states leads to a substantial amount of overprediction. For example, Rhode Island with 87 percent urbanization generated 0.19 million metric wet tons (mmwt) but was predicted to have generated 1.25 mmwt.

The third pattern reveals a group of states with moderate waste generation and 65 to 85 percent urbanization. The states in this pattern include: Florida, Missouri, Massachusetts, Alabama, Georgia, Kentucky, Wisconsin, Arkansas, Mississippi, New Hampshire, Vermont, and North and South Dakota. The residuals suggest that volume generation for states in this group is fairly well predicted by percent urbanization.

Overall, there is not a consistent association between urbanization and waste generation at the state scale. There is, however, a strong association between urbanization and waste sites at the county scale (Chapter 4). While it is not the objective of this chapter to test hypotheses, these correlations are helpful in showing that hazardous waste generation and urbanization, contrary to popular thought, are not strongly associated statistically at the state scale. Indeed, at the state scale, percent urbanization is not a reliable indicator of hazardous waste generation.

## Regional and State Estimates of Hazardous Waste
## Volume Generation: More Rough and Uncertain Estimates

Various hazardous waste inventories were conducted in different regions and states in the late 1970s and early 1980s. These inventories often differ from the national volume estimates in the degree of specificity with which they examine particular industries and types of wastes. In all, nine different estimating procedures are illustrated by six different inventories. Two multi-state regional inventories, one sub-state regional inventory, and three single-state inventories are included. These inventories were also chosen because they represent the spectrum of low-, medium-, and high-concentration waste generation areas in the United States. The states included in these inventories were estimated to produce more than one-third of the total hazardous waste volume in 1980.

### The Delaware River Basin Study

The Delaware River Basin Commission (DRBC) coordinated a survey of industrial establishments in the four Basin states (Delaware, New Jersey, New York, and Pennsylvania) to estimate hazardous waste generation (Carson et al. 1979). The study relied on a selected sample of 335 industrial establishments out of a total of 2,632 plants which represented 138 four-digit SIC categories. The 335 surveyed plants produced about 76 percent of total gross annual sales for the 138 SIC categories in the DRBC region. The survey instrument requested plant representatives to identify the types of hazardous wastes generated and their volumes. The wastes were grouped into four categories of oily wastes, 11 categories of organics, six categories of inorganics, and one category of miscellaneous dilute aqueous wastes (Table 1-7). The estimated volume for these four general groups of wastes was roughly 2.6 million tons annually (based on the 1979 survey). Eighty percent of these wastes were inorganic, and the largest type (41 percent of total wastes) consisted of heavy metal wastes.

## TABLE 1-7

### Surveyed and Extrapolated Industrial Hazardous
### Wastes in the DRBC Region, 1979

| Waste Classification | Reported Volume from Survey in Tons/Year | Extrapolated Quantities In Tons/Year |
|---|---|---|
| *Oily Wastes* | | |
| 0-1 Oily Sludge | 16,250 | 23,740 |
| 0-3 Waste Oil & Oily Material | 13,950 | 17,950 |
| 0-4 Recoverable Oil | 15,560 | 39,530 |
| *Organic Wastes* | | |
| OR-1 Solvent | 23,715 | 33,540 |
| OR-2 Organics | 17,845 | 26,960 |
| OR-2A Organic Rich Aqueous Stream | | |
| except Wastewater Treatment Sludge | 45,905 | 61,050 |
| OR-3 Organics Containing Metal Salts | 18,285 | 20,850 |
| OR-4 Halogenated Solvents | 6,320 | 22,750 |
| OR-5 Biocide, PCB & Alike | 2,115 | 3,930 |
| OR-6 Contaminated Containers, etc. | 16,160 | 26,885 |
| OR-7 Wastewater Treatment Sludges | 41,295 | 55,110 |
| OR-8 Spent Caustic/Acid | 12,195 | 23,260 |
| OR-10 Energy Recoverable Wastes[1] | 16,350 | 25,405 |
| OR-11 Scrap Plastics, Rubbers[1] | 259,055 | 477,125 |
| *Inorganic Wastes* | | |
| 1-1 Inert, Inorganic Waste[2] | 602,045 | 651,125 |
| 1-2 Potentially Recoverable | | |
| Inorganic Waste | 346,015 | 385,465 |
| 1-3 Heavy Metal Waste | 1,061,460 | 1,513.865 |
| 1-4 Water Soluble Inorganics | 5,515 | 7,540 |
| 1-5 Acid/Alkali | 37,670 | 53,520 |
| 1-6 Reactive Inorganic Waste | 3,270 | 4,825 |
| *Miscellaneous Wastes* | | |
| W-1 Dilute Aqueous Waste | 350 | 2,880 |
| | 2,561,325 | 3,477,305 |

Notes: [1]Fifty percent of these wastes may be classified as exotic.

[2]These wastes were excluded from the Exotic Waste Inventory.

Source: Adapted from Carson et al., *Industrial Exotic Waste Program Findings, Conclusions, and Recommendations*, Phase I, Delaware River Basin Commission, February 1979.

Unlike other studies which utilize number of employees to estimate hazardous waste volumes, the DRBC approach assumed that no reliable index is available to extrapolate waste volume proportionately to the rest of the industry for a particular SIC category. Researchers involved with this study decided that gross annual sales figures were just as reliable as total employed to derive proportional volume estimates to the entire industry. Using the gross annual sales for the 335 surveyed firms as a multiplier, it was estimated that roughly 3,480,000 tons per year of hazardous wastes were generated by industries belonging to the 138 SIC categories in the DRBC region (Table 1-7).

The 1979 volume estimates reported in the DRBC study appear to agree with the results in Table 1-4 for inorganic wastes in the Mid-Atlantic region for 1970. However, it may be assumed that the 1979 figures reflect a certain amount of growth in industrial activity in the region since 1970. The 1980 volume estimates shown in Table 1-5 also appear to agree with the DRBC volume estimates since the estimate falls within the one to five million tons per year range.

*Waste Inventory for the New England Region—*
*Arthur D. Little, Inc.*

A waste inventory was developed for the six New England region states (Arthur D. Little, Inc. 1979). Based on surveys of selected industries conducted in each state (Connecticut, Maine, Massachusetts, New Hampshire, Rhode Island, Vermont), wastes were roughly categorized into the following six categories: (1) waste oils, (2) solvents, (3) acids and alkalies, (4) sludges, (5) chemicals, and (6) miscellaneous other wastes. Because individual state inventories were not strictly comparable for all six categories of waste, investigators made approximations as explained in the text. The estimated total volume of wastes was reported to be 73 million gallons per year originating from manufacturing among 15 two-digit SIC industries. Using a conversion figure of 240 gallons per ton, the gallonage figure is equivalent to about 304,000 tons.

Employment statistics were used to extrapolate the inventoried wastes from the state surveys to represent the larger New England hazardous waste stream. The mathematics were performed as follows. The volume of inventoried wastes was multiplied by the ratio of total manufacturing employees per SIC code (numerator) to the number of manufacturing employees per SIC code surveyed (denominator). The following example serves to illustrate the extrapolation method. Total surveyed wastes for Connecticut (all 15 SIC codes) were 68 million gallons per year. This figure was multiplied by the fraction of 392,000 manufacturing employees divided by 267,000 manufacturing employees covered in the survey. The resulting product of 100.1 million gallons per year represents the extrapolated estimated volume of wastes for that state. Since the manufacturing employment is reported by county, it was possible to derive geographically-distributed volume estimates.

Results from applying the extrapolation procedure indicate that the New England region generates from 233 to 333 million gallons of hazardous waste per year (Table 1-8). Converting this to tons implies a range of 958,000 tons to 1.375 million tons of hazardous waste per year. A range is reported because of the uncertainty about the volume of sludges generated as a result of pretreatment programs in the various states. The 0.958–1.375 million ton range represents annual hazardous waste generation based on state industry surveys and employment figures for the mid to late 1970's.

National volume estimates for New England in 1970 suggest this region accounts for three percent of all hazardous wastes, or about 0.275 million metric tons (EPA 1974). Revised estimates for 1974 to 1977 suggest an increase to about 4.2 percent of national volumes, or to about 1.2 million metric wet tons (EPA 1977). This estimate falls within the range reported by A. D. Little, Inc. Estimates for 1980 suggest a declining portion of national wastes at about 2.7 percent, and roughly 1.1 million metric wet tons per year (JRB Associates 1981).

In August of 1982, A. D. Little Inc. (1982) updated hazardous waste generation volumes in the New England states for the New England Council. Looking at 32 specific industry groups including manufacturing and nonmanufacturing (services), it was reported that the estimated total volume could range between 375,000 to 495,000[4] tons per year (Table 1-9). The range was offered because of an impending sludge pretreatment program. Roughly 65 percent of the volume is produced by the chemical industry; and another 20 percent is generated by the fabricated metals, electrical and electronic equipment, and machinery industries. About 10 percent originates from the non-manufacturing industries.

Hazardous waste volume estimates reported here were based on number of employees by SIC code multiplied by a waste generation factor per employee. This is similar to the method utilized in the earlier A. D. Little report. However, the volume reported in 1982 is substantially lower than the earlier estimates produced for NERCOM. The discrepancy is explained by the fact that the earlier estimates were based on wastes proposed for hazardous listing in the December 1978 Federal Register (see footnote 1, reference 1). The latter estimates were based on wastes proposed for listing as hazardous in the May 1980 Federal Register (see footnote 1, reference 3).[5] As a result of comments received by EPA in the interim period, the May

## TABLE 1-8

### Surveyed and Extrapolated Hazardous Wastes
### Generated in the New England Region, Late 1970s
### (Numbers in Million Gallons per Year)

| State | Waste Category | | | | | | |
| --- | --- | --- | --- | --- | --- | --- | --- |
| | Oil | Solvent | Acid/Alkali | Sludges | Chemicals | Other | Total |
| **Connecticut** | | | | | | | |
| Surveyed[1] | 5.2 | 3.9 | 1.5 | 13.6 | 10.6 | — | 34.8 |
| Extrapolated[2] | 18.1 | 5.3 | 6.5 | 70.0 | 1.5 | 6.0 | 107.4 |
| **Maine** | | | | | | | |
| Surveyed | 0.01 | 0.04 | 1.1 | 7.7 | 2.2 | — | 11.0 |
| Extrapolated | 4.8 | 1.5 | 1.8 | 12.7–30.2 | 3.6 | 4.5 | 28.9–46.4 |
| **Massachusetts** | | | | | | | |
| Surveyed | 1.6 | 1.7 | 0.8 | 6.9 | 0.4 | — | 11.4 |
| Extrapolated | 25.3 | 8.1 | 6.0 | 19.3–55.0 | 3.2 | 1.0 | 62.9–98.6 |
| **New Hampshire** | | | | | | | |
| Surveyed | 0.2 | 0.4 | 2.0 | 1.3 | 2.0 | 4.9 | 10.9 |
| Extrapolated | 2.0 | 0.6 | 2.6 | 1.7–17.9 | 2.6 | 6.4 | 15.9–32.1 |
| **Rhode Island** | | | | | | | |
| Surveyed | 0.4 | 0.2 | 1.2 | 1.3 | 0.3 | — | 3.4 |
| Extrapolated | 3.1 | 0.5 | 3.0 | 3.2–23.9 | 0.7 | — | 10.5–31.2 |
| **Vermont** | | | | | | | |
| Surveyed | 0.6 | 0.3 | 0.3 | 0.1 | 0.1 | — | 1.4 |
| Extrapolated | 4.1 | 1.3 | 1.3 | 0.4–7.4 | 0.4 | — | 7.5–14.5 |

Notes: [1]Surveyed 72.9

[2]Extrapolated 233.1–330.2

Source: Arthur D. Little, Inc., *A Plan for Development of Hazardous Waste Management Facilities in the New England Region*, Volume II, Cambridge, Mass.: Arthur D. Little, Inc., September 1979.

## TABLE 1-9

### Estimated Hazardous Wastes Generated in New England, 1982
### (Numbers in Thousand Tons per Year)

| State | *Organic Liquid* | *Organic Solids & Sludges* | *Aqueous Solutions* | *Inorganic Solids & Sludges* | *Total* |
|---|---|---|---|---|---|
| **Connecticut** | | | | | |
| Low[1] | 17.6 | 43.0 | 18.2 | 58.1 | 136.9 |
| High[2] | 17.6 | 49.7 | 18.2 | 58.1 | 143.6 |
| **Maine** | | | | | |
| Low | 1.2 | 2.0 | 0.8 | 2.1 | 6.2 |
| High | 2.1 | 5.3 | 1.3 | 3.0 | 11.7 |
| **Massachusetts** | | | | | |
| Low | 14.4 | 59.5 | 20.3 | 56.3 | 150.5 |
| High | 21.6 | 85.9 | 25.4 | 66.8 | 199.7 |
| **New Hampshire** | | | | | |
| Low | 1.7 | 6.3 | 1.5 | 5.3 | 14.8 |
| High | 3.0 | 8.3 | 2.1 | 6.3 | 19.7 |
| **Rhode Island** | | | | | |
| Low | 1.4 | 17.8 | 2.4 | 6.1 | 27.7 |
| High | 2.4 | 28.6 | 4.7 | 12.6 | 48.2 |
| **Vermont** | | | | | |
| Low | 1.2 | 0.7 | 2.9 | 2.3 | 7.1 |
| High | 2.4 | 1.7 | 3.7 | 3.1 | 10.9 |
| **Total** | | | | | |
| Low | 37.5 | 129.3 | 46.1 | 130.2 | 343.2[3] |
| High | 49.1 | 179.5 | 55.4 | 149.9 | 434.2 |

Notes: [1]Low range option
[2]High range option
[3]The total volume range estimates do not reflect estimated unreported hazardous wastes.

Source: Arthur D. Little, Inc., *Hazardous Waste Generation In New England*, prepared for The New England Council, Boston, Massachusetts, August, 1982.

1980 proposed listing eliminated (or delisted) many categories which had been proposed earlier. The discrepancy also reflects differences in the way the various New England states define and list hazardous wastes.

## State and Sub-State Regional Inventories

*Sacramento Area Council of Governments (SACOG) Region*

The state of California ranked as the third highest hazardous waste generator in the nation in 1982 with about 2.6 million metric wet tons sent off-site for treatment, storage, or disposal (EPA 1982). This figure is considerably higher than the estimated 1.3 million tons of hazardous wastes reported by the University of California-Davis (1981). The discrepancy in estimated volumes is interesting because the University of California report relied on manifest records. This approach involved an investigation of 12,000 transport manifest records, which were obtained from the EPA and are known as the "Part A Database," whereby companies apply for on-site treatment, storage, or disposal permits. The 12,000 records were representative of the amount of hazardous wastes accepted during two "typical months" (September 1979 and May 1980) which totaled some 226,451 tons. This figure was multiplied by six to approximate the annual generation of an estimated 1.3 million tons.

The discrepancy between the two reported volumes is probably due to three factors which are important to consider when using manifest data. First, the manifest data may not include all facilities accepting wastes or generating wastes at this point in time. Second, it is highly likely that some of the wastes are transported to facilities outside of California. Third, the discrepancy may also be influenced by the choice of the two "typical months" used for analysis, which may not be as "typical" as expected; therefore, it would be inappropriate to use a straightforward constant multiplier of six to approximate annual volume.

The SACOG (1982) report makes use of the University of California study to focus on the Sacramento Area and Upper Valley Area which consists of all or part of 18 counties in the SACOG region.[6] The Sacramento Valley area generated about four percent (9,145 tons) of the two-month volume reported. Using the constant of six as a multiplier this area is estimated to generate about 54,870 tons per year. This rather small volume is not particularly of interest except for the fact that it includes about one-half of the sulfur sludges generated in the state, and a considerable portion of hazardous drilling muds and aqueous solutions with organic residues. The local abundance of these types of wastes points out the need for both treatment and disposal facilities in an area that lacks both. Indeed, there are no treatment, storage, or disposal facilities that accept off-site hazardous waste in the Sacramento Valley Region.

## *Illinois*

The EPA estimated that Illinois was the sixth largest state generator of hazardous waste with 2.53 million metric tons in 1982. Patterson Associates (1979) reports a range of annual hazardous waste volume generated in Illinois based on different assumptions. One set of volume ranges was based on extrapolating nationwide estimates down to the state level. Assuming that industrial solid and hazardous wastes are distributed geographically proportionate to the annual industrial value added of products, then Illinois contributes seven percent of U.S. value added and thus generates seven percent of the national industrial waste stream. Further assuming that hazardous wastes comprise roughly 10 percent of all industrial wastes (EPA 1977), a fairly straightforward volume estimate can be extrapolated. Patterson Associates (1979) reviewed a number of national estimates made by EPA and various private contractors. Using either seven percent of value added or 10 percent of total industrial waste, or both, a range of 1.98 to 3.54 million tons per year is reported. These investigators also caution that such extrapolations are not reliable since they do not appreciably consider the unique industrial, demographic, and geographic character of Illinois.

Another volume estimate reported is based on a different set of assumptions. In 1979 a manifest system was imposed by regulation on water reclamation plants and industrial waste pretreatment facilities in the Metropolitan Sanitary District of Greater Chicago (MSDGC). This system tracks industrial residues for five types of hazardous waste loads generated in the sanitary district. The assumptions used to extrapolate from the MSDGC manifest records on volume to an estimate of state volume were as follows. The manifest records comprise roughly one-fifth of the volume of hazardous wastes generated in the MSDGC, and this district generates about 50 percent of the waste volume in the state. Therefore, the 306,728 tons per year tabulated from manifest records account for ten percent of the estimated 3,067,280 tons per year generated in the state of Illinois.

## *Massachusetts*

The Massachusetts Department of Environmental Management, Bureau of Solid Waste Disposal (1982), presents an interesting method for estimating the volume of off-site wastes generated by manufacturing and non-manufacturing activities in the state. The volume estimate reported ranged from 250,000 to 390,000 tons per year in 1981; and it was based on transporter manifest records, reviews of annual reports filed by generators, a selected survey of treatment and storage facilities in the state, and a selected survey of hazardous waste facilities in five states accepting Massachusetts generated hazardous wastes.

The effort referenced here depended on tabulating waste volumes, by type (waste oil, organics, inorganics, special hazard), from specific generators and transporters in the manifest tracking system. The transporter records revealed there were, at a minimum, 1,700 generators shipping 170,000 tons for off-site treatment, storage, or disposal. After reviewing generator and facility reports it was determined that an additional unreported volume of 20,000 tons was transported due to under-reporting of wastes by generators, generators who shipped wastes out of state, and generators failing to report altogether.

The unreported volume was determined by comparing the transporter-generator list against the *Massachusetts Directory of Manufacturers* to determine which firms were potential hazardous waste generating firms based on SIC codes in the Directory. Those firms in the Directory but not on the transporter-generator list were surveyed to determine if they were actually generators. The report details five reasons for the lack of hazardous waste generation reporting. They are that the firms: (1) were sales offices or warehouses, (2) were no longer in business, (3) discharged wastewaters but not hazardous wastes, (4) shipped wastes out of state, and (5) failed to report. Further investigation revealed that the minimum estimated volume of 170,000 tons per year included most of the largest generators in the state. In addition to the estimated 190,000 tons of hazardous waste generated and transported in Massachusetts, the implementation of pretreatment standards in sanitary districts with Publicly Owned Treatment Works (POTW) could raise the annual hazardous waste stream by 60,000 to 200,000 tons per year. Thus, the "minimum" true volume of off-site wastes generated in the state would be 250,000 to 395,000 tons per year.

*New York*

The New York State Department of Environmental Conservation (1979) (NYDEC) used a direct sample survey in order to develop a hazardous waste inventory. The report of the survey findings estimates that roughly 1.1 million tons are generated annually among 14 designated hazardous waste stream categories. The survey further revealed that 100 major firms produced about 90 percent of the total volume, that two counties—Erie and Niagara—produce 44 percent of total volume, and that about 50 percent of total volume is treated or disposed of on-site.

The survey method required that a sample be selected from a list of firms which were potential hazardous waste generators. Like other states, New York relied on a variety of information sources in compiling this list. The *New York State Industrial Directory, 1976*, a list developed by the New York State Department of Labor of manufacturing and mining firms, and SW-14 forms, applications filed for septic tank and industrial waste hauler registration, were consulted to compile the list. When it was completed, the list contained the names of slightly over 4,000 firms, and 1,170 were chosen for the sample. The primary instrument was a questionnaire, followed up by plant visits and/or phone interviews. The reported estimate of about 1.1 million tons is substantially lower than the 2.32 million metric tons suggested by the EPA (1982). However, the survey results were not extrapolated to reflect an estimated total volume for all industry. The survey also did not include nonmanufacturing industry hazardous waste generation. These factors may partially account for the difference in reported estimates by the NYDEC and EPA.

## SUMMARY

The initial step in properly managing hazardous wastes is learning what they are and where they are produced. RCRA defines hazardous wastes and requires the tracking of wastes by type and volume, from point of generation to point of ultimate destination. RCRA is a good first step, albeit as the chapter shows the definition of hazardous waste and the estimates using the manifest system are open to challenge.

Hazardous waste generation as defined under RCRA is strongly spatially-correlated with industrialization. Manufacturing activities are the largest generators. Other generators include the service industries, households, governmental activities, research, accidental spills, and products banned by regulatory action. There are still other hazardous wastes which are regulated under the Clean Air Act, Clean Water Act, and pretreatment standards set by sanitation districts.

Estimating the volume of hazardous waste generated at the national, regional, and state scales is an inexact algebra. The nine estimation procedures briefly discussed in this chapter include: (1) direct survey of industries, (2) examination of manifest records, (3) intense plant or process studies of specific industries, (4) extrapolation from total employed, (5) gross annual sales, (6) number of production workers, (7) value added by manufacturing, (8) number of hours worked, and (9) sales/receipts. Each procedure has advantages and disadvantages. Manifest records and annual reports from generators will probably offer the best source of information at the state level in the future. Allowances should be included to account for unreported and under-reported waste volumes and contributions to the waste stream from small and household generators. As will be seen in Chapter 6, this information is critical for the development of facility capacity and facility location decisions. It will also provide an instructive data base from which to infer the location and contents of illegal dumping and abandoned dumpsites.

## NOTES

1. The seven Federal Registers with lists of hazardous wastes are as follows:
  (1) *U.S. Federal Register*, 40 CFR Part 250, December 18, 1978, pp. 58946–58975.
  (2) ——, 40 CFR Part 116, February 16, 1979, pp. 10270–10278.
  (3) ——, 40 CFR Part 261, May 19, 1980, pp. 33084–33137.
  (4) ——, 40 CFR Part 261, July 16, 1980, pp. 47832–47836.
  (5) ——, 40 CFR Part 261, November 12, 1980, pp. 74884–74891.
  (6) ——, 40 CFR Part 261, November 25, 1980, pp. 78532–78550.
  (7) ——, 40 CFR Part 261, January 16, 1981, pp. 4614–4620.
2. U.S. Federal Register, 40 CFR Part 261, May 19, 1980.
3. Solids are converted to liquid equivalents assuming 10 pounds equals a gallon. This relationship will in fact vary with respect to particular wastes.
4. The lower total volume range estimates in Table 1-7 do not reflect estimated unreported hazardous wastes.
5. Telephone interview with Dr. Joan Berkowitz, Arthur D. Little, Inc., December 12, 1982.
6. The 18 counties in the SACOG region comprise the Sacramento Valley Area and the Upper Valley Area; see SACOG-1982.

## REFERENCES

Arthur D. Little, Inc. *A Plan for Development of Hazardous Waste Management Facilities in the New England Region.* Volume II, *Hazardous Waste Management Program of the New England Regional Commission.* Cambridge: Arthur D. Little, Inc., September 1979.

Arthur D. Little, Inc. *Hazardous Waste Generation in New England.* Prepared for the New England Council, Cambridge: Arthur D. Little, Inc., August 1982.

Booz-Allen & Hamilton, Inc., and Putnam, Hayes & Bartlett, Inc. *Hazardous Waste Generation and Commercial Hazardous Waste Management Capacity.* SW-894, Washington, D.C.: U.S. Environmental Protection Agency, December 1980.

Carson, John T., Jr., Moore, Clark D., and Bhatla, M. N. *Industrial Exotic Waste Program Findings, Conclusions and Recommendations Phase I, Final Report.* Delaware River Basin Commission, February 1979.

Council on Environmental Quality. *Environmental Quality—First Annual Report of the CEQ.* Washington, D.C.: U.S. Government Printing Office, 1970.

JRB Associates Inc. *Solid Waste Data: A Compilation of Statistics on Solid Waste Management Within the United States*. Springfield, VA: National Technical Information Service, 1981.

Massachusetts Department of Environmental Management, Bureau of Solid Waste Disposal. *Hazardous Waste Management in Massachusetts: Statewide Environmental Impact Report*. Boston: Massachusetts Department of Environmental Management, August 1982.

New York State Department of Environmental Conservation. *An Inventory of Industrial Hazardous Waste Generation in New York State*, June 1979.

Ollis, D. F., Chin, P. C., and Coffey, D. *Hazardous Waste Generation and Off-Site Disposal Patterns in California*. University of California at Davis, Chemical Engineering Department, September 1981.

Patterson Associates, Inc. *Hazardous Wastes Management in Illinois*. Project No. 40.047, Doc. No. 79/32. Chicago: Illinois Institute of Natural Resources, October 1979.

Pierson, K. M. *A Guide to the Safe Use and Disposal of Hazardous Household Products*. Boston: Metropolitan Area Planning Council, 1982.

Sacramento Area Council of Governments. *Hazardous Waste in the SACOG Region*. Sacramento, California: SACOG, February 1982.

United States Bureau of the Census. *Statistical Abstracts of the United States 1981*. Washington, D.C.: U.S. Government Printing Office, December 1981.

United States Environmental Protection Agency. *Report to Congress: Disposal of Hazardous Wastes*. SW-115, Washington, D.C.: U.S. Government Printing Office, 1974.

United States Environmental Protection Agency. *State Decision-Makers' Guide for Hazardous Waste Management*. SW-612, Washington, D.C.: U.S. Government Printing Office, 1977.

United States Environmental Protection Agency. "Hazardous Waste Generation Estimates." Memorandum prepared by E. Pappajohn, State Programs Branch, 1982.

# 2

# The Conditions for the Creation of a Wide Credibility Gap: Private and Public Control of Hazardous Waste and Waste Sites

A little over a decade ago, hazardous wastes and waste sites were a relatively obscure public health and land use issue. Isolated incidents of public controversy over municipal "sanitary" landfills were reported in the media, and less frequently in the corpus of professional and academic circles. The controversy usually centered on malodorous gaseous emissions, infestation by microbial organisms and rodent vectors, open pit fires, and aesthetically displeasing appearance. While these concerns are well justified as public health and land use issues, they are dwarfed by over four decades of improperly managing hazardous wastes. The improper management of hazardous waste has not only created public health and environmental impacts, but it also has left a deep psychological imprint of mistrust in the minds of the public that threatens to undermine efficacious management programs.

The new controversy over hazardous wastes has expanded from problems with methane emissions to concerns over toxic emissions, from vector infestation to groundwater contamination, and from open pit fires to chemical fires and explosions spewing forth contaminated plumes. A body of literature has arisen which documents the potential (and sometimes, the actual) route of contaminant migration from both controlled and uncontrolled waste sites (see Chapter 3). Consequently, hazardous waste management has become a major environmental issue with serious implications for land use planning, protection of public health, and natural resource management.

The purpose of this chapter is to review private and public efforts to control waste sites. We begin with a brief discussion of past state-of-the-art hazardous waste management practices and the typical pattern of damage incidents associated with these practices. These damage incidents are partially a result of stricter regulation of air and water pollution due to other environmental legislation. Next, we review the current federal strategy for controlling hazardous waste and waste sites. This includes an introduction to the Resource Conservation and Recovery Act (RCRA), and the Comprehensive Environment Response, Compensation, and Liability Act (CERCLA, or otherwise known as "Superfund" legislation). Together, these laws are designed to shape current state-of-the-art hazardous waste management practices and address issues of siting new facilities (RCRA) and to provide a mechanism to prioritize problematic waste sites and take remedial action to contain, detoxify, or remove them. Neither of these laws is totally ill-conceived. But they do not provide a panacea for hazardous waste management problems. They are, essentially the first, in what will hopefully prove to be a series of incremental steps, toward resolving hazardous waste and waste site problems.

## HAZARDOUS WASTE MANAGEMENT: PRIVATE CONTROL AND PAST STATE-OF-THE-ART PRACTICES

The potential for extensive damage incidents related to hazardous wastes became alarmingly clear when EPA recognized that 80 to 90 percent of hazardous wastes were being disposed of without adequate safeguards to protect human health and natural resources (EPA 1977a; EPA 1979a.) Documentation of damage incidents allowed EPA to tabulate their type and frequency. A list of over 400 such incidents was reported by the EPA (1977b) with the following six disposal/damage mechanisms (starting with the highest frequency): (1) leachate and groundwater contamination; (2) runoff and surface water contamination; (3) burning and air pollution; (4) direct contact poisoning; (5) indirect poisoning from crop contamination; (6) fire and explosion. A detailed discussion of these prototypical damage incidents appears in Chapter 3 along with the respective routes of contaminant migration through the air, soil and water.

The primary actors responsible for hazardous waste management in the private sector are generators, transporters, and handlers. Generators are firms (both manufacturing and non-manufacturing) and institutions that produce hazardous wastes as defined and discussed in Chapter 1. It is not uncommon to find that large quantity generators handle their wastes on the same property where they are produced. This is known as on-site hazardous waste management, and accounts for roughly 80 to 95 percent of hazardous waste volume (this excludes additional waste not covered under the RCRA definition). Roughly 5 to 20 percent of hazardous wastes are transported to off-site commercial hazardous waste management facilities.

Transporters of hazardous waste most frequently utilize the tanker-truck (commercially nicknamed the "18-wheeler"). Transporters may be independent or unionized, or they may be incorporated as a component of the waste-generating or commercial waste-handling firm. Technically speaking, if a generator produces hazardous waste at one facility and transports it to another facility which it owns, it is considered off-site hazardous waste management.

Commercial hazardous waste handlers are involved with recycling and treatment, storage and disposal methods (these are also called TSDFs). The number of firms receiving and handling hazardous wastes is insignificant compared to the number of waste generators. While there is a substantial market for providing hazardous waste management services, the industry faces the dilemma of trying to create new facility capacity in a climate of stiff public opposition to facility development proposals (see Chapters 6, 7 and 8).

Hazardous waste sites, per se, can be grouped into three general categories. The first, and most ignominious, is the abandoned or so-called "orphan" site (see Chapters 4 and 5). These are so termed because there usually is no legally responsible owner or operator to be found. The second category consists of existing sites — for want of a better term. These include operating sites (with a license or a permit) and sites not in operation, but not abandoned. In other words, clear legal responsibility for these sites is understood. The third category consists of accidental spill sites and surreptitious dumping sites.

Much attention has been focused on the commercial, off-site hazardous waste handlers. Excluding very small waste handling firms (e.g., those that only use incineration), there were about ten regional waste processing plants in the nation in 1974 (EPA 1974). These plants were operating at about 25 percent capacity and processed roughly 2.3 million metric tons per year. The EPA (1974) estimated that the industry, working at full capacity, could at best process one-quarter of the 1973 volume of generated wastes. Within a few years, the number of firms accepting hazardous wastes for treatment, storage or disposal had grown to slightly over 109 (Strauss 1977). By 1980, roughly 127 commercial facilities were in operation (Booz-Allen & Hamilton, Inc. 1980); with nine firms emerging as the industry leaders with control of 46 separate installations in operation during 1981 (Booz-Allen & Hamilton, Inc. 1982).

The historical record of hazardous waste damage incidents shows that the commercial off-site landfill and the industrial on-site landfill and surface impoundment present the most critical problems for health and resources.

Fields and Lindsey (1975) reported that the storage, treatment or land disposal of hazardous wastes (other than radioactive and pesticide wastes) was essentially unregulated by state and federal governments. The glaring absence of hazardous waste management regulations created a permissive atmosphere for private sector generators to discard their wastes at cheapest cost. Consequently, hazardous wastes were commonly disposed of in conventional sanitary landfills as well as chemical waste dumpsites.

The past state-of-the-art landfill technology was quite primitive. Rarely were liners (synthetic or soil) used to prevent leachate from migrating into groundwater resources. Thus, contaminated leachate has become a chronic pollution event. Waste site selection decisions often ignored simple planning criteria designed to segregate this form of land use from wetlands, floodplains, surface water supplies, population centers, and endangered species habitats (Anderson and Greenberg 1984). Landfill operators generally did not segregate wastes potentially subject to hazardous reactions. Essentially, landfills and dumpsites were poorly designed, operated and sited.

The same criticisms have been made with respect to surface impoundments (EPA 1978; Stein and Noyes 1981). These consist of pits, ponds, and lagoons constructed to retain process waste-waters before eventual discharge into the environment. Surface impoundments are widespread and numerous with an estimated 132,000 operational or abandoned in the United States (EPA 1978). They are used primarily by industry, publicly owned treatment works, agriculture and mining. The vast majority of surface impoundments are on-site operations since they involve an enormous volume of liquid and semi-liquid solvents and sludges.

Like the landfill and dump site, the surface impoundment was rarely lined to prevent leachate from contaminating ground water resources. Indeed, some impoundments were intentionally designed to filter out organics and heavy metals by leaching through the soil which supposedly served as a filtering mechansim. This was an accepted state-of-the-art practice by waste generators. Not only is it common to find surface impoundments located over groundwater aquifers, it is also common to find withholding lagoons adjacent to streams, lakes and estuaries (Bowley 1980). These lagoons periodically released contaminants into adjacent water bodies as a routine and permitted discharge, and are also prone to unregulated mixture with water bodies under conditions of prolonged precipitation events and flood episodes.

Storage of hazardous wastes in portable containers, tanks, and waste piles at site of generation and at off-site commercial facilities has been documented to contribute both sudden and chronic damage incidents. The portable container has often been associated with the non-sudden, chronic contamination of ground water. Portable containers include pesticide bags, cardboard boxes, and metal drums with a maximum volume equal to 110 gallons. The metal drum was widely used to package wastes for transportation. Drums were often disposed of in landfills, where they eventually corroded and released their waste content. Drum storage also presents a potential non-sudden, leakage event. If drums are stored above ground without a cement pad and roof enclosure, they are likely to come into contact with precipitation which expedites the corrosion-leakage cycle.

The past state-of-the-art in drum storage could also lead to explosion and fire, a sudden damage event readily sensationalized by the media. The Chemical Control Corporation explosion in Elizabeth, New Jersey drew attention to the common practice of not segregating drums containing volatile wastes prone to chemical reaction (see Chapter 3).

Tanks used for the storage of hazardous wastes have been determined to present both sudden and non-sudden damage incidents. Some portion of the Chemical Control Corporation explosion and fire included wastes stored in above-ground tanks. This incident makes manifest the danger of storing ignitable and reactive wastes without safe separation distances or appropriate engineering design controls. Above-ground tanks have also been observed to breach or crack and leak the waste content slowly over time and create a non-sudden damage event via contaminated run-off or leachate.

Underground tanks used for storage of hazardous wastes have frequently been noted to present a chronic, leakage problem (Pierson 1982). Underground tanks usually have a useful life of 40 years (American Petroleum Institute 1981). These tanks are subject to stress from the freeze-thaw cycle of the soil and from land subsidence, corrosion and cracking (especially around fittings). The potential for leakage is exacerbated by the fact that many local fire ordinances require that tanks containing flammable liquids be placed underground. While this requirement substantially limits damage from explosion and fire it does little to protect groundwater resources.

Waste piles, which have been identified as containing hazardous wastes, are another form of hazardous waste storage that have caused damage incidents. Waste piles are common to mining and agricultural operations, but they are also found in conjunction with manufacturing operations. It has not been standard practice to place waste piles on cement pads with roof covering and enclosure. Thus, the piles have been exposed to direct contact with precipitation and have subsequently contributed toxic contaminants to run-off.

Incineration of hazardous wastes has presented a potential health hazard for some time (EPA 1980a). Open-pit burning and open incineration are the worst practices. These two types of incineration have no air pollution control devices to limit toxic emissions. As the toxic constituents eventually settle out of the atmosphere they are a potential cause of direct contact poisoning of humans; or as they bioaccumulate in crops, they are a potential cause of indirect poisoning. Other forms of incineration such as rotary kiln, multiple hearth and fluidized bed combustion may have pollution control devices, but they have not been shown to consistently and effectively destroy or remove organic hazardous constituents from stack emissions.

Another form of private control over hazardous wastes and waste sites derives from the insurance underwriters industry. Underwriters are very sensitive to potentially costly liability litigation. Humpstone (1979) explains that the comprehensive general liability (CGL) policy offered to firms dealing with toxic materials was standardized in 1965 by the insurance industry such that coverage policies would be comparable among competing carriers. The standard CGL policy, at that time, did not distinguish coverage according to sudden and non-sudden categories. However, Humpstone argues that widespread concern among underwriters led to deletion of non-sudden coverage in policies in 1971 because of court ordered liability awards to victims of the Minimata Bay, mercury poisoning incident in Kuamoto, Japan. Roughly 1,500 people had been afflicted with the mercury poisoning from eating fish exposed to the mercury, and were subsequently awarded between $77,000 and $87,000 apiece. Fearing a similar rash of litigation, especially with regard to hazardous waste sites, the insurance industry would not provide non-sudden coverage until about 1974. It was at this time that the insurance industry began once again to insure firms against the chronic damage event, and policies that were written were subject to a number of important exemptions and a risk analysis (these are discussed later in this chapter).

The private sector has suffered from a number of other deficiencies with regard to controlling waste and waste sites. In terms of abandoned waste sites, industry has not conducted long-term surveillance after the useful life of the site (EPA 1974; Fields and Lindsey 1975; EPA 1977b). Existing sites as well as abandoned sites, and some fraction of hazardous waste generators followed the common practice of externalizing the costs of appropriate hazardous waste management because of the absence of regulatory controls. The volume of wastes was increasing by roughly three to ten percent (or more) per year.

Summarizing, due to the poor siting of waste disposal sites, the primitive technology employed, the haphazard management procedures, and the increase in chemical production, it was only a matter of time before some of the toxic contaminants re-emerged as a critical environmental problem.

## PUBLIC CONTROL OF HAZARDOUS WASTE
## MANAGEMENT AND WASTE SITES: AN OVERVIEW

It would be too easy and indeed misleading to blame industry alone for the hazardous waste problem. The household unit, as pointed out in Chapter 1, contributes to the hazardous waste stream, as do the public sector activities of government. Industry, the public, and the government are tied together by the product-oriented economy of the American consumer.

Federal regulation of toxic and hazardous substances in the environment has been an incremental process. At times, Congress has been influenced by warnings concerning the widespread diffusion of pesticides (Carson 1964) and the "closing circle" of chemical contaminants which threaten human health and the environment (Commoner 1971). Consequently, legislation has been enacted by Congress to address the contamination of air, land, and water resources. Controlling hazardous substances in any one of these areas has had the effect of increasing the volume of hazardous residues in other areas. For example, restricting the toxic content of industrial wastewater dischargers with pre-treatment requirements causes an increase in the volume of toxic sludges generated which have to be treated or land disposed. As air and water pollution legislation limited the emissions from the stack and pipe, the volume and constituents of waste residues increased and diversified into an essentially unregulated class of potentially dangerous land pollutants.

Public control of hazardous waste had been difficult for a number of reasons. One reason was the lack of a clear definition of hazardous wastes until the enactment of RCRA. While various agencies controlled hazardous substances, there was no clear statutory authority to control hazardous wastes. What is now defined as hazardous waste under authority of RCRA often slipped through the gaps in Congressional legislation and the regulatory authority of federal agencies. Table 2-1 shows various legislation and administering agencies for hazardous substance control. These laws have been discussed elsewhere in detail and therefore will not be reviewed here (see Table 2-1). An analogy to these laws regulating hazardous waste can be made to Baram's (1979) description of environmental carcinogens and how they slip through the regulatory cracks.

> Each of these agencies has statutory authority to regulate the use and emission of *some* of the substances, from *some* of the sources, in *some* of the pathways, for the purposes of protecting *some* of the population under *some* circumstances.

## TABLE 2-1

## Federal Legislation Addressing Hazardous Substances

---

AIR POLLUTION LEGISLATION

Clean Air Act 1963

Authorized Federal government to control air pollution. (Department of Health, Education and Welfare)

Clean Air Act Amendments 1970, 1977

Authorizes the Environmental Protection Agency to set national ambient air quality standards (health-based standards), and an implementation program through air quality control regions. Also allows EPA to regulate emissions from mobile and stationary sources. Control of point source emission of hazardous air pollutants.

WATER POLLUTION LEGISLATION

Water Pollution Control Act 1948

Temporary Federal authorization to provide sewage, and water-treatment facility low interest loans.

Water Quality Improvement Act 1970

Authority for Federal control of hazardous contaminants, and oil spills from vessels and drilling operations.

Marine Protection, Research, and Sanctuaries Act 1972

Also known as the Ocean Dumping Act, allows the EPA to regulate ocean disposal of sludges and hazardous materials.

Safe Drinking Water Act 1974

Allows EPA to set health based standards for hazardous substances such as trihalomethanes, synthetic organics, and inorganic elements in public water supplies. Regulation of underground injection of materials. Provides authority to develop federal-state control of groundwater resources.

Clean Water Act Amendments 1972, 1977

Provided EPA with authority to establish limits for point and non-point discharges of contaminants into waterways. Also provides authority for EPA to develop water quality standards indicating water quality criteria and water use designation. Establishes mechanism for statewide planning for prevention, reduction, and elimination of pollution.

LEGISLATION ADDRESSING PESTICIDES, FOODS, CONSUMER PRODUCTS, THE WORKPLACE, AND THE GENERAL ENVIRONMENT

Federal Food, Drug and Cosmetic Act 1958, 1962

Authorizes the Food and Drug Administration of the Health and Human Services Administration to require safety and performance testing of new food, drug, and cosmetic products. The Delaney Amendment specifically bars the use of substances in foods which have shown carcinogenic potential based on animal tests.

Federal Insecticide, Fungicide and Rodenticide Acts 1972, 1975

## TABLE 2-1 (Continued)

### Federal Legislation Addressing Hazardous Substances

Authorizes the EPA to require the registration of all pesticides; establish guidelines for their use, storage, transportation, and disposal. Also authorizes EPA to require the registration of establishments that produce pesticides.

Consumer Product Safety Act 1972; and the Federal Hazardous Substances Act 1960, 1969

Authorizes the Consumer Product Safety Commission to prevent or limit public exposure to hazardous substances in consumer products. The act does not extend to tobacco, food, drugs, or cosmetics.

Occupational Health and Safety Act 1970

Authorizes the Occupational Health and Safety Administration of the Department of Labor to set workplace exposure standards so that employees will not suffer impairment of health or functional capacity. Also established the National Institute for Occupational Safety and Health to conduct research to develop workplace exposure standards.

Atomic Energy Act 1954

Established the Nuclear Regulatory Commission to regulate release of radioactive wastes into the environment.

National Environmental Policy Act 1969

Authorizes EPA to require the preparation of Environmental Impact Statements to document short-term and long-term impacts of "significant Federal actions."

HAZARDOUS WASTES AND HAZARDOUS SUBSTANCES
RELEASE LEGISLATION

Resource Conservation and Recovery Act 1976

Authorizes EPA to establish requirements for generators, transporters, and managers of hazardous waste facilities. Establishes a cradle-to-grave tracking system for hazardous wastes. Establishes minimum national criteria for the design and operation of treatment, storage, and disposal facilities. Requires a national listing of waste sites.

Comprehensive Environmental Response, Compensation, and Liability Act 1980

Authorizes the EPA to amend the National Contingency Plan with a hazardous substance response plan. Establishes a National Priority List of waste sites requiring removal or remedial action. Establishes the $1.6 billion "Superfund" to provide money for taking action vis-à-vis the National Priority List.

Toxic Substances Control Act 1976

Authorizes EPA to require pre-market toxicological testing of new chemicals. Also authorizes EPA to require registration of all existing chemicals and allow selected testing requirements. EPA is delegated broad discretion for banning or limiting the use of substances which pose an "unreasonable risk to human health or the environment."

Sources: Adapted from the cited acts; supplemented with adaptations from Baram 1976; Lippmann and Schlesinger 1979; Sassnet 1978; Task Force On Environmental Cancer and Heart and Lung Disease 1978 (see References).

RCRA was enacted in 1976 as another step in the incremental process to control hazardous pollutants, this time with specific emphasis on defining and regulating hazardous waste. This was another step toward closing the circle to protect human health and the environment.

Hailed as a comprehensive planning strategy, The Resource Conservation and Recovery Act of 1976 (RCRA) was soon criticized because it primarily addressed existing and new generators, transporters and handlers but failed to anticipate the need for controlling abandoned sites (Jorling 1979). As is often the case with complex environmental problems, the intended "comprehensive" legislation is eventually revealed to be an incremental step. In 1980 Congress enacted the Comprehensive Environmental Response, Compensation, and Liability Act (CERCLA) to deal with abandoned waste sites. The next two sections deal with RCRA and CERCLA, respectively. Each law is described with respect to its goals and objectives, implementation strategies, and implications for protecting human health and the environment.

## CONTROLLING EXISTING AND NEW HAZARDOUS WASTE GENERATORS, TRANSPORTERS, AND HANDLERS: RCRA

The major goal of RCRA is to replace past state-of-the-art hazardous waste techonology and management practices prone to damage incidents with a standardized technology and management system that will substantially diminish, if not eliminate, the potential for damage events. The objectives selected by EPA to achieve the goal of RCRA are primarily based on a "pathway approach" of control (EPA 1977b). The underlying philosphy of this approach is that a system can be created to develop adequate treatment and disposal capacity, to minimize cost to society while protecting human health and the environment, to recover materials and energy, and to assign the costs of such a system efficiently and equitably to generators. EPA (1977b; 1980b) prioritized the following waste management control options: (1) waste reduction; (2) waste separation and concentration; (3) waste exchange; (4) energy and material recovery; (5) waste incineration and/or treatment; and last in priority but unfortunately not last in practice, (6) secure storage and/or disposal.

A critical characteristic of EPA's pathway approach control philosophy is that it essentially relies on market mechanisms to realize the goal of the law. EPA, and where appropriate, the corresponding state regulatory agencies are responsible for identifying, defining, and enforcing a management system designed to protect the integrity of air, land, and water pathways.

But generators, transporters, and handlers of hazardous wastes are allowed much freedom in choosing options within the system to achieve compliance. The underlying rationale of the policy is that the regulatory effort should concentrate on channeling the wastes to "safe" or "environmentally adequate" processes and facilities; the corporate manager and technical decisionmaker can choose the most economic option. It is also suggested that the regulated system will spur generators and handlers to devise innovative, cost-efficient management alternatives consistent with protecting the integrity of environmental pathways. Like many other regulatory schemes, RCRA has been subject to good use and abuse by virtue of its underlying philosophy and the harsh reality of implementation. Some of these issues are considered in this chapter and in Chapter 8. We now turn to an overview of the key provisions of RCRA and its implementation schedule and strategy.

Public Law 94-580, the Resource Conservation and Recovery Act of 1976 contains eight subtitles. Subtitle C — Hazardous Waste Management, is most relevant to planners at the state, county and local level.

RCRA, Subtitle C is comprised of thirteen separate sections (Table 2-2).

### TABLE 2-2

### RCRA Subtitle C — Hazardous Waste Management

| Section: | Title |
|----------|-------|
| 3001 | Identification and Listing of Hazardous Waste |
| 3002 | Standards Applicable to Generators of Hazardous Waste |
| 3003 | Standards Applicable to Transporters of Hazardous Waste |
| 3004 | Standards Applicable to Owners and Operators of Hazardous Waste Treatment, Storage, and Disposal Facilities |
| 3005 | Permits for Treatment, Storage, or Disposal of Hazardous Waste |
| 3006 | Authorized State Hazardous Waste Programs |
| 3007 | Inspections |
| 3008 | Federal Enforcement |
| 3009 | Retention of State Authority |
| 3010 | Effective Date |
| 3011 | Authorization of Assistance to States |
| 3012 | State Inventory Programs |
| 3013 | Monitoring Analysis and Testing |

The first seven sections form the critical provisions designed to overhaul hazardous waste management in the United States. EPA has promulgated regulations to implement these sections. The definition of hazardous waste as stated in Chapter 1 is found under Subtitle A — General Provision, Section 1004 (5).

### Section 3001: Identification and Listing of Hazardous Wastes

This section of RCRA was briefly discussed in Chapter 1. Essentially, it is the mechanism for categorizing which wastes are to be regulated by definition. To reiterate, solid wastes, which include solids, semi-solids, liquids, and contained gases, may be considered hazardous wastes if listed under 40 CFR Part 261.31 to 261.33. These hazardous wastes and waste streams are listed in Subparts C and D. As of July 1, 1983 there are many listed categories, and a single category may contain a waste stream with dozens (or more) of individual hazardous constituents. Wastes which are regulated as hazardous wastes but are not listed are included by virtue of identifying their ignitable (261.21), corrosive (261.22), reactive (261.23), or toxic (261.24) characteristics (see Chapter 1, figure 1-1).

There are a number of issues concerning identification and listing of hazardous wastes and waste streams. One issue concerns the categories of wastes that are excluded from regulation under RCRA. There are ten major categories of excluded wastes (Table 2-3) as outlined under 40 CFR Part 261.4. The rationale for exclusion is waste stream specific. However, there are three basic rationales. One rationale is that certain waste streams are already regulated, such as industrial point source discharges which are regulated under the Clean Water Act. A second rationale is that not enough evidence is available to provide persuasive proof that the waste stream is hazardous. This is currently the case for fly ash and bottom ash from coal combustion processes. It should be noted that EPA may rescind such exclusions in the future, provided a preponderance of evidence shows that the waste stream exhibits any of the four characteristics mentioned above. The third rationale is that streams such as household wastes are so numerous and contain such a constellation of constituents that it would be humanly impossible to regulate the entire volume.

A second issue concerns what is called the small generator exemption. The preamble to the federal regulations states that over 90 percent of the hazardous waste stream is produced by roughly 10 percent of all generators and that regulation of all generators (roughly 700,000 industrial and business activities) would be near impossible. Consequently small quantity generators are relieved of a majority of (but not all) regulatory requirements.

## TABLE 2-3

## Waste Categories Excluded From RCRA Regulation

Wastes excluded because they are not defined as "solid wastes."

1.  Domestic sewage (untreated sanitary waste) and mixtures of domestic sewage that pass through a sewer system to a publicly owned treatment works.

2.  Point source industrial wastewater discharges regulated under Section 402 of the Clean Water Act.

3.  Irrigation return flows.

4.  Radioactive wastes and radioactive by-products defined by the Atomic Energy Act of 1954.

5.  Materials subjected to in-situ mining extraction processes that are left in the ground.

Solid wastes not regulated as hazardous wastes.

1.  Household wastes such as garbage, trash, and sanitary wastes in septic tanks generated by single and multiple residences, hotels, and motels.

2.  Solid wastes returned to the soil as fertilizers from the growing and harvesting of agricultural crops and the raising of animals (including animal manures).

3.  Mining overburden returned to the mine site.

4.  Fly ash waste, bottom ash waste, slag waste, and flue gas emission control waste generated from coal or fossil fuel combustion.

5.  Drilling fluids and other wastes from exploration, development, or production of crude oil, natural gas, or geothermal energy.

---

A small quantity generator as defined by RCRA is a person who produces less than 1,000 kilograms (1 metric ton: equivalent to 2205 pounds) in a calendar month of any listed or characteristic hazardous wastes. An exception is made for acute hazardous wastes (261.33 (e)), whereby a small quantity generator is any person who produces less than 1 kilogram in any given calendar month. However, if a generator accumulates over 1,000 kilograms of hazardous wastes or more than 1 kilogram of acute hazardous wastes in any given calendar month, even though these wastes may have been generated over a period of months, the generator is not eligible for exemption as a small quantity generator. RCRA has been criticized because it encourages firms to get rid of their wastes before they accumulate in excess of the regulatory cut-off volumes. The problem caused by this policy is that the generator may send the small quantity waste stream to a licensed hazardous waste facility; a re-use, reclamation, or recycling facility; or an industrial or municipal solid waste facility. The municipal solid waste facility may be ill-equipped to adequately manage the long-term storage or disposal of these wastes.

The states have varied their approach to setting small quantity cut-off volumes. Some states are more demanding than the EPA (Table 2-4).[2] California, New Hampshire, New Jersey, New York, and some other New England and Mid-Atlantic states allow small-quantity generator exemptions to persons generating under 100 kilograms of hazardous waste in a calendar month. Massachusetts sets the cut-off at 20 kilograms per month. California and Rhode Island do not allow exemption; cut-off volumes in these states are 0 kilograms.

Another issue related to Section 3001—Identification and Listing of Hazardous Wastes—involves special consideration for reusable and recyclable waste streams. Since reuse and recycling of hazardous wastes is a preferred management option compared to destruction or disposal, the EPA has written regulatory language to encourage its use. The regulation specifies that any listed hazardous waste in Subpart D is subject to: notification to EPA (Table 2-2: Section 3010), standards for transportation, and storage before reuse or recycling.[3] The same regulation allows wastes (other than sludges) deemed hazardous because of characteristic criteria to be exempt from Subtitle C if they are to be "beneficially used or reused or legitimately recycled or reclaimed."[4] The disadvantages of this policy are discussed in Chapter 8.

There are at least three other issues related to Section 3001. First, EPA has determined that the mixture of hazardous wastes with other forms of solid waste, regardless of the concentration of the hazardous waste constituent, renders the entire waste stream subject to Subtitle C. Second, the regulations also allow petitions for delisting wastes in two ways. One way is for a generator to have them removed from the Subpart D list (Appendix A) by arguing that the waste stream produced is different from the listed waste stream.[5] The other way to avoid regulatory inclusion is by showing the EPA analytical technique accepted for determining hazardous characteristics of a waste was faulty.[6] The third issue concerns "empty" containers and the specifications for allowable residues and requirements for rinsing.[7]

## Section 3002: Standards Applicable to Generators of Hazardous Waste

Regulations designed to set standards for generators are found in Part 262[8] which is comprised of five Subparts. These regulations constitute the second basic method used to implement the pathway control strategy. The first method was the Section 3001 classification of hazardous wastes. This second method introduces the cradle-to-grave manifest system which is designed to track hazardous wastes from their point of generation to their

## TABLE 2-4
## State Hazardous Waste Management Program Characteristics

| State | Estimated[1] Volume Generation (MMT) | Small[2] Generator Exemption (KG) | Phase 1 State[2] Interim Authorization | Number[3] Of Active/Inactive Waste Sites | Federal[3] Support For Inventories ($1000) |
|---|---|---|---|---|---|
| *Region I* | | | | | |
| Connecticut | 0.61 | 1000 | 4/21/82 | 197 | 128 |
| Maine | 0.13 | 200 | 3/18/81 | 67 | 43 |
| Massachusetts | 0.82 | 20 | 2/25/81 | 321 | 208 |
| New Hampshire | 0.10 | 100 | 11/3/81 | 54 | 35 |
| Rhode Island | 0.19 | 0 | 5/29/81 | 46 | 30 |
| Vermont | 0.03 | 100 | 1/15/81 | 20 | 25 |
| *Region II* | | | | | |
| New Jersey | 3.12 | 100 | 2/2/83 | 663 | 430 |
| New York | 2.32 | 100 | | 1008 | 667 |
| Puerto Rico | 0.56 | 1000 | 10/14/82 | 136 | 88 |
| *Region III* | | | | | |
| Delaware | 0.30 | 1000 | 2/25/81 | 61 | 40 |
| Maryland | 0.59 | 1000 | 7/8/81 | 143 | 93 |
| Pennsylvania | 2.55 | 1000 | 5/26/81 | 748 | 486 |
| Virginia | 1.22 | 1000 | 11/3/81 | 231 | 150 |
| West Virgina | 0.79 | 1000 | | 153 | 99 |

**TABLE 2-4 (Continued)**

**State Hazardous Waste Management Program Characteristics**

| State | Estimated[1] Volume Generation (MMT) | Small[2] Generator Exemption (KG) | Phase I State[2] Interim Authorization | Number[3] Of Active/Inactive Waste Sites | Federal[3] Support For Inventories ($1000) |
|---|---|---|---|---|---|
| *Region IV* | | | | | |
| Alabama | 0.73 | 1000 | 2/25/81 | 392 | 254 |
| Florida | 0.96 | 1000 | 5/19/82 | 260 | 169 |
| Georgia | 0.70 | 1000 | 2/3/81 | 534 | 347 |
| Kentucky | 0.70 | 1000 | 4/1/81 | 244 | 158 |
| Mississippi | 0.34 | 1000 | 1/7/81 | 233 | 151 |
| North Carolina | 1.33 | 1000 | 12/18/80 | 628 | 408 |
| South Carolina | 1.14 | 100 | 2/25/81 | 111 | 72 |
| Tennessee | 1.82 | 1000 | 7/16/81 | 573 | 372 |
| *Region V* | | | | | |
| Illinois | 2.53 | 1000 | 5/17/82 | 543 | 353 |
| Indiana | 1.28 | 1000 | 8/18/82 | 435 | 282 |
| Michigan | 1.99 | 100 | | 824 | 405 |
| Minnesota | 0.36 | 1000 | | 198 | 129 |
| Ohio | 2.57 | 1000 | | 764 | 496 |
| Wisconsin | 0.63 | 1000 | 1/15/82 | 202 | 131 |
| *Region VI* | | | | | |
| Arkansas | 0.37 | 1000 | 11/18/80 | 227 | 147 |
| Louisiana | 1.25 | case-by-case basis | 12/19/80 | 293 | 190 |

## TABLE 2-4 (Continued)

### State Hazardous Waste Management Program Characteristics

| State | Estimated[1] Volume Generation (MMT) | Small[2] Generator Exemption (KG) | Phase 1 State[2] Interim Authorization | Number[3] Of Active/Inactive Waste Sites | Federal[3] Support For Inventories ($1000) |
|---|---|---|---|---|---|
| New Mexico | 0.06 | 1000 | | 144 | 93 |
| Oklahoma | 0.23 | 1000 | 1/14/81 | 406 | 263 |
| Texas | 3.01 | 1000 | 12/24/80 | 1043 | 677 |
| *Region VII* | | | | | |
| Iowa | 0.30 | 100 | 1/30/81 | 299 | 194 |
| Kansas | 0.35 | 100 | 9/21/81 | 261 | 169 |
| Missouri | 0.91 | 100 | | 426 | 277 |
| Nebraska | 0.12 | 1000 | 5/14/82 | 169 | 110 |
| *Region VIII* | | | | | |
| Colorado | 0.18 | 1000 | | 239 | 155 |
| Montana | 0.05 | 1000 | 2/26/81 | 79 | 51 |
| North Dakota | 0.03 | 1000 | 12/20/80 | 31 | 25 |
| South Dakota | 0.01 | 1000 | | 40 | 26 |
| Utah | 0.11 | 1000 | 12/12/80 | 101 | 66 |
| Wyoming | 0.04 | 1000 | | 65 | 42 |
| *Region IX* | | | | | |
| Arizona | 0.16 | 1000 | 8/18/82 | 140 | 91 |
| California | 2.63 | 0 | 6/4/81 | 860 | 558 |
| Hawaii | 0.03 | 1000 | | 72 | 47 |
| Nevada | 0.05 | 1000 | | 113 | 73 |

## TABLE 2-4 (Continued)

## State Hazardous Waste Management Program Characteristics

| State | Estimated[1] Volume Generation (MMT) | Small[2] Generator Exemption (KG) | Phase 1 State[2] Interim Authorization | Number[3] Of Active/Inactive Waste Sites | Federal[3] Support For Inventories ($1000) |
|---|---|---|---|---|---|
| *Region X* | | | | | |
| Alaska | 0.13 | 1000 | | 93 | 60 |
| Idaho | 0.20 | cooperative arrangement | | 107 | 69 |
| Oregon | 0.38 | case-by-case ruling | 6/16/81 | 159 | 103 |
| Washington | 0.08 | sliding scale-degree of hazard | | 402 | 261 |

Notes: [1]See Chapter 1, Table 1-6.
[2]Footnote 2, Chapter 2; and Simcoe, B.: State Small Quantity Hazardous Waste Generator Survey, Association of State and Territorial Solid Waste Management Officials, September, 1983.
[3]48 FR P. 5688 (February 7, 1983).

ultimate destination. Quarles (1982) points out that the "clear purpose of the statute is to place. . .primary responsibility on the waste generators." The various Subparts define who is a generator; what procedures are to be used to determine waste stream regulatory inclusion; manifest and pre-transport requirements; recordkeeping; and special considerations.

EPA defined generator as "any person, by site, whose act or process produces hazardous waste identified or listed in Part 261."[9] This was later refined to place responsibility on the person who "first" causes the waste to become subject to the regulation (Quarles 1982). One implication of this definition is that a number of persons may actually handle the waste, such as the generator, transporter, and handler. Legal responsibility may fall solely on the generator, or all three persons if they enter into a special agreement. Generators who treat, store, or dispose of hazardous wastes on-site are subject to most of the regulations under Section 3002, except for the manifest requirement, since the waste does not leave the site of generation.

The generator is required to obtain an EPA identification number before handling hazardous waste on-site or sending it off-site.[10] Generators are also responsible for making the initial determination of whether the waste is hazardous.[11] The hazardous determination procedure usually consists of checking for waste category exclusion; and if the waste is not excluded from regulation, the generator must determine if the constituent is a listed waste or characteristic waste. To determine if the constituent is a characteristic waste, the generator must test for such characteristics using methods prescribed by EPA,[12] or an equivalent test. A generator may assume characteristics to be present based on knowledge of either the material or processes used.

The manifest requirements are outlined under Subpart B.[13] The manifest is similar to a shipping docket or bill-of-lading. The information required is the name and address of a permitted facility designated to receive the waste; an alternative permitted facility (in case of emergency); a manifest document number; the generator's name, address, and EPA identification number; EPA identification number of the transporter; and the description and quantity of each waste. The manifest must also be signed and dated to show a good-faith effort to comply with the regulation.

Hazardous wastes to be transported off-site are subject to pre-transport requirements.[14] The regulations refer specifically to packaging, labeling, and placarding according to standards set by the Department of Transportation.

The EPA regulation regarding accumulation period specifies a 90-day limit for generators. If a generator stores hazardous waste on-site, the wastes must be placed in containers, labeled, and marked with the date just as if the wastes were being sent off-site. Generators may store wastes up to

90 days, beyond which they must be permitted as a treatment, storage, or disposal facility (TSDF). This requirement forces a distinction between the generator and TSDF unless the generator is also an on-site, permitted, TSDF.

The standards for generators also include requirements for recordkeeping and reporting.[15] Both manifest records and records of test results used to determine if wastes are hazardous are to be kept on file by generators for a period of three years. Generators are also required to submit an annual report to EPA or an authorized state agency by March 1 for the preceding year. The annual report requires generators shipping wastes off-site to specify the types and quantities of wastes and transporters used and to identify the designated receiving facilities. Provision is made for exception reporting, whereby the generator who does not receive a signed copy of the manifest from the designated TSDF within 35 days of shipment has another ten days to report on the disposition of the waste and the efforts made to determine such disposition.

There are two special conditions under Section 3002.[16] First, generators intending to export hazardous wastes to a foreign country or to import hazardous wastes from a foreign country must notify the EPA (this authority is not delegated to state agencies). The notification must include information on waste type, volume, destination, and point of departure. The second condition applies to farmers disposing of waste pesticides which are hazardous wastes. Farmers are not subject to regulations for generators if empty containers are triple rinsed, or if residues are disposed of consistent with instructions on the pesticide label.

### Section 3003: Standards Applicable to Transporters of Hazardous Waste

Three Subparts appear under this Section.[17] The first Subpart requires that transporters of hazardous waste obtain an EPA identification number prior to accepting any hazardous wastes for shipment. The actual shipment process is regulated by virtue of regulations promulgated by the Department of Transportation pursuant to the Hazardous Materials Transportation Act.[18]

The second Subpart requires transporters to comply with the manifest system. This applies primarily to wastes that go to off-site destinations. Transporters are also required to maintain signed copies of manifest records for a period of three years. The transporters' manifest copies are required to accompany the actual shipment except when wastes are delivered by rail or water (bulk shipment). In these cases the signed manifest may be sent to the receiving TSDF independent of the waste shipment. Transporters may store shipments for no longer than ten days; beyond that period a transporter would have to obtain a permit as a TSDF.

The final Subpart of Section 3003 outlines the actions required of transporters in the event of uncontrolled discharges.[19] The transporter is required to take immediate action by notifying local, state or federal authorities. The transporter is also required to clean up the uncontrolled discharge so that it no longer presents a hazard to human health or the environment. However, the actual clean-up process is not specified in the regulations, perhaps because of the wide variety of substances and conditions existing at a spill or leakage site. Massachusetts, for example, requires transporters to carry the Department of Transportation *Emergency Response Guidebook* (1980) which spells out initial actions such as evacuation and containment of spills to protect human health.[20]

### Section 3004: Standards Applicable to Owners and Operators of Hazardous Waste Treatment, Storage, and Disposal Facilities

The intent of Section 3004 is to control the handling of hazardous wastes by TSDFs. Often referred to as the "technology forcing" mechanism of RCRA, Section 3004 incorporates performance, design and operations standards. Regulations for this Section apply to "new" TSDFs. Facilities already constructed and in operation (existing facilities) will eventually be required to comply with these regulations. Existing facilities were not constructed nor are they managed to the rigorous standards outlined under Section 3004. Indeed, the EPA and appropriate state authorities would have to close most existing facilities if the "new" TSDF regulations were applied to existing facilities.

Such an action would be disastrous for both the environment and the economy. The EPA utilized a provision in Section 3005 (e) to allow many facilities to continue operations under interim status. This provision requires that owners or operators of TSDFs notify EPA and apply for a permit according to regulations written under Section 3005. Roughly 10,000 notifications were filed by November, 1980 (Quarles 1982).

Currently, regulations for Section 3004 appear in: 40 CFR Part 264, May 19, 1980; 40 CFR Part 264, July 1, 1982; and, 40 CFR Part 264, July 26, 1982. There are 15 Subparts to Part 264. A brief discussion of these lengthy regulations follows. A more detailed discussion is available in Quarles (1982) and in the preamble to the Federal Registers mentioned above.

*Standards of Performance and Operations—Subparts A–H*

Subpart A of 264 states that the purpose of these regulations is to "establish minimum national standards which define the acceptable management of hazardous waste."[21] The regulations apply to all TSDFs except those facilities which handle only excluded wastes or meet the requirements of a small quantity generator exemption. As stated above, facilities in compliance with regulations specified in Part 265 are under interim status and final approval of their permit applications may occur by the latter part of 1983. At any time, however, the EPA Administrator may bring suit against an owner or operator of any facility that poses an imminent hazard by virtue of uncontrolled spills or leakage of hazardous waste into the environment.

Several general facility standards are outlined under Subpart B. Like generators and transporters, TSDFs are required to obtain an EPA identification number. Owners or operators must notify EPA before receipt of hazardous waste from a foreign source. Notification in writing must be made by owners or operators of TSDFs to generators who send their waste off-site that they have procured appropriate permits.

The general waste analysis requirements are also outlined under Subpart B. The analysis includes a detailed chemical and physical characterization of the waste based on a representative sample before the waste is transported. Owners or operators must include in the analysis a description of the treatment, storage or disposal processes to be utilized. Both testing and sampling protocols have been selected by EPA, but alternative approaches may be used upon successful petition to the EPA.[22]

Other performance standards covered in Subpart B include provision for security to keep unauthorized personnel from entering the active portion of the facility and disrupting the wastes. General inspection for facility malfunction or deterioration, erratic operation practices, and uncontrolled discharges must be made according to a written schedule, and an inspection log must be kept for at least three years. Personnel training is required to ensure effective response to emergencies including operations shutdown.

Location standards are listed under Subpart B.[23] The EPA promulgated only two location standards from an original proposed list of eight (see Chapter 6).[24] Location standards are designed to aid facility siting decisions by specifying areas that are prone to hazard conditions and are to be avoided. A more general class of siting criteria (which are somewhat similar to location standards) are discussed at length in Chapter 7.

The first location standard refers to seismic considerations. The regulation specifies that new TSDFs must not be located within 200 feet of a fault which has experienced displacement in Holocene times (roughly the last 11,000 years). EPA has determined that all states are in compliance with this standard by virtue of their geographic location except all or parts of the following Western and Pacific States: Alaska, Arizona, California, Colorado, Hawaii, Idaho, Montana, Nevada, New Mexico, Utah, Washington, and Wyoming.[25] Those of us who have experienced earthquakes on the East Coast have to wonder about this regulation.

The second location standard is focused on the 100-year floodplain. Rather than banning facilities from these areas, EPA requires that owners or operators design, construct and operate the facility such that washout of any wastes is prevented. An alternative to this requirement is allowed if it can be demonstrated that the wastes can be safely removed before contact with flood waters and that the place chosen to move the wastes to is a permitted facility. Again, we have to question the wisdom of relying on engineering designs to control floodwaters.

Subparts C and D deal with preparedness and prevention requirements and contingency plan and emergency procedures, respectively. Subpart C requires that a facility be designed and operated to "minimize the possibility of a fire, explosion, or any unplanned sudden or non-sudden release" of hazardous waste into air, soil, or surface water.[26] Specific equipment is required under Subpart C such as: internal communication or alarm systems; telephone or two-way radio to contact outside agencies/authorities; portable fire extinguishers, spill control and decontamination equipment; and adequate water volume and pressure to sustain hose streams. Arrangements must also be made, or an attempt must be made, to familiarize local police and fire departments with the types of wastes handled at the facility and the types of emergency response necessary to control an unplanned release.

Subpart D is designed to spell out the contingency plan and appropriate emergency procedures. The contents of the contingency plan include: facility personnel actions in the case of an unplanned sudden or non-sudden release; arrangements with local police and fire departments, hospitals, contractors and emergency response teams; name, address and phone numbers of persons qualified to act as emergency coordinators; a list of all emergency equipment; and an evacuation plan for facility personnel. The emergency procedures requirement outlines how the contingency plan should be operationalized.

Subpart E includes requirements for maintaining the manifest system, recordkeeping, and reporting. These requirements apply to both on-site and off-site facilities. The manifest documents for owners or operators of TSDFs are the same as for generators and transporters. Owners or operators of facilities are required to sign copies of the manifest documents and give them to the transporter and return a copy to the generator within 30 days. Shipments that have significant discrepancies with manifest specifications must be noted and the owner or operator must attempt to reconcile such discrepancies with the generator or transporter.

Owners or operators of facilities are required under this Subpart to submit an annual report by March 1 of each year to describe the activities of the facility for the previous year. The annual report must include: facility EPA identification number; the EPA identification number of all generators from which the facility has accepted wastes; the quantity and types of wastes received; the method of treatment; storage or disposal for each waste; and the most recent facility closure and post-closure cost estimates.

The EPA proposed groundwater protection regulations appear under Part 264, Subpart F, issued on July 26, 1982, which became effective in January of 1983. A similar Subpart is found under Part 265 authorized by Section 3005 and is applicable to TSDFs under the interim status period. Interim status applies to facilities that applied for operating status under RCRA before the final regulations were issued. Such facilities could be issued an interim operating status, but not a final operating permit. There are three key elements to Subpart F of Part 264 regulations: (1) contaminant detection monitoring; (2) compliance monitoring; and (3) a corrective action program. The thread which ties these three elements together is the groundwater protection standard specified in the facility permit and the focus on leachate and the contamination plume. Notwithstanding the requirements of these regulations, the success of any groundwater protection scheme is tenuous at best (see Chapters 3, 7 and 8 for further discussions).

Subpart F of Part 264 applies to both new and existing facilities; specifically it applies to surface impoundments, landfills, waste piles, and land treatment units. However, some facilities are exempt from this requirement if they can demonstrate a very low or a nonexistent threat of groundwater contamination. Other facilities are exempt if they choose the more stringent pollution control approach which includes a leachate detection, collection and removal system.

The major focus of this requirement is on leachate which carries hazardous constituents. There are about 380 hazardous constituents identified under Part 261 that are included under this requirement.[17] Presently, only 14 of these hazardous constituents have established concentration limits,[28] based on maximum concentration limits set under the Safe Drinking Water Act. Facility permits may specify all or part of the listed hazardous constituents which must be monitored according to a detection monitoring plan.

General groundwater monitoring requirements stipulate that owners and operators must install a sufficient number of wells (see discussion of Part 265, Subpart F) at locations and at sufficient depth so that an accurate representation of background water quality upgradient of the facility and the quality of water passing through the point of compliance can be determined. The monitoring program must include a description of sample collection procedures and the analytical techniques employed. A written document must also include the groundwater surface elevation of each sample, and this document is to be submitted with the annual report due March 1 of each year.

This Subpart also requires owners or operators to establish a hazardous constituent detection monitoring program to determine if leakage is occurring. Detection of indicator parameters such as pH, specific conductance, total organic carbon, or total organic halogen, as well as other constituents specified in the permit must be conducted according to a schedule. Statistical tests of significance must be employed to determine if contamination by hazardous constituents is statistically greater than background levels.

The warning mechanism explicit in this regulation is detection of leakage. If leakage containing hazardous constituents is higher than background levels (using tests of statistical significance), a permit modification incorporating a groundwater protection standard may be required with a compliance monitoring program. The groundwater protection standard states that hazardous constituents entering the uppermost aquifer underlying the waste management area beyond the point of compliance should not exceed concentration limits established under §§264.94.[29] The waste management area includes the horizontal plane of the area where the waste is stored or disposed. The point of compliance is specified in the facility permit and will most often be located at the outer edge of the waste management area, oriented such that it will be in the path of groundwater flow. This is where the groundwater monitoring well is situated, and it includes the vertical distance from the land surface to the uppermost aquifer underlying the waste management area.[30]

The compliance monitoring program is indeed flexible and will most likely be arranged on a case-by-case basis. Allowable concentration levels for hazardous constituents may be set at background levels, at maximum concentration limits set for the 14 constituents specified by the Safe Drinking Water Act, or at alternate concentration limits. This means that EPA or state permitting authorities have much discretion in amending permits. For example, hazardous constituents detected at significantly higher levels than background, yet lower than maximum concentration limits, may or may not require a corrective action program. Similarly, since there are no maximum concentration limits for the overwhelming majority of hazardous constituents, what benchmarks will be used to determine acceptable concentrations, alternate concentrations, or whether a corrective action program should be required? Very little research has been completed at the present time on these hazardous constituents (EPA 1979b.)

The compliance monitoring program lasts from the initial permit amendment through the active life of the waste management area and facility closure. If a corrective action is ongoing at the time of closure, the compliance program may be extended until the protection standard has not been exceeded for a period of three consecutive years.[31]

The goal of the corrective action program is to force compliance with the groundwater protection standard. This may require the removal or treatment in-place of hazardous constituents at excessive concentration levels. The corrective action program may be extended beyond the active life of a facility. However, owners or operators are only responsible for cleaning up a contamination plume (or part of a contamination plume) up to the property boundary. Contamination plumes migrating beyond the property boundary are subject to regulation under CERCLA.

Provisions regarding closure and post-closure care of TSDFs are particularly important for planners. Subpart G of Section 3004 specifies that all TSDFs are required to follow closure plans,[32] and owners or operators of all disposal facilities (as well as persons responsible for surface impoundments and waste piles who intend to remove the wastes at closure) must follow post-closure plans.[33] The closure performance standard may be very stringent. It requires owners or operators to control, minimize or eliminate "to the extent necessary" the post-closure escape of hazardous waste.[34] The stringency of this requirement will likely rest on the interpretation of the phrase "to the extent necessary." This implies a ministerial responsibility on the part of owners or operators and is unlike other environmental regulations which rely on phrases such as "to the extent possible."

Owners or operators are required to maintain a written closure plan on the premises. The plan has numerous inclusions, and they are all conditions of the permit. Three major inclusions are: (1) plans to partially or completely close the facility at any point during the operating life of the facility; (2) estimated maximum inventory of wastes in storage and treatment; and, (3) a 180-day notification period before beginning closure.

The post-closure care period is 30 years and applies to owners or operators of surface impoundments, waste piles, landfills, and land treatment facilities.[35] During this period, which may be extended or reduced as part of the permit, the owner or operator is required to continue groundwater monitoring and reporting and to maintain waste containment equipment. Requirements outlined under Subpart F — groundwater monitoring and protection—may be invoked as necessary during the post-closure period.

The future status of the affected property is of particular interest to planners. Regulation 264.117 (c) states that post-closure use of the property must "never be allowed to disturb the integrity of the final cover, liner(s), or any other components of any containment system" unless it is determined necessary for the proposed property use, or necessary to protect human health or the environment. The determination is to be made by either the EPA regional administrator or the appropriate state permitting authority. There is great potential for conflict here with local land use authority and traditional home-rule powers. Essentially, legal authority to reuse such properties is vested in government officials who may be far removed from the affected communities. The terms by which these officials determine reuse questions are not spelled out anywhere under RCRA (see Chapter 8).

Other planning aspects of closure and post-closure include notification and submission requirements. A plat prepared and certified by a professional surveyor must be submitted within 90 days of closure completion to the local zoning or land use authority. The plat must indicate the location and dimensions of disposal areas with respect to permanently surveyed benchmarks. The plat must also display a note stating the owner or operator's obligation to restrict site disturbance. A separate report must also be submitted which states the type, quantity and location of hazardous wastes in each landfill cell or disposal area. Finally, the property deed or other instrument examined in a title search must, in perpetuity, notify any future purchaser of the property that the land has been used to manage hazardous wastes and has restricted use. This notation may only be removed if all wastes, liners, contaminated soils, etc. are removed. Whenever such items are removed, the person responsible must enter the manifest system as a generator.

An innovative feature of Part 264 regulations is found in Subpart H — financial requirements. The objective of this regulation is to make sure that appropriate funds are available for facility closure and post-closure care and that owners or operators obtain at least minimum liability coverage for third party compensation claims. Theoretically, the financial responsibility requirements are designed to prevent new and existing facilities from becoming "Superfund" sites in the future. However, there has been some criticism to the effect that specified minimum liability insurance limits are too low (see Chapter 8).

Closure and post-closure financial responsibility must be spelled out as a permit condition for each TSDF. A written estimate of these costs, with annual inflationary adjustments, must be included as part of the closure plan (Subpart G). A variety of options are available by which owners or operators must establish financial assurance for closure or post-closure (Subpart H). The various states with authorized RCRA programs may or may not accept the full range of options outlined by EPA under this regulation. However, the options or instruments specified by state programs must be at least equivalent in coverage to the options set forth by EPA.

Liability requirements are specified for sudden and non-sudden accidental occurrences. Owners or operators of TSDFs are financially responsible to compensate third parties for bodily injury or property damage related to facility operations and accidental environmental exposure. The EPA has introduced some degree of certainty in the insurance underwriting industry by setting minimum liability coverage levels. For sudden accidental occurrences all owners or operators of TSDFs must maintain at least $1 million per occurrence, and $2 million as an annual aggregate. Legal defense costs are excluded from these amounts. For non-sudden accidental occurrences, owners or operators of surface impoundments, landfills, or land treatment facilities are required to maintain coverage at a minimum of $3 million per occurrence, and an annual aggregate of $6 million (exclusive of legal defense costs).

To this point, the discussion of Part 264 has focused on the first eight Subparts which primarily address standards of performance and operations. The next seven Subparts integrate technological standards of design and engineering along with management and operations standards for owners or operators of facilities.

*Use and Management of Containers—Subpart I*

Regulations regarding containers apply to all owners or operators of hazardous waste facilities who use them to store hazardous wastes. When containers are used to store free-standing liquid hazardous waste, they must be in good condition (free of leaks, structural defects, and severe rusting), and they must utilize compatible liner materials to avoid a chemical reaction. Containers must remain closed unless waste is entered or removed, and weekly inspections for leakage and corrosion are required.[36]

Engineering and design standards with respect to containers are found in the requirements for containment systems and closure. The design and operation standards for containment systems are a direct response to the haphazard past usage of containers for storage. Container storage areas must have an impervious base, with slope for drainage into a collection and removal system. If there is a leak, accidental spill, or accumulated precipitation, it must be removed, and if it is a listed or characteristic mixture, it must be managed as a hazardous waste. The capacity of the containment system is required to be "10% of the volume of containers or the volume of the largest container, whichever is greater."[37] The closure requirement entails complete removal of containers, and the owner or operator becomes responsible for the removed containers as any other hazardous waste generator. The regulatory intent of these requirements is to prevent container storage areas from becoming abandoned chemical dump sites.

*Tanks—Subpart J*

Regulation of tanks used to treat or store hazardous waste applies to above-ground tanks and directly addresses the poor record of past tank storage practices. Unfortunately, the regulations do not apply to below-ground tanks. At time of closure, owners or operators must remove all hazardous waste from tanks.

Design, operating, and inspection requirements under these regulations have great potential for eliminating much of the past sudden and non-sudden damage incidents.[38] Tanks are required to incorporate design standards with respect to shell strength, thickness, foundation, seams and pressure controls. Operating requirements include the following: exclusion of incompatible wastes that could react or corrode the tank; use of inner liners; controls to prevent overfilling; and for uncovered tanks, adequate freeboard to prevent overtopping. Inspection requirements for tanks are similar to those for containers, with slight differences resulting from unit design. Daily monitoring of temperature, pressure data and overfill control equipment, and weekly inspection of structural integrity and immediate surrounding area are required inspection standards.

*Surface Impoundments—Subpart K*

New surface impoundments used to treat, store or dispose of hazardous wastes are required to install a liner composed of synthetic material or a soil based mixture designed to prevent waste migration into subsurface soil and ground or surface water. Impoundments must also be designed to prevent overfilling and overtopping; and they must utilize dikes designed to prevent massive failure. However, if an owner or operator can demonstrate that alternative design, operating practices, and location characteristics will prevent hazardous constituents from migrating into ground or surface water, he is exempt from the above requirements.

Surface impoundments with double-liners are exempt from the Subpart F groundwater protection requirements. The liners and impoundment must be above the seasonal high water table. A leak detection and removal system must be in operation between the upper and lower liners.

Other requirements involve inspections, emergency repairs, closure, and post-closure care.[39] Inspections are required during and after construction or installation of the liner to assess its integrity. Weekly inspections (and inspections after storms) are required to detect overtopping, sudden liquid level drops, and liquids in the leak detection system. Owners or operators are also required to conduct weekly inspections to assess the integrity of any dikes used to contain the impoundment and its contents. Emergency repairs are required when inspections show rapid liquid loss or dike leakage. The facility contingency plan must show the ability of the owner or operator to shut off additional wastes immediately and to stop or contain leaked materials. Options for facility closure involve either removal or decontamination of waste residuals, liners, contaminated sub-soils, structures, and equipment; or removal of free liquids and stabilization of remaining wastes, installation of final covers, and implementation of post-closure monitoring and maintenance requirements.

### Waste Piles—Subpart L

Regulations under this Subpart apply to owners or operators who treat, store, or dispose of hazardous waste in piles. Facilities using piles that are enclosed by structures and which do not generate runoff or leachate are not subject to these requirements. In a regulation similar to that applying to surface impoundments, owners or operators may be exempt from these requirements if they can demonstrate prevention of waste migration.[40]

Waste piles must incorporate a liner with a leachate collection and removal system immediately above it. The waste pile must be designed to prevent runoff from at least the 25-year storm event from flowing on the active portion of the pile. Facilities using the double liner system with leachate detection, collection and removal under the waste pile are exempt from Subpart F ground water protection requirements. Exemption from Subpart F requirements may also be obtained if the pile and liner are fully above the seasonal high water table, the liner maintains its integrity, and the wastes are periodically removed to inspect the condition of the liner.

Closure requirements offer two alternatives. Owners or operators may remove or decontaminate waste residuals, liners, and other equipment; or if it is impractical to remove or decontaminate subsoils, the owner or operator may close the facility and follow post-closure care requirements applicable to landfills.

### Land Treatment—Subpart M

Owners or operators of facilities that treat or dispose of hazardous waste in land treatment units are required to design a treatment program, demonstrate its effectiveness, and monitor soil contamination in the unsaturated zone. The treatment program must be designed to degrade, transform or immobilize hazardous constituents in the treatment zone. The treatment zone can be no farther than five feet in depth, and it must be at least three feet above the seasonal high water table. Owners or operators must demonstrate the effectiveness of land treatment techniques with the aid of field tests, laboratory tests, available data, and in the case of existing facilities, with operating data. The rate and method of waste application, as well as the type and quantity of wastes, are specified as conditions of the permit.

Monitoring the unsaturated zone under the land treatment unit is similar to monitoring groundwater, except, in this case the soils are tested rather than the water. Owners or operators must monitor soil-pore liquid movement. Soil tests must also be taken. Like water quality tests, the soil tests must show that concentrations of hazardous constituents in the treatment zone are not statistically significantly higher than background levels at time of closure. Rather than test the soil for all hazardous constituents, principal hazardous constituents (PHCs) are specified as part of the permit. The performance standard requires that the most difficult hazardous constituent to treat "considering the combined effects of degradation, transformation, or immobilization" will serve as a PHC, and other wastes will be more manageable by comparison. If hazardous constituent concentrations in the treatment zone soil are not significantly different from background levels, then post-closure care is not required, proved a vegetative cover is maintained.

Special consideration is made in this Subpart for future use of the active portion of the land treatment unit.[41] Reusing treatment zone land for the growth of food-chain crops is not prohibited. However, the owner or operator must demonstrate that crops will not adversely affect human health. Land used to grow tobacco and leafy vegetables and root crops for human consumption must not exceed an annual application of 0.5 kilograms per hectare for cadmium. For other crops, the cadmium level begins at 2 kilograms per hectare and is scheduled to be reduced to 0.5 by January of 1987.


## Landfills—Subpart N

Owners and operators of new landfills are required to construct or install a synthetic or soil-based liner to prevent migration of hazardous wastes. A leachate collection and removal system is also required, unless an owner or operator can demonstrate that alternative design, operations or location characteristics can prevent migration. The use of a double-liner system for a landfill may exempt such facility from the Subpart F requirements.

Surveying, recordkeeping and post-closure care requirements are of special interest to planners. Owners or operators are required to specify on a map the permanently surveyed benchmarks showing the exact location and dimensions of each landfill cell. The operating record must contain a list of the contents of each cell. The post-closure care requirements, which last for 30 years, were discussed earlier in this chapter. Briefly, these requirements entail the construction of a final cover, continued maintenance and monitoring, and a leak detection system.

*Incinerators—Subpart O*

Owners and operators of facilities designed to incinerate hazardous wastes are subject to the regulations detailed in this subpart. The actual hazardous wastes that can be incinerated in a particular incinerator are specified in Part B of the facility permit. The permit also requires a waste analysis including a trial burn and a demonstration that waste fed into the incinerator is within the physical and chemical composition limits specified.

Similar to land treatment regulations which focus on a principal hazardous constituent, the incinerator regulations focus on what is called the principal organic hazards constituents (POHCs). One or more POHCs may be specified because they exhibit the "greatest degree of difficulty of incineration."[42] The strategy pursued here is that if you design for the most difficult incineration operations, the less difficult hazardous organic constituents to incinerate will subsequently meet all performance standards set for the more difficult incineration activities.

There are three basic performance standards.[43] First, incinerators must achieve 99.99 percent destruction and removal efficiency (DRE) for each POHC designated in the permit, and for each waste feed. Second, stack emissions of hydrogen chloride (HC1) must not exceed the larger amount of either four pounds per hour or one percent of HC1 gas in the stack before entering pollution control equipment. The third performance standard requires owners or operators to limit particulate emissions to 0.08 grains per dry standard cubic foot.

Monitoring requirements involve keeping an operating record of combustion temperature, waste feed rates, and carbon monoxide (CO) concentration prior to release from the stack. The incinerator must be demonstrated to have an emergency waste feed cut-off system in working order. The incinerator and emergency cut-off system are to be visually inspected on a daily basis for leaks, spills, fugitive emissions, or signs of tampering. Closure of the facility requires removal of all hazardous waste and residues, including ash, scrubber water, and scrubber sludge.

**Section 3005: Permits for Treatment, Storage or
Disposal of Hazardous Waste**

This section outlines the standards and requirements which must be met
in order to obtain a permit for TSDFs. It is almost identical to Section 3004
and Part 264 regulations, with a number of important differences. Rather
than close down existing facilities, Section 3005 (e) allows the EPA to grant
interim status for their continued operation. Owners or operators of facilities in existence on or before November 19, 1980 (the effective date of this
regulation) are eligible for interim status provided they comply with the
following two criteria. First, owners or operators had to notify EPA that
they were handling hazardous wastes that come under regulation. This requirement is authorized under Section 3010 (a) of Subtitle C. Second, Part
A of the permit application had to be filed by November 19, 1980. Facilities
that handle specific wastes which eventually will come under regulation of
Subtitle C must also apply for interim status subsequent to the waste regulation period. The permit process is discussed at greater length in the next
section. This section is concerned with some essential differences between
requirements for existing TSDFs (Part 265) and requirements for new
TSDFs (Part 264).

Part 265 is designed to set management and operation standards for existing facilities in order to establish minimum national standards for acceptable hazardous waste management during the interim status period. Part
264, by contrast, requires specific design and performance standards with
which only new facilities can comply, as well as more rigorous management
and operation standards. For example, Subpart F of Part 265 requires
owners or operators of landfills to monitor for contamination migration,
while Part 264 requires not only monitoring but also a protection program
incorporating corrective action. Another example would be the number of
design standards for tanks, waste piles, and surface impoundments included
in Part 264 but not in Part 265. Still other examples include the location
standards and considerations scattered in Part 264 which are applicable to
new facilities but are often only partially applicable to existing facilities.

Another striking contrast between standards for existing and new TSDFs
is the absence of Subparts P, Q, and R from regulations for new facilities.
Part 265 existing facility permit regulations include: Subpart P — Thermal
Treatment; Subpart Q—Chemical, Physical, and Biological Treatment; and
Subpart R — Underground Injection. Thermal treatment of hazardous
waste by processes other than incineration and conditions for the open
burning and detonation of waste explosives are found in section 265 Subpart P.[44] EPA intends to merge this Subpart with Part 265 Subpart O — In-

cinerators.[45] There are twelve or more possible technologies for incineration and thermal treatment processes recognized by EPA in operation at existing facilities (see Table 2-5).

Chemical, Physical, and Biological Treatment (Subpart Q) in Part 265 is not required under Part 264. In Part 265 the regulation applies to facilities that use the treatment techniques itemized in Table 2-5; but it does not apply to tanks, surface impoundments, land treatment facilities, or incinerators. The difficulty which arises is that alternative treatment in forms other than in the facilities mentioned here are often waste-specific process, and therefore extremely diverse (e.g., centrifugation, distillation, filtration, ion exchange, reverse osmosis).[46] It is perhaps too complex to regulate all processes at this time. Parts of these 265 regulations are incorporated in the chemical, physical, and biological treatment requirements under the 264 Subparts dealing with containers, tanks, surface impoundments, waste piles, land treatment facilities, landfills, and incinerators. The EPA expects to establish more specific standards under a separate subpart.

The interim status regulations applying to underground injection of hazardous waste (Subpart R) have been altered for both new and existing underground injection facilities. Underground injection wells are also regulated under the Safe Drinking Water Act and are required to obtain an underground injection control (UIC) permit from the EPA. The EPA has ''promulgated a permit-by-rule for injection wells.''[47] This is essentially an arrangement to share the responsibility of regulating one activity which overlaps the jurisdictions of two laws. If a facility has an approved UIC permit under authority of the Safe Drinking Water Act, it can satisfy the requirements of RCRA by notification, obtaining an identification number, entering the manifest system, recordkeeping, and reporting as specified in Part 264.

Regulations specifying the permit application and review processes are listed in Parts 122, 123, and 124.[48] Part 122 contains the basic requirements of the permit application which is divided into two stages — Part A and Part B. Part A of the permit application covers certain general informational items required by EPA Forms 1 and 3. This information includes a description of the facility and its operations, types and volumes of waste processed, other items related to site location, and the names and addresses of owners and operators. Part A of the permit applications also includes the recordkeeping, maintenance and operation requirements detailed in Part 265 for existing facilities.

Part B of the permit application requires much more detailed information than that required in Part A. For example, Part B of the application requires specific information on the waste analysis plan, the inspection

## TABLE 2-5

### Hazardous Waste Treatment, Storage, and Disposal Methods

| EPA Handling Code | Treatment, Storage, Disposal Technique | EPA Handling Code | Treatment, Storage, Disposal Technique |
|---|---|---|---|
| Storage | | Chemical Treatment | |
| S01 | Container (barrel, drum, etc.) | T19 | Absorption mound |
| | | T20 | Absorption field |
| S02 | Tank | T21 | Chemical fixation |
| S03 | Waste pile | T22 | Chemical oxidation |
| S04 | Surface impoundment | T23 | Chemical precipitation |
| S05 | Other | T24 | Chemical reduction |
| | | T25 | Chlorination |
| Treatment and Thermal Treatment | | T26 | Chlorinolysis |
| | | T27 | Cyanide destruction |
| T06 | Liquid injection incinerator | T28 | Degradation |
| T07 | Rotary kiln incinerator | T29 | Detoxification |
| T08 | Fluidized bed incinerator | T30 | Ion exchange |
| T09 | Multiple hearth incinerator | T31 | Neutralization |
| T10 | Infrared furnace incinerator | T32 | Ozonation |
| T11 | Molten salt destructor | T33 | Photolysis |
| T12 | Pyrolysis | T34 | Other |
| T13 | Wet air oxidation | | |
| T14 | Calcination | Physical Treatment (separation of components) | |
| T15 | Microwave discharge | | |
| T16 | Cement kiln | | |
| T17 | Lime kiln | T35 | Centrifugation |
| T18 | Other | T36 | Clarification |
| | | T37 | Coagulation |
| | | T38 | Decanting |
| | | T39 | Encapsulation |
| | | T40 | Filtration |
| | | T41 | Flocculation |
| | | T42 | Flotation |
| | | T43 | Foaming |
| | | T44 | Sedimentation |
| | | T45 | Thickening |
| | | T46 | Ultrafiltration |
| | | T47 | Other |

**TABLE 2-5 (Continued)**

**Hazardous Waste Treatment, Storage, and Disposal Methods**

| EPA Handling Code | Treatment, Storage, Disposal Technique | EPA Handling Code | Treatment, Storage, Disposal Technique |
|---|---|---|---|
| (Removal of specific components) | | Biological Treatment | |
| T48 | Absorption-molecular sieve | T67 | Activated sludge |
| T49 | Activated carbon | T68 | Aerobic lagoon |
| T50 | Blending | T69 | Aerobic tank |
| T51 | Catalysis | T70 | Anaerobic lagoon |
| T52 | Crystallization | T71 | Composting |
| T53 | Dialysis | T72 | Septic tank |
| T54 | Distillation | T73 | Spray irrigation |
| T55 | Electrodialysis | T74 | Thickening filter |
| T56 | Electrolysis | T75 | Trickling filter |
| T57 | Evaporation | T76 | Waste stabilization pond |
| T58 | High gradient magnetic separation | T77 | Other |
| T59 | Leaching | T78–79 | (Reserved) |
| T60 | Liquid ion exchange | Disposal | |
| T61 | Liquid-liquid extraction | | |
| T62 | Reverse osmosis | D80 | Underground injection |
| T63 | Solvent recovery | D81 | Landfill |
| T64 | Stripping | D82 | Land treatment |
| T65 | Sand filter | D83 | Ocean disposal |
| T66 | Other | D84 | Surface impoundment (closed as landfill) |
| | | D85 | Other |

Source: 40 CFR Part 264 Appendix I, Table 2, pp. 461–462, 1982.

schedule, the contingency plan, etc. Permit applicants may voluntarily submit Part B applications, or EPA may call them in any time after promulgation of Part 264 regulations (effective January 26, 1983).

As mentioned in the discussion on Section 3004, facility permits may be modified, be used to exact certain conditions, or be revoked if owners or operators fail to comply with the required standards. In this way, EPA or the approved state authority may use the permitting power to control the impacts of the hazardous waste management industry. When both Parts A and B of the application are submitted to EPA, the review process begins. EPA may state an intent either to deny or approve the permit. Thirty days from statement of intent, the public may submit written comment on the proposal. If written notice of public opposition is submitted, a public hearing may be required. Following procedures described in Part 124, EPA or the appropriate state authority must issue a final permit decision which becomes effective immediately.

### Section 3006: Authorized State Hazardous Waste Programs

The implementation strategy and schedule for RCRA extends to authorized state hazardous waste management programs. An "authorized program" is defined as a state program that is "equivalent" to the federal program (it addresses all regulatory sections) and is at least as stringent (but may be more stringent). The requirements for authorization of a state program are listed in Part 123, Subpart A.

The EPA has developed a two-phased schedule for states to assume authority over all or part of the required hazardous waste management regulations. Under Subpart F of Part 123, states may apply for "interim authorization" to administer and enforce their own programs in lieu of the federal program. Phase I of interim authorization requires a state to have enabling legislation and regulations that are "substantially equivalent" to and as stringent as the requirements specified for identification and listing (Part 261) and the standards for generators (Part 262), standards for transporters (part 263), and preliminary standards for interim status TSDFs (Part 265 and Part A of the permit application). Phase II allows states with interim authorization to establish a permit program for TSDFs in lieu of the federal program. Phase II requirements correspond to Part 264 requirements for new facilities and incorporate Part B of the permit application for new and existing facilities into the requirement.

The timetable and sequence of state activities is as follows: Phase I of the interim authorization began on November 19, 1980, when proposed rules for Parts 261, 262, 263, and 265 became effective. Phase II, the interim final regulations of Part 264, became effective on January 26, 1982. Together, Phases I and II comprise the interim authorization period. This period is scheduled to last up to 24 months (or until January 26, 1985) when "all interim authorizations automatically expire and EPA shall administer the federal program in any state which has not received final authorization."[49] By March, 1983, 36 states had received Phase I interim authorization (see Table 2-4), and ten states had received Phase II interim authorization.

Final authorization of a state program may occur any time after initial promulgation of Phase II regulations. However, the state regulations are required to be "equivalent" to RCRA regulations as interpreted by the EPA. The EPA does not require that the two phases follow a strict timetable. For example, a state may receive final authorization, if its program satisfies all requirements, by submitting the Phase I and II regulations all at one time. Some states may wish to administer only a partial program, and they can obtain authorization for parts of the overall program, deferring to EPA to administer remaining portions. The EPA has 90 days to review final authorization applications submitted by a state and issue an approval, modification, or denial.

A total of 8,906 Part A applications have been filed for TSDF interim status permits. Also under Phase I, 51,334 generator notifications and 12,559 transporter notifications have been filed and have obtained EPA identification numbers (Gale 1983). The various EPA regional offices have been selectively calling in TSDF Part B permit applications during 1983.

## Sections 3007–3011

Sections 3007 through 3011 involve various requirements for generators, transporters and handlers. Section 3007 establishes authority for EPA to inspect properties and operations of generators, transporters and handlers. Section 3008 authorizes the EPA or appropriate State authorities to suspend or revoke permits when facilities are non-complying. This section also carries provision for criminal penalties that may be invoked if a person acts in violation of RCRA regulations. A $25,000 fine or one-year prison term may be imposed on anyone transporting hazardous wastes to a TSDF without securing appropriate permits; anyone who treats, stores, or disposes of hazardous waste without a permit; and anyone who makes false statements or misrepresentations concerning labels, manifests, records, etc. Section 3009 allows States to assume implementation of RCRA, as long as EPA determines that the State program is not less stringent than the Federal RCRA requirements. Section 3010 specifies effective dates for notification and beginning of the regulatory period. Finally, Section 3011 authorized $25 million to be appropriated during 1978 and 1979 to aid the states in their development of hazardous waste programs.

## Section 3012: Hazardous Waste Site Inventory

Section 3012 authorized financial assistance for state inventory programs. The inventory program entails an inspection and assessment of hazardous waste sites and an inventory of storage and disposal sites.[50] While

$20 million was authorized by Congress[51] to assist states in developing such programs, only $10 million was appropriated from the Superfund as a one-time nonrecurring allocation.[52]

The purpose of the inventory is to help complete the listing of active and inactive waste sites called for under the Comprehensive Environmental Response, Compensation and Liability Act (CERCLA). Roughly 15,000 potential uncontrolled sites have been listed under CERCLA via the Emergency and Remedial Response Information System (ERRIS) (which is discussed at length in Chapter 4). Financial grants to states are allowed for preliminary assessments, site inspections, responsible party searches, inventory completion, and special attention to selected sites. States may choose to assume all or part of these activities. Financial allotments to states are based partially on how much of the inventory activities they assume, and the number of sites currently under the ERRIS (see Table 2-4).

There is some overlap among RCRA Sections 3004, 3012, 3014, and 7003, especially as they apply to inactive hazardous waste sites and their potential for threatening human health. By and large, however, RCRA is essentially a preventative law, directly addressing existing and future public control of hazardous waste management and waste sites. CERCLA, on the other hand, is primarily concerned with the removal of hazardous waste from active and inactive sites which do or may pose a threat of harm to human health or the environment. We now turn to a discussion of the elements and requiremnts of CERCLA.

## CONTROLLING HAZARDOUS WASTE MIGRATION FROM ACTIVE AND INACTIVE WASTE SITES, AND ACCIDENTAL RELEASES: CERCLA

The Comprehensive Environmental Response, Compensation, and Liability Act of 1980 (CERCLA), also known as the "Superfund" legislation, establishes authority, delegated to the EPA, to respond to past, present, or potential releases of "hazardous substances" into the environment. The mandate to the EPA is indeed broad. The scope of the statute goes beyond dealing with hazardous wastes regulated under Section 3001 of RCRA to a more broadly defined group of hazardous substances. In addition to hazardous wastes regulated under RCRA, the definition of "hazardous substance" under CERCLA includes substances designated under Section 311 (b) (2) (A) of the Federal Water Pollution Control Act; toxic pollutants listed under Section 307(a) of the Federal Water Pollution Control Act; hazardous air pollutants under Section 112 of the Clean Air Act; imminently hazardous chemicals specified in Section 7 of the Toxic

Substances Control Act; and other substances which may be designated pursuant to Section 102 of CERCLA.[53]

Congress intended to provide EPA with emergency powers to respond to sudden releases of these hazardous substances, to clean up inactive hazardous waste sites, and to establish mechanisms for assigning liability and compensation for cleanup costs. Congress also directed EPA to revise and republish the National Contingency Plan (NCP) to include a national hazardous substance response plan to accomplish the objectives of CERCLA. By July of 1982 the EPA promulgated revisions to the NCP and in December of the same year amended the NCP with Appendix B which established the National Priorities List of known and threatened releases of hazardous substances (see discussion in Chapter 4).

CERCLA is comprised of three titles. Title I (see Table 2-6) defines the constellation of hazardous substances and releases that are regulated. It also provides authority for EPA to respond itself, or to order those responsible to respond to hazardous substance releases into the environment according to a planned procedure and with specific requirements for financial responsibility. Title II establishes a tax on crude oil, specific petroleum products and 42 chemical feedstocks to provide a $1.6 billion Hazardous Substance Response Trust Fund. The Fund is to be used to finance response actions, the cost of which will be recovered from those responsible having financial resources. This Title also provides for a Post-Closure Tax and Trust Fund,

## TABLE 2-6

### Title I—Hazardous Substances Releases, Liability, Compensation

| | |
|---|---|
| Section 101 | Definitions |
| Section 102 | Reportable Quantities and Additional Designations |
| Section 103 | Notices, Penalties |
| Section 104 | Response Authorities |
| Section 105 | National Contingency Plan |
| Section 106 | Abatement Action |
| Section 107 | Liability |
| Section 108 | Financial Responsibility |
| Section 109 | Penalty |
| Section 110 | Employee Protection |
| Section 111 | Uses of Fund |
| Section 112 | Claims Procedure |
| Section 113 | Litigation, Jurisdiction and Venue |
| Section 114 | Relationship to Other Law |
| Section 115 | Authority to Delegate, Issue Regulations |

whereby a $2.13 per ton tax is imposed on hazardous waste disposed of in a disposal facility permitted under Subtitle C of RCRA. Title III contains a variety of miscellaneous provisions, including requirements for reports and studies evaluating the effectiveness of responses and the experience of recovering response costs from liable parties, and identifing options for overcoming obstacles to siting new TSDFs.

### Title I: Hazardous Substances Releases, Liability, Compensation

There are 15 sections under Title I. Selected sections (of special interest to planners and others who work at local government scales) are described in this discussion. Other sections are certainly important, but less relevant to planners, so they are not addressed here.

Section 101 is intended to define the terms referred to in the remaining portions of the Act. The definition of hazardous substance has already been described. However, there are exclusions for natural gas, natural gas liquids, liquefied natural gas, and synthetic gas used as fuel.[54] Also, federally permitted releases of toxic and hazardous substances regulated under other environmental laws are not subject to response actions under CERCLA.

Other terms of interest defined under Section 101 include "facility"[55] and "release."[56] A "facility" is defined to include any building, structure, installation, equipment, pipe (including a pipe into a sewer or POTW), pit, pond, lagoon, impoundment, ditch, container, motor vehicle, rolling stock, aircraft, or any site where a hazardous substance has come to be located. Excluded under the definition are workplace environment, vessels, and consumer products. A "release" is defined to include any form of discharge, dumping, or disposing of hazardous substances into the environment. Certain releases are excluded from regulation. These include federally permitted releases, releases from federal facilities, workplace releases, engine exhaust emissions, nuclear emissions from a nuclear incident, and fertilizer applications. These exclusions represent releases regulated under other legislation or Executive Order. Despite the large number of exclusions from the definitions of hazardous substance, facility, and release, the inclusions cover a broad array of contaminants discharged into the environment which have an extraordinary potential for entering complex routes of migration (see Chapter 3).

Releases of hazardous substances which may present substantial danger to public health, welfare, or the environment must be reported to the EPA. The specific substances included are those listed by definition (101(14)), others authorized under Section 102, and others to be determined by the EPA.[57] In effect, a release of one pound or more, or any amount specified by other statutes (an amount which may be greater or less than one pound), are considered "reportable quantities."[58] Section 103 applies the requirement to notify the National Response Center (NRC: 800-424-8802) of first knowledge of release of reportable quantity from current operations by operators of vessels, offshore or onshore facilities.[59] Failure to comply with immediate notification may result in a $10,000 fine or one year of imprisonment.[60]

Section 103 also requires past and present owners or operators of TSDFs, and transporters who hauled hazardous substances to TSDFs to notify the EPA of their existence, location, characteristics (e.g., type, volume, and form of hazardous substances), and potential for releases.[61] This requirement does not include facilities granted a permit or interim status under RCRA, Subtitle C. Notification was due by June of 1981, and this provided some of the early data base with regard to a national waste site inventory (see Chapter 4).

Section 104 establishes authority for EPA to respond to releases or threatened releases of hazardous substances and any "pollutant or contaminant." The response authority is broadly defined to include remedial actions and even removal of contaminants from natural resources. EPA has taken response actions to control inactive hazardous waste sites (EPA 1982). Quarles (1982) has aptly described the intended chief purpose of CERCLA:

> . . .to provide for the cleanup of contaminated groundwater caused by old dump sites which in many instances had been closed or abandoned.

If hazardous substances migrate to groundwater, for example, the groundwater itself becomes a "pollutant or contaminant," which is defined to include any substance which may "reasonably be anticipated to cause death, disease, behavioral abnormalities, cancer, genetic mutation, physiological malfunctions . . . or physical deformations."[62] As will be discussed in Chapters 3 and 8, the implementation of the response authority has been quite controversial, and there will likely remain a substantial amount of confusion about it until it is possible to evaluate key elements of the response program over time.

Section 104 contains other important provisions which directly affect resource expenditures for response actions and cost-sharing agreements with states and which provide for monitoring and analysis of public health impacts. EPA may respond to a release only if public health, welfare, or the environment is threatened and if other assistance is not likely to occur on a timely basis. Any response by EPA is halted after six months of activity, or by the time $1 million is spent on response actions. The activity may be extended if the state involved agrees to cooperate with the action, assumes all future maintenance costs after completion of the response, and substances removed from the site are taken to a TSDF in compliance with Subtitle C of RCRA. There are additional cost-sharing agreements that are necessary. The affected state must agree to pay either ten percent of the response costs or 50 percent or more if the waste site is related to a state or local government activity.[63]

Section 104 also establishes the Agency for Toxic Substances and Disease Registry as part of the Public Health Service.[64] This Agency, in cooperation with other administrative agencies and the various states, is required to establish and maintain a registry of persons exposed to toxic substances, a registry of serious diseases and illness, and an inventory of health effects related to toxic substances. The Agency is also required to assist states in conducting periodic survey and screening programs to determine the relationship between exposure to toxic substances and illness. An additional provision requires the Agency to establish a national list of areas closed or restricted to public use because of contamination.

Implementation of response activities by EPA has been controversial during 1982 and 1983, especially in the area of recovering costs for response activities. The choice of sites for response actions has also been the subject of much public debate (see discussion in Chapters 4, 5 and 8). The main thrust of the response activities has centered on remedial and removal strategies. This is appropriate since containing or removing hazardous substances from an uncontrolled waste site is advisable. However, there is little systematic knowledge concerning the health impacts around such sites. There is also a glaring absence of concern with respect to CERCLA about other important social and economic effects from these sites (see Chapter 5). The lack of attention under CERCLA to these concerns underscores a substantial shortcoming in the waste control legislation.

Section 105 provides the authority for EPA to develop the modus operandi for taking response actions. The EPA was directed under Section 105 to amend the National Contingency Plan established under Section 311 of the Federal Water Pollution Control Act to respond to oil spills with the inclusion of a national hazardous substance response plan. The purpose of the amendment is to establish standards and procedures for responding to hazardous substance, pollutant or contaminant releases. Section 105 is comprised of nine separate provisions. Relevant provisions are discussed here, as they are defined by regulation in the Federal Register of July 16, 1982.

The actual response structure of the NCP was left intact. The EPA had developed an effective response strategy for oil spills, and it broadened the strategy to accommodate hazardous substance releases. This is defined under Subpart F of the NCP.

Section 105 of CERCLA requires that the NCP contain methods to discover and inventory facilities that have handled hazardous substances. Five methods have been specified under Subpart F of the NCP. They are (1) notification as specified by CERCLA Section 103; (2) investigations authorized under CERCLA Section 104; (3) notification by a permit holder (as required by the permit; (4) inventory efforts or random observation by government officials or the public; and, (5) other sources.[65] The inventory of releases and their characteristics provide the data base for evaluating the magnitude of danger and is the first of seven phases involved in investigating releases.

The second phase (Phase II—Preliminary Assessment)[66] involves an evaluation process. First, the lead agency (state or EPA) must determine the nature of the release, its source, and whether responsible parties can and will undertake a response. Next, the EPA may require the generation of additional data to complete the evaluation.[67] Finally, a determination must be made whether the release (and its quantity) justifies a CERCLA response.

Section 105 also requires that the determination of appropriate response be based on an evaluation of each release. EPA categorizes responses under the assumption that "the less imminent the threat, the greater the time available for the evaluation process."[68] Phase II regulations[69] involve releases requiring immediate removal.

The Phase III—Immediate Removal regulations give EPA broad discretion in ordering or undertaking a response to prevent or mitigate immediate and significant risk to human health or the environment. In addition to removal of hazardous substances to approved TSDFs, the EPA can fence off uncontrolled sites, provide alternative water supplies, recommend evacuation, place physical barriers to deter the spread of release, etc. These immediate removal responses are limited to the statutory $1 million expenditure or six-month time lapse. However, immediate removal actions may in some instances exceed the statutory limits until abatement of the hazard is achieved. EPA policy requires that a letter requesting exemption from the statutory limits be submitted to the Office of Solid Waste (OSW). The OSW may specify certain conditions and may extend either the $1 million dollar limit, the six-month limit, or both.

Phase IV of Subpart F[70] establishes a priority of response actions after completion of preliminary assessments and immediate removal actions. These response actions are called "planned removals" and "remedial actions." The major objective is to determine if an immediate danger exists for persons living or working near the release. This Phase also requires that EPA, along with the states, evaluate and establish a National Priority List

(NPL) of immediate removal, planned removal, and remedial action sites. The list is to include about 400 such sites, with the first 100 consisting of at least one site designated by each state as its worst uncontrolled waste site. Federally owned facilities will not be included in the NPL.[71] The targets of 100 and 400 have been reached. But we are not confident about the results. Issues related to establishing the NPL are discussed at length in Chapter 4.

Phase V addresses planned removal actions. It should be noted that planned removals may occur at sites not on the NPL. These sites will be considered for action by the EPA if the Governor of the State affected makes a request for action. The time frame of the planned removal action is similar to that of the immediate removal action; it continues until abatement of risk to public health or to the environment.[72]

Remedial action requirements and limitations are detailed under Phase VI.[73] Remedial actions usually entail long-term actions to mitigate threats to public health or the environment. This category of actions has captured the media spotlight which has sensationalized the occurrence of uncontrolled waste sites. A typical example of a remedial action is one in which some hazardous substances are removed from a site and action continues either to clean contaminated groundwater sources or to utilize engineering controls to impede contaminant migration. Initial experience has shown that the problems of cleaning up abandoned sites are extremely complex and the solution expensive. Many initial efforts have not been successful (EPA, 1981).

The nature and extent of remedial actions are subject to specific requirements found under Subpart F. Alternative actions are screened based on economic, engineering and environmental criteria.[74] Only feasible engineering alternatives can be considered as part of the remedial action. Screening among these engineering alternatives to choose one technique requires that the EPA rule out techniques that are more costly than others and do not provide "substantially greater public health or environmental benefit."[75] In addition, EPA places constraints on the extent of remedy and choice of remedial action by limiting them to:

> . . .the lowest cost alternative that is technologically feasible and reliable and which effectively mitigates and minimizes damages to and provides adequate protection of public health, welfare, or the environment.

The evaluation of "reliable," "effective," and "adequate" is subjective and nowhere defined by CERCLA or the amended NCP. Determinations of what is "reliable," "effective," and "adequate" are likely to be made on an ad hoc basis and to be the result of a political process whose outcome will depend on the particular waste site and release and the strength of actions by responsible government and private parties and potentially impacted neighbors. See Chapter 8 for a discussion of the issue of how to define what is clean.

Other provisions under Subpart F include recovery of costs and a listing of technical approaches for remedying releases. Documentation of response costs are required in order to expedite the recovery of such costs.[76] This is the seventh phase of the Subpart F response action. Along with documentation of costs, the lead agency must account for impacts (real or potential) on public health and the environment. Subpart F also lists a broad (but not exhaustive) array of engineering methods for on-site response actions[77] to control air, ground, and surface water emissions; technologies for treating the wastes; and provisions for transporting contaminated materials to off-site locations. Subpart F — § 300.70 provides authority for the EPA to distribute alternative water supplies to communities with contaminated water. This may include individual treatment units, a new pipe system, new wells or deeper wells, bottled or treated water, or upgrading treatment of existing water distribution systems. These alternatives (each with a different cost structure) have been exercised by EPA at uncontrolled waste sites.

Temporary or permanent relocation of residents, businesses, and community facilities may also be ordered by EPA when it becomes necessary to evacuate the area surrounding a site contaminated by release of hazardous substances. This discretion on the part of the EPA administrator has been relatively little used in the past. When it has been used, it has caused much publicity. Concern is certainly appropriate since the criterion used to make the decision in favor of evacuation and permanent relocation is that a clear and present danger to public health exists, and relocation would be both environmentally preferable and more cost-effective than other remedial actions.[78] This action, when invoked, requires the use of the police powers to condemn the affected area, to restrict public use, and to add the area to the Agency for Toxic Substances and Disease Registry list of areas closed to the public. Since the police power is well-established in questions arising from public health, safety, and welfare, the focus of legal attention is shifted to questions concerning property rights, just compensation for a taking, and other land use issues.

Section 107 specifies the parameters of liability related to releases of hazardous substances. Liable parties include owners and operators of vessels, past and present owners and operators of facilities, hazardous waste generators who contracted to remove wastes, and transporters who accepted wastes and selected a TSDF. Liability extends to costs for response actions under the NCP, payment for damages, and even punitive damages in certain cases, but it does not provide for third party damages as RCRA does. Liability applies to releases of hazardous substances, and liable parties are responsible for all response action costs and up to $50 million for injury or damage to natural resources. If the releases result from willful misconduct or violation of standards, the liability limit may be raised above $50 million. Punitive damages of three times the amount of response costs may be exacted against liable parties for refusal to cooperate with response actions. See Chapter 8 for a further discussion of the serious issue of liability for hazardous waste disposal.

Other sections under Title I are related to provisions found under Title II. Title II establishes the authority to raise money for the "Superfund" designed to finance response actions. We now turn to a discussion of Title II, how it works, and how it is related to Title I.

### Title II: Hazardous Substance Response Revenue Act of 1980

Title II is comprised of three subtitles and numerous sections. These subtitles contain authorization for the imposition of taxes and establishment of a hazardous substance response trust fund (Superfund). Title II also authorizes the imposition of taxes on hazardous wastes that are permanently disposed of in landfills, and it creates a liability fund that can be used in the future to address cleanup costs.

Subtitle A essentially amends the Internal Revenue Code of 1954 (IRC) (establishing Chapter 38 — Environmental Taxes, under Subtitles C and D of the IRC) by imposing a tax on crude oil, petroleum products, and certain chemicals. Crude oil is taxed at 79 cents per barrel. This tax is paid by owners and operators of United States refineries. Petroleum products are also taxed at 79 cents per barrel, and this tax is paid by importers who "enter" them into the United States for consumption, use, or warehousing.[79] Certain chemicals (Table 2-7) sold by manufacturers, producers or importers are taxed at amounts varying from $0.24 to $4.87.

The revenues received under the imposition of these taxes are set aside for use in response actions. After a lengthy debate in which this tax was opposed by industry and the amount of tax monies was greatly reduced, the tax took effect on April 1, 1981. It is scheduled for termination on September 30, 1985. Provision is made under Subtitle A to allow termination of the tax in 1983 or 1984 if the unobligated balance of the Hazardous Response Trust Fund exceeds $900 million and will exceed $500 million on September 30 of the following year. Chapter 8 argues that the fund should be continued beyond 1985.

Subtitle B established the Hazardous Substance Response Trust Fund (Response Trust Fund).[80] This part of CERCLA provides the mechanism for using the taxes imposed under Subtitle A in response actions authorized

## TABLE 2-7

### Hazardous Substance Response Revenue Act of 1980: List of Tax on Certain Chemicals

| Chemical | Tax Per Ton ($) | Chemical | Tax Per Ton ($) |
|---|---|---|---|
| 1. Acetylene | 4.87 | 22. Chromite | 1.52 |
| 2. Benzene | 4.87 | 23. Potassium dichromate | 1.69 |
| 3. Butane | 4.87 | 24. Sodium dichromate | 1.87 |
| 4. Butylene | 4.87 | 25. Cobalt | 4.45 |
| 5. Butadiene | 4.87 | 26. Cupric sulfate | 1.87 |
| 6. Ethylene | 4.87 | 27. Cupric oxide | 3.59 |
| 7. Methane | 4.87 | 28. Cuprous oxide | 3.97 |
| 8. Naphthalene | 4.87 | 29. Hydrochloric acid | 0.29 |
| 9. Propylene | 4.87 | 30. Hydrogen fluoride | 4.23 |
| 10. Toluene | 4.87 | 31. Lead oxide | 4.14 |
| 11. Xylene | 4.87 | 32. Mercury | 4.45 |
| 12. Ammonia | 2.64 | 33. Nickel | 4.45 |
| 13. Antimony | 4.45 | 34. Phosphorous | 4.45 |
| 14. Antimony trioxide | 3.75 | 35. Stannous chloride | 2.85 |
| 15. Arsenic | 4.45 | 36. Stannic chloride | 2.12 |
| 16. Arsenic trioxide | 3.75 | 37. Zinc chloride | 2.22 |
| 17. Barium sulfide | 2.30 | 38. Zinc sulfate | 1.90 |
| 18. Bromine | 4.45 | 39. Potassium hydroxide | 0.22 |
| 19. Cadmium | 4.45 | 40. Sodium hydroxide | 0.28 |
| 20. Chlorine | 2.70 | 41. Sulfuric acid | 0.26 |
| 21. Chromium | 4.45 | 42. Nitric acid | 0.24 |

Source: Public Law 96–510, 26 USC 4661.

under Section 104 according to procedures detailed in the National Contingency Plan. The Response Trust Fund is financed largely by the imposed taxes. It also derives funds from general revenues, from money recovered from response actions and actions under Section 311 of the Clean Water Act, and from penalties and punitive damages assessed under Title I of CERCLA.[81] The estimated total amount of the Fund is roughly $1.6 billion. Congress decided that an amount equal to about one-eighth of the Fund should be derived from general revenues. The remaining seven-eighths is derived from the sources mentioned above.

Expenditures from the Response Trust Fund are limited to actions defined by Section III — Uses of Fund, under Title I. This includes costs incurred for removal and remedial actions as specified in Section 105; costs for assessing damages to natural resources; costs involved with restoring or replacing natural resources; and costs of doing epidemiological studies and maintaining a registry of persons exposed to hazardous substances released into the environment. Expenditures are not allowed for claims of personal injury. Additionally, 85 percent of the Fund is reserved for uses found in Section 111 of Title I and payment of debt incurred for advances borrowed under authority of the Fund. Roughly 15 percent of the Fund is devoted to accidental spills.

Subtitle C provides for the imposition of a tax on land disposal facilities and establishes a liability fund for closed land disposal facilities. The tax imposition, again, amends the Internal Revenue Code of 1954 to include a charge of $2.13 per dry weight ton of hazardous waste disposed of at a qualified facility.[82] A qualified hazardous waste disposal facility is one that has received either a permit issued pursuant to Sections 3004 and 3005 of RCRA, or one that has received interim status solely under Section 3005 of RCRA. The tax is paid by owners or operators of such facilities and applies only to hazardous wastes remaining in landfills after closure. The tax was effective beginning September 30, 1983. It remains in effect as long as $200 million can be maintained in a Post-Closure Liability Trust Fund. Hence, the tax may be discontinued and reinstated as long as landfilling is considered a feasible, economically acceptable hazardous waste management option.

The purpose of the Post-Closure Liability Trust Fund is to raise revenues that can be used to respond to hazardous substance releases from permitted hazardous waste landfill facilities. The post-closure care period is defined by RCRA as 30 years, with some adjustment short of and beyond 30 years based on specified criteria. The Post-Closure Liability Trust Fund will be available, perhaps long, after termination of Superfund activities, to take response actions. The careful wording used to define the scope of permissible expenditures from this Fund allows broad discretion in taking response actions,[83] but limits the use of the Fund to facilities closed in accordance with an approved closure and post-closure agreement containing requirements established under Subtitle C of RCRA.

### Title III: Miscellaneous Provisions

Provisions requiring a number of reports and studies are specified in Section 301 of Title III. A comprehensive report describing the experience with implementing CERCLA is scheduled for submission by EPA in late 1984.

The scope of the report contents is broad. It includes an evaluation of the effectiveness of response actions to control impacts related to releases; a summary of Response Fund expenditures and success with cost recovery efforts; a projection of future expenditures to control hazardous waste sites and hazardous substance releases; and an assessment of a tax schedule based on the potential dangers posed by various hazardous substances. The language in the statute expresses a clear interest on the part of Congress to monitor CERCLA and evaluate its usefulness as a policy to control hazardous substances. Congress has also directed the EPA to consult with the Secretary of the Treasury and recommend tax rates for the Post-Closure Liability Fund. In a related, but distinct, study, Congress has asked EPA to assess the necessity for and adequacy of revenues raised for the Post-Closure Liability Fund.

Two other studies are required under Section 301. One study, which was due for submission in 1982, involves an estimate of TSDF capacity and demand on a regional and state basis. This report was to be issued by EPA in November of 1983 as part of the overall regulatory impact analysis. It was not issued. The second report, which is available in two volumes,[84] involves a legal review of common law and statutory remedies for harm to humans with respect to releases of hazardous substances.

## SUMMARY

The objective of this chapter was to review some of the more typical problems with controlling chemical hazardous waste and waste sites and to examine private and public sector involvement. Both RCRA and CERCLA are comprised of rules and regulations explicitly addressing a broad array of control strategies. However, the efficacy of these laws and regulations depends ultimately on private and public sector cooperation and sincerity. In the final analysis, the two laws and their implementation will be judged on how well they remedy or prevent the impacts of hazardous substances on man and environment. The laws will also be judged on what they fail to do and what they do not attempt to control.

The control of hazardous waste sites and the control of hazardous wastes and other hazardous substances are a complex task. Yet, many of the policies set forth under RCRA and CERCLA are based on incomplete knowledge and on political bargains. Hazardous waste management is extremely research dependent, but this essential research is often hampered by obstacles not easily overcome. In particular, there are serious problems with assessing contaminant migration and ground water pollution; with evaluating the social, economic, health and environmental effects of uncontrolled waste sites; and with finding acceptable sites for new facilities. The remaining chapters of this volume concentrate on these three problems and offer some alternative approaches for formulating policy and conducting research that can offer helpful guides for future policy.

## NOTES

1. 40 CFR § 261.5, 1982.
2. Adapted from EPA memorandum to Hazardous Waste Branch Chiefs, "Summary of State Differences From the RCRA Program," State Programs Branch, Washington, D.C., September 27, 1982.
3. 40 CFR § 261.6, 1982.
4. Ibid. § 261.6 (a) (1).
5. Ibid. § 260.22
6. Ibid. § 261.21
7. Ibid. § 261.33 (c)
8. Ibid. § 262.
9. Ibid. § 260.10.
10. Ibid. § 262.12.
11. Ibid. § 262.11.
12. Ibid. § 261 Subpart C.
13. Ibid. § 261 Subpart B.
14. Ibid. §§ 262. 30–33.
15. Ibid. §§ 262. 40–43.
16. Ibid. § 262 Subpart E.
17. Ibid. § 263.
18. 49 U.S.C. §§ 1801–1812, 1978.
19. 40 CFR § 263 Subpart C, 1982.
20. Massachusetts Register 310 (MR GL-21C) 30.415.
21. 40 CFR § 264.1, 1982.
22. Ibid. § 261, Appendix I.
23. Ibid. § 264.18.
24. *U.S. Federal Register* 40 CFR § 250.43–1, 1978.
25. 40 CFR § 264 Appendix VI, 1982.
26. Ibid. § 264.31.
27. Ibid. § 261 Appendix VIII.
28. Ibid. § 264 Table 1.
29. Ibid. § 264.92.
30. Ibid. § 264.92.
31. Ibid. § 264.96 (c).
32. Ibid. § 264.110.
33. *U.S. Federal Register* 40 CFR § 264.110, July 26, 1982.
34. 40 CFR § 264.111 (b) 1982.
35. *U.S. Federal Register* 40 CFR § 264.117 (a) (1) July 26, 1982.
36. 40 CFR §§ 264.170–174, 1982.
37. Ibid. § 264.175 (b) (3).
38. Ibid. §§ 264.191–192, 264.194.
39. *U.S. Federal Register*, 90 CFR § 264, §§ 226–228, July 26, 1982.

40. Ibid. § 264.278 (a) (2).
41. Ibid. § 264.276.
42. Ibid. § 264.342.
43. Ibid. § 264.343.
44. Ibid. §§ 265.370–382.
45. Karen Gale, RCRA/CERCLA Hotline, telephone interview, Summer 1983.
46. 45 Fed. Reg. 33217 May 1980.
47. 47 Fed. Reg. 32281 July 1982.
48. 45 Fed. Reg. 33290 June 1980.
49. 45 Fed. Reg. 33479 May 1980.
50. 48 Fed. Reg. 5684 February 1983.
51. 42 U.S.C. 6933, Section 3012, 1980.
52. 48 Fed. Reg. 5684, February 1983.
53. 42 U.S.C. § 101 (14).
54. Ibid. § 101.
55. Ibid. § 101 (9).
56. Ibid. § 101 (22).
57. Ibid. § 102 (a).
58. Ibid. § 102 (b).
59. Ibid. § 103.
60. Ibid. § 103 (b) (3).
61. Ibid. § 103 (c).
62. Ibid. § 104 (a) (2).
63. Ibid. § 104 (c).
64. Ibid. § 104 (i).
65. 47 Fed. Reg. § 300.63, 32214, July 1982.
66. Ibid. § 300.64.
67. Ibid. § 300.64 (b).
68. Ibid. at 31181.
69. Ibid. § 300.65.
70. Ibid. § 300.66.
71. Ibid. § 300.66 (e) (2).
72. Ibid. § 300.67 (d).
73. Ibid. § 300.68.
74. Ibid. §§ 300.68 (h) (1–3).
75. Ibid. at 31182.
76. Ibid. § 300.69.
77. There are five EPA publications with relevant information concerning removal and remedial response activities:
    (1) *Closure of Hazardous Waste Surface Impoundments*, SW-873, September 1980.
    (2) *Remedial Action at Waste Disposal Sites*, EPA-625/6-82-006, June 1982.
    (3) *Superfund*, HW-1, December 1982.
    (4) *Environmental Response Team*, HW-2, April 1982.
    (5) *EPA's Emergency Response Program*, HW-3, November 1982.
78. 47 Fed. Reg. § 300.70.
79. 42 U.S.C. Title II, § 4611.
80. Ibid. § 4661.
81. Ibid. § 221 (b) (1).
82. Ibid. § 231.
83. Ibid. § 232.
84. These are available through National Technical Information Service.

## REFERENCES

American Petroleum Institute. *Recommended Practice for Abandonment or Removal of Used Underground Service Station Tanks*. API, Bulletin 1604, 1981.

Anderson, R. and Greenberg, M. "Siting Hazardous Waste Management Facilities: Theory versus Reality." In *Solid, Hazardous and Radioactive Wastes*, Vol. II, edited by Majumdar S. Pennsylvania Academy of Sciences, 1984, pp. 170–186.

Baram, M. "Regulation of Environmental Carcinogens: Why Cost-Benefit Analysis May be Harmful to Your Health." *Technology Review*, July/August, 1976, pp. 40–42.

Booz-Allen & Hamilton, Inc. and Putnam, Hayes and Bartlett, Inc. *Hazardous Waste Generation and Commercial Hazardous Waste Management Capacity*. Washington, D.C.: U.S. Environmental Protection Agency, SW-894.1, 1982.

Bowley, D. R. *Surface Waste Impoundments in Massachusetts — A Survey Report*. Boston, Massachusetts: Department of Environmental Quality Engineering, 1980.

Carson, Rachael. *Silent Spring*. Greenwich, Connecticut: Fawcett Publications, 1964.

Commoner, Barry. *The Closing Circle*. New York: Alfred Knopf, 1971.

Fields, T. and Lindsey A. *Landfill Disposal of Hazardous Wastes: A Review of Literature and Known Approaches*. Cincinnati, Ohio: U.S. Environmental Protection Agency, SW-165, 1975.

Gale, K. RCRA/CERCLA Hotline, telephone interview, Summer 1983.

Humpstone, C. S. "Hazardous Waste Criteria: Fulfilling Financial Requirements." *Waste Age*, December, 1979.

Jorling, T.C. "Managing Hazardous Wastes." *EPA Journal*, Vol. 5, 1979, pp. 2, 7.

Lippman, M. and Schlesinger, R. B. *Chemical Contamination in the Human Environment*. New York: Oxford University Press, 1979.

Pierson, K. *Underground Fuel Storage Manual*. Boston, Massachusetts: Metropolitan Area Planning Council, 1982.

Quarles, J. *Federal Regulation of Hazardous Wastes — A Guide to RCRA*. Environmental Law Institute, 1982.

Sasnett, S. K. *A Toxics Primer*. Washington, D.C.: League of Women Voters, 1978.

Stein, R. B. and Noyes, J. A. "Groundwater Contamination Potential at 21 Industrial Waste-Water Impoundments in Ohio." *Groundwater*, Vol. 19, 1981, pp. 70–80.

Strauss, Matthew A. *Hazardous Waste Management Facilities in the United States—1977*. Cincinnati, Ohio: U.S. Environmental Protection Agency, EPA/530/SW-146.3, 1977.

Task Force on Environmental Cancer and Heart and Lung Disease. *Environmental Pollution and Cancer and Heart and Lung Disease—First Annual Report to Congress*. Washington, D.C.: U.S. Environmental Protection Agency, 1978.

U.S. Department of Transportation. *Hazardous Materials—1980 Emergency Response Guidebook*. Washington, D.C.: U.S. Department of Transportation, DOT-P 5800.2, 1980.

U.S. Environmental Protection Agency. *Report to Congress: Disposal of Hazardous Wastes*. Washington, D.C.: U.S. Government Printing Office, SW-115, 1974.

U.S. Environmental Protection Agency. *The Report to Congress: Waste Disposal Practices and Their Effects on Ground Water*. Washington, D.C.: U.S. Environmental Protection Agency, SH-656, 1977a.

U.S. Environmental Protection Agency. *State Decisionmaker's Guide for Hazardous Waste Management*. Washington, D.C.: U.S. Government Printing Office, SW-612, 1977b.

U.S. Environmental Protection Agency. *Surface Impoundments and Their Effects on Ground-Water Quality in the United States — A Preliminary Survey*. Washington, D.C.: U.S. Environmental Protection Agency, EPA 570/9-78-004, 1978.

U.S. Environmental Protection Agency. "Hazardous Waste Fact Sheet." *EPA Journal*, 5:2, 1979a.

U.S. Environmental Protection Agency. *Water Related Environmental Fate of 129 Priority Pollutants*, Vol. 1. Washington, D.C.: Environmental Protection Agency, EPA 440/ 4-79-029a, 1979b.

U.S. Environmental Protection Agency. *Damages and Threats Caused by Hazardous Material Sites*. Washington, D.C.: U.S. Environmental Protection Agency, EPA/430/9-80/004, 1980a.

U.S. Environmental Protection Agency, *Research Summary — Controlling Hazardous Wastes*. Cincinnati, Ohio: U.S. Environmental Protection Agency, EPA - 600/8-80-017, 1980b.

U.S. Environmental Protection Agency. *Remedial Actions at Hazardous Waste Sites: Survey and Case Studies*. Washington, D.C.: U.S. Environmental Protection Agency, 1981.

# 3

# The Uncertain State of Knowledge About the Effects of Hazardous Waste Sites

Everything must go somewhere.

Barry Commoner, 1971

Improper hazardous waste management is the most serious environmental problem facing our nation today. It is the environmental issue of the 80's.

Congressman James Florio, D-New Jersey, 1981

Each group of wastes, and often individual pollutants, exhibits different rates of migration, different effects on biota and public health, and requires different site containment, remedy and restoration procedures.

U.S. Environmental Protection Agency, 1980a

For many years the chemical and biological by-products of our technological age have been discarded with little thought and care about their potential impact on public health and the environment. Abandoned dumpsites are the most prominent manifestations of this practice and hence are treated first in this book. Horror stories about dumpsites are common. The growing awareness of what occurred at these sites has led many Americans to conclude that hazardous waste management is the most serious environmental problem and that something must immediately be done. The call for action is so recent that those who must prepare national or state policies for cleaning up existing and locating new facilities and those who must decide what to do at each site do not have an established scientific foundation to draw upon.

This chapter presents an overview of what is known and not known about the actual and potential impacts of hazardous waste sites on public health, the environment, and the economy of communities. In order to show that spectacular effects are not the norm, the most popular media images of effects are compared to the initial evidence of damages as reported by the U.S. EPA. After this brief comparison, the key scientific and social scientific issues concerning negative local impacts of sites are considered.

## INITIAL EVIDENCE OF DAMAGE

On April 21, 1980, residents of east and central New Jersey and New York City witnessed a spectacular demonstration that the atmosphere can be a path for the venting of uncontrolled hazardous waste. Thousands of drums exploded and were burned in a fire at the Chemical Control Corporation that was vividly described by David Weinberg (1980) in his article "We Almost Lost Elizabeth."

> There, growing in the night sky, were 100 square yards of flame, an enormous, fluid organism that seemed to be expanding thirty or forty feet a minute.

While other cases may have been less spectucular than the Chemical Control conflagration, there is ample qualitative and quantitative evidence that damage has occurred at many sites. From the East Coast ("Landfill Threatens Atlantic City Water," *New Jersey Hazardous Waste News* 1981) to the West Coast ("Silicon Valley's Love Canal," *SCCOSH News* 1981) local environmental groups have described the impacts of disposal sites on their regions.

But more than any other environmental issue, the hazardous waste disposal problem has not been confined to the pages of local environmental newsletters. On September 22, 1980 the cover story of TIME magazine was "The Poisoning of America: Those Toxic Chemical Wastes." The cover was less subtle than the title, depicting a human head partially submerged in water. The part out of water was normal, the submerged part was a skull. A reporter, Michael Brown, was nominated for three Pulitzer prizes for his numerous spellbinding stories on hazardous waste sites, especially Love Canal. Lois Gibbs, a resident of the Love Canal area, will probably not be nominated for a Pulitzer prize for writing her story (1982) depicting the horrors of Love Canal; but her book will undoubtedly sell, and she will probably sell some of the Love Canal T-shirts that are advertised in the book.

In their efforts to find catchy titles for stories about water contamination, authors have reached out to the "Rhyme of the Ancient Mariner." One author, Jacqueline Warren (1981), borrowed "Water, Water Everywhere"; a second, Grace Singer (1981), "Nor Not a Drop to Drink." Catchy pictures also abound. On the one hand, some of the industries involved in creating hazardous waste sites have identified, filmed, and widely publicized sites which have benefited, or at least, not harmed the environment. On the other hand, the U.S. Environmental Protection Agency (1975, 1980b) has displayed equally spectacular pictures of the physical damage at sites—pictures described by the senior author's then 10-year-old son in a single word: gross.

A catchy title and a spectacular picture may be worth a thousand words, but the authors of this book will deliberately refrain from introducing emotionally stimulating pictures and phrases which stress unduly the spectacular appearance of hazardous waste sites and get in the way of evaluating the evidence about their true impact. Apropos of this decision, this section will examine two initial tabulations by the U.S. Environmental Protection Agency of damages caused by mishandling of hazardous materials.

The first tabulation is of 421 damage reports made during the 1970s (Table 3-1). Haphazard disposal on vacant properties and farmlands and spray irrigation account for almost half of the cases; and landfills/dumps and surface impoundments account for most of the remaining cases. Groundwater pollution occurred in about 60 percent of the cases, with wells affected in one-third of the cases. Surface water pollution occurred in 40 percent of the cases. A minority of cases reported impacts which did not affect water: direct contact poisoning, 12 percent; air pollution, 4 percent; and fires/explosions, 4 percent.

The second data set (U.S. EPA, 1980a) was based on readily available data on 350 sites (Table 3-2). The following substances were identified at more than 10 percent of the sites: chlorine and chlorinated compounds; benzene; ethylene; toluene; methane; sodium hydroxide; sulfuric acid; and waste oil and other petrochemicals.

The cover of the volume reporting the second data set featured a picture of the Chemical Control mess, and, indeed, the data in these tables and in Chapter 4 show that mishandled hazardous waste can explode and pollute the air as they did in the Chemical Control case. The wastes can also accumulate in the food chain, poisoning people and animals; probably causing cancer, birth defects, and genetic damage; and undoubtedly causing property to be devalued. In fact, however, both Tables 3-1 and 3-2 and the tables in Chapter 4 show that water contamination is the most recurrent impact, not spectacular fire and explosion.

These tables show why elected officials and government agencies like the U.S. EPA (1980b), the Council on Environmental Quality (1980), and the U.S. Comptroller General (1978) have joined a growing list of scientists and public research interest groups who perceive hazardous waste as a serious threat to public health and the environment, perhaps the most serious existing threat. However, the scientific evidence needed to justify and to develop a plan for the expenditure of tens of billions of dollars at tens of

## TABLE 3-1

## Impacts of Hazardous Waste Land Disposal:
## 421 U.S. EPA Damage Reports, 1977

| Impact | Disposal Method[1] | | | | | | | | | | |
|--------|------------------|----|-----------------------------|----|-----------------|----|-----------------------------------|----|------------------------|----|-------|----|
| | Landfills, dumps | | Surface impound- ments | | Waste storage | | Smelting, slag, mine tailings | | Other[2] disposal | | Total | |
| | No. | % | No. | % | No. | % | No. | % | No. | % | No. | % |
| Ground- water pollution | 64 | 64 | 57 | 64 | 10 | 67 | 11 | 73 | 117 | 58 | 259 | 61 |
| Wells affected | 28 | 28 | 32 | 36 | 4 | 27 | 2 | 13 | 74 | 36 | 140 | 33 |
| Surface water pollution | 49 | 49 | 42 | 47 | — | — | 8 | 53 | 71 | 35 | 170 | 40 |
| Direct contact poisoning | 6 | 6 | 1 | 1 | 5 | 33 | — | — | 40 | 20 | 52 | 12 |
| Air | 5 | 5 | 3 | 3 | — | — | — | — | 9 | 4 | 17 | 4 |
| Fires, explosions | 11 | 11 | — | — | — | — | — | — | 3 | 1 | 14 | 4 |
| Total | 99 | — | 89 | — | 15 | — | 15 | — | 203 | — | 421 | — |

Notes: [1] Column sums do not equal the column totals because many cases involved multiple impacts.
[2] Includes disposal on vacant properties, farmlands and spray irrigation.
Source: U.S. EPA, *Waste Disposal Practices and Their Effects on Groundwater, Report to
Congress*, Washington, D.C.: U.S. Govt. Printing Office, 1977.

thousands of inactive, active, and proposed sites across the United States is
far from what is needed.


## HEALTH, ENVIRONMENTAL, SOCIAL AND
## ECONOMIC EFFECTS: THE UNCERTAIN EVIDENCE

Hazardous waste disposal sites are a veritable alphabet soup of chemicals
and biological materials. Without knowledge of what went into a site and
what has come out, it has to be assumed that during the course of the next
several decades the full range of effects can result. These effects are as
follows:

*People*
immediate death
life-shortening
  exposures
acute illness
severe disability
chronic illness
chronic disability
minor and temporary illness
emotional illness

*Environment*
ecosystem elimination
elimination of species
reduction of diversity
reduction of species
reduction of biomass
loss of water source

*Social*
disruption of existing
  communities
negative effects distributional:
  fall primarily on
  disadvantaged people;
  on specific types of
  communities; future
  generations

*Economic*
severe damage of man-made
  structures
severe devaluation of
  property
reduced appreciation of
  property values
loss of productivity
  of the land
local taxpayers pay for cleanup, security, and other maintenance of site

Acute and chronic public health effects have been the major concern. Much less research has been done on ambient environmental damage, albeit initial monitoring at disposal sites (see Tables 3-1 and 3-2 and Chapter 4) and studies of the fate and impacts of chemicals in the environment (Eisler et al. 1979, Reese et al. 1972, Schimmel, et al. 1979, Lassiter 1978) imply that it can be serious. Little attention has been paid to social and economic effects, although they may be easier to document than health and environmental problems. Because social and economic effects are of critical importance to planning, they are stressed here.

## Health and Environmental Effects

In order to estimate risk from hazardous waste sites accurately, the amount and nature of the wastes must be known; the movement of wastes from sites must be predictable; and the effects of escaping substances on people must be known.

## TABLE 3-2

### Impacts of Hazardous Waste Disposal: 350 Sites, 1980

| Impact | Number of cases | Number of impacts/ Number of cases (350) |
| --- | --- | --- |
| Well closures | 468 | 1.34 |
| Ground and surface water pollution | 168 | .48 |
| Habitat destruction[1] | 74 | .21 |
| Major soil contamination | 43 | .12 |
| Human health[2] | 27 | .08 |
| Fish kills | 12 | .03 |
| Livestock[3] | 7 | .02 |
| Sewerage system[4] | 6 | .02 |
| Other impacts[5] | 29 | .08 |

Notes: [1]Waters or fields destroyed or changed.
   [2]Kidney malfunction, respiratory difficulty, or death.
   [3]Killed by ingestion of contaminated water or vegetation.
   [4]Treatment works or sewers rendered unsafe or inoperable.
   [5]Includes crop and wildlife damage; air pollution; fire or explosions.
Source: U.S. EPA, *Damages and Threats Caused by Hazardous Material, Spills*, Washington, D.C.: The Agency, 1980.

## Hazardous Waste Sources

In order to get an accurate picture of what has been discarded in existing sites and to plan new sites, information about waste producers and transporters is needed. Little was known about generators, waste sources, transporters, or waste stream destination until the early 1970s when the U.S. EPA began to gather information as background material for legislation. More than two dozen studies were made of hazardous waste generation and management practices of such industries as rubber and plastics (Kushnir, Nagy 1978); pharmaceuticals (U.S. EPA 1976); pesticides (Atkins 1972, Wilkinson et al. 1978); and metal smelting and refining (Leonard et al. 1977). These studies formed the basis for some of the material presented in

Chapter 1. Other studies were made of the contents and operations of land-fills containing hazardous waste (Eichenberger et al. 1978; Ghassemi, Quinlivan 1975) and the compatibility of different hazardous wastes (Hatayama et al. 1978).

The data gathered from these studies along with the RCRA manifest system should greatly enhance the capability of managing wastes at active and proposed sites. In addition, less mixing of wastes is expected in the future which should reduce the complication of analyzing the health effects of complex mixtures. Nevertheless, there are tens of thousands of existing sites and impoundments containing wastes which are not known or have only been generally characterized.

## Major Pathways for Chemical Waste Pollutants

Exposures to hazardous chemicals occur in workplaces, in homes, and in the outdoor environment. But exposure to hazardous chemical wastes is likely to occur only if one lives near a site which has experienced an accidental incident or a deliberate dumping of waste, or is in contact with contaminated air, water, soil, and food. The soil, air, and especially water are the major pathways. Their interaction with one another and with people, animals, and plants is illustrated in Figure 3-1.

*Soil.* Soil is usually the first point of contact. Direct contact by grazing animals and crop intake with subsequent human and animal ingestion are one concern. The second is the passage of hazardous wastes through the soil to water by leaching and overland flow and to the air through volatilization.

Research has focused on soil as a conduit of hazardous substances from land disposal sites to groundwater. Pesticides and heavy metals have received most of the attention (Fuller 1977; Copenhaver, Wilkinson 1979a, 1979b). A typical example is research done at the University of Arizona by Fuller (1978). The movement and retention of arsenic, berrylium, cadmium, cyanide, chromium, copper, mercury, lead, selenium, vanadium, and zinc through eleven soils were studied in a laboratory. Leachate movement was found to be influenced by the chemical, biological, and physical properties of the chemical; by the level of clay, lime, and hydrous iron oxides in the soil; and by soil permeability.

A substantial amount of research has been done. But much more is needed, especially of chemical mixtures derived from disposal sites, in order to predict how much hazardous waste will be transported through and over the soil, and if it will be substantially transformed by contact with the soil and soil biota.

**FIGURE 3-1**

**Major Pathways for
Hazardous Chemical Wastes**

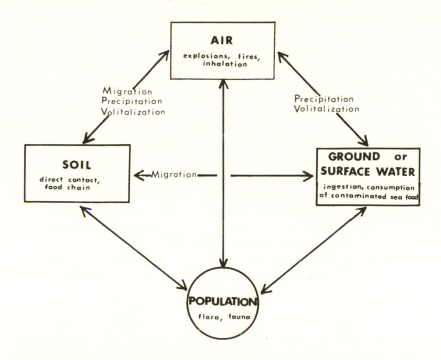

*Air.* Fires and explosions involving hazardous waste can carry particles and gases into the lungs or onto the skin and can injure by combustion, heat, and concussion and by the impact of debris. Chronic emissions from sites can pollute neighborhoods and water supplies.

The federal government has been legally involved with the regulation of air quality for almost two decades. Nearly all of the studies have been of the initially regulated criteria pollutants, not of the plethora of chemicals and chemical mixtures that can be emitted from a hazardous waste land disposal site or an incinerator. The U.S. EPA is studying the monitoring of, the fate of, and public health impacts of selected, usually ubiquitous, hazardous chemicals in the atmosphere (Jones and Leber 1979, Suta 1982, Schuetzle 1979, Josephson 1981, Air Pollution Control Association 1981). For example, Cupitt (1980) reported on the tropospheric lifetimes and fates of 46 materials. Theoretical mathematical models of chemical and physical removal processes were developed and applied to such hazardous chemicals as acrylonitrile, benzo(a)pyrene, and halogenated chemicals. With respect to the drift of toxic materials from incinerators, Freudenthal et al. (1979)

developed a mathematical model that predicts the percentage of people affected by the drift of different pathogens and toxics from cooling tower plumes. These studies, however, are largely exploratory and more than anything point out the enormous gap in our knowledge of the spread of hazardous substances through the air.

*Water*. Since about 80 percent of hazardous waste has been disposed of in landfills, lagoons, pits, and ponds, the migration of chemicals from land disposal sites through soil into water is the key path for hazardous wastes. The processes are complex.

Contaminants passing into the groundwater may be biologically, physically, or chemically transformed beyond transformations that occurred while they were in contact with the atmosphere and the soil. Once the contaminants are in the ground, a plume of polluted water is formed, the size, shape and chemical contamination level of which depends upon the nature of the bedrock, the amount and location of water, and other factors summarized below. Groundwater moves slowly, thereby limiting dilution. Diffusion and dilution occur much more rapidly in surface water. It is not surprising that Page (1981) found low-level concentrations more often in surface than in groundwater, but the highest concentrations were in groundwater.

One of the first important empirical studies of contaminant migration from disposal sites was by the firm of Geraghty and Miller (Miller, 1977a) for the U.S. EPA. The study measured the prevalence of subsurface migration of hazardous chemicals at 50 land disposal sites located in humid areas of the United States east of the Mississippi River. The 50 facilities included abandoned and active landfills, lagoons, and combinations of both. Waste disposal had been practiced at these sites for at least three years, and no groundwater contamination had been reported prior to use of the site for waste disposal. Substances tested for included cyanide, arsenic, selenium, heavy metals (other than iron and manganese), and organic substances. Migration of at least one of the substances was found at 43 of the 50 sites. Cyanide, arsenic and/or selenium migrated from 30 sites; heavy metals from 40 sites; and organics from 27 sites.

Much more research (such as the Geraghty and Miller study summarized above) has been done on the extent of groundwater contamination by toxics than on any of the other paths (Scalf et al. 1973, Miller et al. 1974, Van der Leeden et al. 1975, Miller et al. 1977b, U.S. EPA 1977) and on the monitoring of toxics in groundwater than on the surface water, air, and land (Crouch et al. 1976, Everett et al. 1976, Hampton 1976, Wehran Engineering Corporation and Geraghty and Miller 1976, Fungaroli and Steiner 1979,

Miller 1980, Wang and Anderson 1981). Yet David Miller (in Lowrance 1981, pp. 28, 36) whose firm Geraghty and Miller has done a good deal of the research, in commenting on geohydrological surveys at chemical disposal sites, stated that:

> The lack of monitoring at tens of thousands of sites where there is potential for contamination, along with the lack of full-scale analysis of water quality at tens of thousands of wells, rule out the possibility for a reliable determination of the extent and severity of groundwater degradation and associated health risks in the United States.

Furthermore, Miller added:

> The monitoring industry is in its infancy. There is no consensus on drilling methods, sampling frequency and protocol, standard quality assurance procedures, or numbers of wells needed to define the problem.

Groundwater research emphasizes the great complexity of predicting the movements of chemical wastes at disposal sites. Many factors influence the rate of migration and the quality of a contaminated plume. First, the extent and type of lining at the disposal site will influence the rate of leakage. The rate of migration will also be affected by whether the waste is deposited in containers (corrosion will have to occur before it can escape), and in dry or wet form (dry waste will have to reach the field capacity which is the moisture content at which it transmits water). Site-specific geohydrological conditions are a third factor. For example, on the one hand, groundwater moving in a limestone channel will probably move rapidly with little interaction with surrounding materials. On the other hand, unconsolidated sediments with low permeability will allow only slow movement. In general, silt and clay tills slow migration more than do coastal plain sands. Fourth, the amount and frequency of precipitation, extent of soil freezing, and other conditions that depend on local meteorology are important. Lastly, the amount of pumping of the aquifer is a key determinant influencing the shape of the plume and the speed with which it moves.

The chemical quality of leachate or percolate reaching the water table also depends upon the types of chemicals disposed at the site. Not only do they vary in toxicity, but also in solubility in water, in pH, and in other physical properties. The greater the mixture of substances, the more likely an unanticipated mixture is to reach the water table. Miller (in Lowrance 1981, p. 35) succinctly summarizes the problem:

> plume shapes, lengths, rates of movement, and concentrations over time cannot always be predicted accurately, even with extensive study.

New sites with secure landfills would presumably not permit subsurface migration, or would they? A good deal of research has been focused on the suitability of different liners (Haxo et al. 1977). Josephson (1982) reported that the permeability of clay liners changes when in contact with certain classes of organic fluids (e.g., basic [aniline]; neutral [methanol]). Montague (1982) argues that there is no such thing as a secure landfill and that the best landfills only retard migration. Likening a secure landfill to a bathtub with an umbrella on top, he argues that even if a liner or double-bottom liner remains intact, and if humans do not build on top of or near the site, that natural forces (erosion, vegetation planted on the umbrella, animals, sunlight and subsidence) will destroy the cap after human attention wanes. U.S. EPA (1982c) groundwater monitoring regulations for landfills present a strategy for detecting leakages with the understanding that leakage will occur and that monitoring is only a first line of defense.

The last decade has witnessed striking advances in the monitoring of hazardous chemicals; greatly improved testing methods and assay methods; and improvement in mathematical modelling of pollutants moving through the air, water, and ground. The epitome of these developments with respect to hazardous waste sites in our opinion was the multimedia transfer study by the U.S. EPA of, not surprisingly, Love Canal. Approximately 6,000 air, water, soil, biota, and sediment samples were taken. Unlike many previous studies, a careful quality assurance program was implemented to estimate the accuracy of the data and to document all of the procedures (U.S. EPA 1982a). The 1980 study also included a major geohydrologic investigation.

There will likely be further improvements in scientific knowledge of what, where, when and how to monitor along with new monitoring approaches (e.g., environmental monitors, biological, and biochemical indicators). Yet our baseline of knowledge is low and the substances and sites are so different that it is hard to be sanguine about science providing the equivalent of a yellow brick road for predicting the spread of contaminants. Like most others who write and speak about the subject of environmental monitoring at hazardous waste sites, we see research as a long-term endeavor, while decisive actions at some sites are needed now.

## Health Effects of Hazardous Waste

Effects on health are the most undesirable outcomes of hazardous waste disposal and have drawn most of the attention of the research community. Indeed, the following presentation draws heavily upon three conferences which were entirely or partially devoted to research on the health effects of hazardous chemical wastes (Lowrance 1981; Bloom 1981; Environmental Influences on Fertility, Pregnancy and Development 1982). Despite the importance of being able to predict outcomes of the disposing of hazardous chemical wastes, uncertainty about data, methods, and effects was the most obvious theme of all three conferences. Acute effects from damage incidents like fires and explosions and injury from debris are obvious. But an abnormal number of cancers, adverse reproductive outcomes (e.g., birth defects, low birth weights, spontaneous abortions), and other acute and chronic effects are more difficult to detect and even more difficult to attribute to hazardous wastes.

There are three main causes of uncertainty. One is that the hazardous character of most chemicals is not known because there are so many chemicals and because methods of testing chemicals and of extrapolating the results to endpoints of exposure are debatable. Excellent summaries of the effects of chemicals and books on how to assess the effects of chemicals are available (Sitting 1980, Sax 1978, Lewis and Tatkin 1979, Lee 1980, Conway 1979, Rizwanul 1980, and Cornaby 1981). Yet, relatively few chemicals have been tested for toxicity, and still fewer for mutagenesis, teratogenesis and carcinogenesis. The argument that because relatively few chemicals dominate the market, only these few need attention does not hold for hazardous waste sites because they have been the repositories for all chemicals, not just those that have been widely marketed.

It is infeasible to test all chemicals with epidemiological or animal tests. Only the use of short-term tests (e.g., Ames) holds out the possibility of testing many chemicals in the near future. The difficulties of extrapolating the short-term tests as well as animal tests to human populations are well-known to readers who have followed the saccharin controversy. Neel (in Bloom 1981) succinctly summarized the problem: "There is a wide band of uncertainty in our efforts to screen out mutagens and/or extrapolate from an experimental setting to effects on human populations."

Most, but not all, substances that have been classified as mutagens and/or carcinogens by animal bioassay and short-term mutagen test have been classified as carinogens in epidemiological studies. Voytek (in Lowrance 1981) argues that if one protects for carcinogens, then one is also protecting against sterility and other human reproductive hazards. While his claim is debatable, if it is correct and were applied to the testing of chemicals escaping from chemical waste sites, then the testing backlog would be reduced.

However, even if every chemical did not have to be separately tested for every effect, conclusive assessments of chemicals are retarded by the difficult problem of estimating the effects of chronic, low-dose exposures. Data that can be used to calculate the lower segment of dose-response curves are badly needed. In the absence of data, scientists debate the relative validity of linear dose-response models that produce considerably more health effects than do models that assume that there is a lower threshold before an effect will occur. For example, the Committee on the Biological Effects of Ionizing Radiation of the National Academy of Sciences (1980) reported a great polarity of views about the shape of the dose-response curve to estimate cancer and finally settled upon a hybrid of several types of models. The U.S. EPA, in a controversial decision, has decided to use linear models that assume no threshold before effects occur to estimate the health effects of chemicals.

Some chemical substances have been widely tested, and yet, scientists are reluctant to predict their impact. For example, as the basis for regulatory action, the U.S. EPA recently released a report on population risk of leukemia due to exposure to benzene (Albert 1981). Reading the report, one has the impression that the EPA carcinogen assessment group wished that it had considerably more evidence than the three epidemiological studies that were the foundation for the study.

Trihalomethanes (chloroform, fluoroform, bromoform) are another unproven threat that has received widespread attention because they are thought to be ubiquitous by-products of the interaction of chlorinated water and organic material in drinking water. After a detailed review of the literature, the Safe Drinking Water Committee of the National Academy of Sciences (1977, 1980) concluded that:

> The methodological complexities inherent in epidemiological studies of human populations exposed to multiple contaminants at low concentrations (ppb) in drinking water make it virtually impossible to establish a causal link between THM's (trihalomethanes) and an increase in cancer of the bladder or of any other site.

Statements of equivocation or infeasibility have been made about many other widely studied and ubiquitous substances like acryonitrile, polycyclic aromatic hydrocarbons, and cadmium. Furthermore, most chemicals either have not been tested for any health effects or have only received initial testing.

New protocols and procedures are being developed for specific problems such as acute toxicity (Normandy and Reynolds 1979) and effects on the immune system (Dandliker et al. 1979). The U.S. EPA (1982b) has published a set of documents that provide test guidelines for 39 health effects (e.g., specific tissue and organ toxicity, neurotoxicity, and mutagenicity). However, at this time, we cannot say how much danger is associated with exposure to a part per billion, part per million or part per thousand of most chemicals. A massive effort is needed to determine the risk associated with tens of thousands of chemicals.

If our ability to assess the impact of relatively simple and common chemicals is inadequate, then the inability to predict the effect of complex substances and mixtures such as those disposed of in chemical waste sites or formed in chemical waste sites greatly retards what can be inferred about the risk posed by living near a waste site. The toxicity of some substances is enhanced by mixing, while the effects of others may be reduced by mixing with other chemicals and by coming into contact with the contents of the soil and ground. In one of the few studies of chemicals derived from wastes, Epler (1980) reported a multidisciplinary effort to test seventeen solid waste extracts roughly representative of different types of industry and arsenic-contaminated groundwater. Much of the report was devoted to testing different approaches for characterizing the wastes. Perhaps major groups of mixtures, rather than each possible mixture, can be characterized; but such a notion is probably wishful thinking. Characterizing the substances emanating from hazardous waste disposal sites will probably require a long-term and expensive research effort.

A third major cause of uncertainty about the impacts of hazardous waste disposal sites on public health is variations in human receptivity. Empirical studies show that toxics are found in many Americans, but that there are wide variations in their effect on health (Jenkins 1979; Holleman and Hammons 1980). Among the plausible reasons for these variations are that some people smoke, consume substantial volumes of alcohol and drugs, and maintain nutritional habits that would lead to relatively high levels of hazardous chemicals in their bodies, and work or live near sources of hazardous chemicals, while others do not. A high body burden of hazardous chemicals does not necessarily lead to a noticeable health effect and vice versa. Some humans are extremely sensitive to substances (e.g., young, elderly, pregnant women), others are not (Friedman 1981). Finally, with respect to hazardous chemical waste sites, the widely varying types of chemicals and paths that they may take make it difficult to predict chronic, low dose exposure rates.

In summary, the diversity or total absence of knowledge about the hazardous character of substances at chemical waste sites, the diversity of site characteristics that can enhance or retard the migration of substances, and the diversity of the human population result in a wide range of susceptibility to chemical exposures from chemical hazardous waste sites and great uncertainty about public health effects.

*Love Canal: An Illustration of Uncertainty*

The continuing controversy over health impacts at Love Canal illustrates the high degree of uncertainty about health impacts. More money has been spent studying Love Canal than any other site. Yet more than five decades after it began to be used for a chemical disposal site and years after it became a household horror story, there is no definitive statement of what the health impacts have been or are likely to be. The articles and the book by Michael Brown (1979) lead one to believe that severe health impacts had occurred and would continue to occur. Brown's research was supported by a researcher at Roswell Park Memorial Institute who reported birth-related problems and by an EPA cytogenetics study (*Environmental Science and Technology* 1980, Smith 1980).

The New York State Department of Health has found much less evidence of health effects. Janerich et al (1981) studied cancer incidence rates in the census tract surrounding Love Canal for the period 1955–1977. Since waste burial began in the 1920s, the liver, lymphoma, and leukemia rates for the period 1955–1977 should have shown an excess of incidence, assuming that migration was not a confounding factor. Rates in the area were usually among the highest in the Niagara Falls area, which, in turn, were higher than the remainder of New York State (excluding New York City). But the authors conclude that the registry data show "no evidence for higher cancer rates associated with residence near Love Canal."

Vianna (1980), a well-known epidemiologist with the State of New York, compared spontaneous abortions, low birthweights, and congenital defects in that part of the Love Canal area that was flooded during high water periods and therefore in contact with chemical wastes with that part that was not flooded. He reported that rates of spontaneous abortions and congenital defects were higher in the flood-water area than they were in the non flood-water area, albeit the excess was not statistically significant. The percentage of low birthweight babies was higher in the flood-water area, and Vianna refers to the birthweight data as the most reliable result. However, he cautions that the results are tentative because of the type of data that was used (recall by patients) and because of uncontrolled, confounding factors (e.g., smoking, social status).

In late 1980, a panel of scientists appointed by New York Governor Hugh Carey and headed by Lewis Thomas of Memorial Sloan-Kettering Institute released a report that questioned the evidence of health effects among Love Canal residents (Smith 1980; Environmental Science and Technology 1980). The essence of their report was that the early tests of acute effects were poorly designed (especially the human chromosome test) and there were no good studies of chronic effects. Cantlon (1980), then chairman of the Environmental Studies Board of the National Academy of Sciences, called the chromosome study "a classic case of how not to do an operation."

Most recently, responding to the observation that the Thomas committee report has been used to write off the Love Canal case as one of hysterical overreaction, Levine (1982) sharply criticized the Thomas report as hurried, incomplete, and disparaging of all the studies that showed health effects, often on the grounds of minor methodological and data problems. In summary, the existing Love Canal studies are inconclusive and may remain so for one or more decades, if, indeed, conclusive findings can ever be made.

## Social and Economic Effects

Numerous news stories and a small amount of empirical research provide evidence that abandoned sites and proposed sites will drive people out of communities or at least keep out new people and depress land values. But the evidence is anecdotal and not unequivocal.

New stories are common. Brown (1979, p. 12) describes the plight of one Love Canal family:

> The Schroeder backyard, once featured in a local newspaper for its beauty, now had degenerated to the point where it was unfit even to walk upon.

Stories like those of the Schroeders abound in local newspapers. Homeowners are reportedly trapped in neighborhoods which have been psychologically debilitated, if not physically disfigured, by an abandoned chemical waste site.

The survey research, while limited in size and almost exclusively related to municipal solid waste sites, shows that Americans do not want to discuss the subject of solid waste and certainly do not want a site in their neighborhoods. Moore and Ishler (1980) show that solid waste is not a major public issue. They found solid waste management to be at the bottom of a list of 49 priority issues (followed by post-high school education) in a 1980 survey of almost 10,000 Pennsylvania residents.

A community that gets a facility is perceived as an undesirable place to live. For example, about 200 persons in Erie County, Pennsylvania (Commissioners of Erie County 1972), were asked their reactions to the siting of a municipal solid waste facility near their homes. Less than 6 percent were willing to accept the facility, and another 6 percent were undecided. Almost two-thirds were unequivocally opposed and another one-fourth would fight unless they could be convinced that the landfill would be carefully operated. Coughlin et al. (1973) reported that only 4 percent of sampled residents who lived near a relatively well-run Pennsylvania landfill found any positive influence on the neighborhood. Many of the objectors in Coughlin's study knew very little about the operations at the site and listed "just the fact that it is there" as the major objection.

At a symposium entitled "The Not-In-My-Backyard Syndrome" (1983), the subject of psychological impacts was directly addressed by Reverend Ted Creen. A member of the Board of Directors of Home Support Services of Whitchurch-Stoufville, Canada, he related his insights on stress and depression among families as a result of a prolonged confrontation between residents and government officials over a proposed expansion of a landfill. Analogies were made by Reverend Creen to the psychological stress experienced by family members in the Love Canal area. Specific symptoms of the Canadian families were anxiety over the uncertain impacts of hazardous waste in the landfill, the tendency for married couples to disagree strongly about the level of public opposition to the proposal, unpredictable behavior exhibited by children in the town who do not fully understand the problem and react to community confrontation, and domestic disharmony.

Even direct economic benefit does not guarantee acceptance of a new site. Philipovich (1968) and Pollock (1974) reported that proposals to place baled solid waste in abandoned, Pennsylvania coal mines were rejected. In one case $35-40 million in direct revenues had been forecasted for a poor community. The proposal was rejected by voters by a 2 to 1 margin because the citizens did not want their town to become the "garbage spot" of Pennsylvania.

A lack of knowledge and fear are characteristic of the public's perceptions. Resources for the Future (Council on Environmental Quality 1980) asked more than 1,500 people how they felt about living near five types of facilities: a 10-story office building; a large factory; a coal-fired power plant; a nuclear power station; and a new chemical waste disposal site. Less than 30 percent of the people were willing to accept either of the last two facilities within 10 miles of their homes. In comparison, more than 60 percent were willing to have a 10-story office building, large factory, and coal-fired power plant within 10 miles of their homes. Their views about living near a chemical waste site were not based on knowledge of what happened at Love Canal. Resources for the Future found that 74 percent of respondents knew what had happened at Three Mile Island, but only 22 percent knew what had happened at Love Canal. The respondents knew more about acid rainfall and oil production than they did about what happened at Love Canal.

Bealer et al. (1981) summarize the public's reaction to proposed waste sites as:

The acticipation of "pain" may very well far exceed its reality. But facts be damned. It is one of the oldest of sociological axioms that if the person defines a situation as real it will be real in its consequences for him or her.

The well-known study of 21 hazardous waste sites by Centaur Associates (1979) suggests that the best way of finding a new site is to keep a very low profile, one that does not contribute to any fears. Strong opposition occurred in cases where a new site was proposed in an area that was not industrialized and had to undergo a complex licensing process. The four sites that were approved with the least opposition were sites in already industrialized areas, on private property with a relatively simple licensing process. Much more will be said about the public's perceptions of new sites in Chapters 6 and 7.

The impact of solid waste sites on property values has received limited attention, but the little it has shows that the impact is not always negative. Massey (1978) reported that in his sample of 454 people in the states of Illinois, Indiana, and Wisconsin, of those who thought that landfills had an effect on property values, virtually everyone assumed that the effect was negative. However, the majority of respondents did not think that it had any effect. Persons with higher property values were more likely to be opposed than persons with lower property values, probably because they had more to lose. Coughlin (in Stevens, 1974) reported a study in which little effect was noticed near a Philadelphia landfill. Massey (1978) suggested that the property value issue was invoked as a defense against new sites because the strongest protests about property impacts were in places threatened with sites.

## SUMMARY

More than anything else, this chapter has shown that generalizing about the effects of hazardous waste sites from the few spectacular examples is inappropriate. The need for conclusive statements about the health, environmental, social, and economic effects of existing and proposed chemical waste sites has not been met, nor is it likely to be met in the immediate future. The contents of the existing sites are not known because records of what was put in and the extent of mixing are not known. Predicting the exit routes of chemical wastes is a site-specific task requiring data, most of which has not been collected. The lack of data and agreed-upon models to calculate the effects of chronic, low-dose exposures does not allow firm inferences about potential health effects. Social and economic effects are presumed to be negative, but have not been systematically studied. Absent clear scientific conclusions that can be explained to them and can counter media sensationalism, the public believes the worst about every abandoned, existing and proposed site, thereby widening further the already chasm-like credibility gap created by a lack of information on generation of wastes and a lack of proper waste management control.

## REFERENCES

Air Pollution Control Association. *Toxic Air Contaminants, Health Effects, Monitoring and Control.* Pittsburgh: The Association, 1981.

Albert, R. *Carcinogen Assessment Group's Final Report on Population Risk to Ambient Benzene Exposure.* Springfield, VA: National Technical Information Service, 1981.

Atkins, P. *The Pesticide Manufacturing Industry: Current Waste Treatment and Disposal Practices.* Springfield, VA: National Technical Information Service, 1972.

Bealer, R., Martin, K., Crider, D. *Sociological Aspects of Siting Facilities for Solid Wastes Disposal.* University Park, PA: Department of Agricultural Economics and Rural Sociology, Pennsylvania State University, 1981.

Bloom, A., ed. *Guidelines for Studies of Human Population Exposed to Mutagenic and Reproductive Hazards.* White Plains, NY: March of Dimes Birth Defects Foundation, 1981.

Brown, M. *Laying Waste: The Poisoning of America by Toxic Chemicals.* New York: Pantheon Books, 1979.

Cantlon, J. "Science and EPA." *EPA Journal*, Vol. 6, 1980, pp. 25–27.

Centaur Associates, Inc. *Siting of Hazardous Management Facilities and Public Opposition.* Washington, D.C.: U.S. Environmental Protection Agency, 1979.

Commissioners of Erie County, Pennsylvania. *Solid Waste Directed Information and Education Program.* Erie, PA: Great Lakes Research Institute, 1972.

Committee on the Biological Effects of Ionizing Radiation, National Research Council. *The Effects on Populations of Exposure to Low Levels of Ionizing Radiation.* Washington, D.C.: National Academy of Sciences Press, 1980.

Commoner, B. *The Closing Circle.* New York: Bantam Press, 1971.

Conway, R., ed. *Environmental Risk Analysis for Chemicals.* New York: Van Nostrand, 1979.

Copenhaver, E. and Wilkinson, B. "Movement of Hazardous Substances in Soil: A Bibliography." Vol. 1, *Selected Metals.* Springfield, VA: National Technical Information Service, 1979a.

———. "Movement of Hazardous Substances in Soil: A Bibliography." Vol. 2, *Pesticides.* Springfield, VA: National Technical Information Service, 1979b.

Cornaby, B., ed. *Management of Toxic Substances in Our Ecosystems: Taming the Medusa.* Woburn, MA: Ann Arbor Science Pub., 1981.

Coughlin, R., Newburger, H., and Seigner, C. "Perceptions of Landfill Operations Held by Nearby Residents." Philadelphia, PA: Regional Science Research Institute., Discussion Paper Series, No. 65, 1973.

Council on Environmental Quality. *Environmental Quality, the Eleventh Annual Report of the Council on Environmental Quality.* Washington, D.C.: Superintendent of Documents, U.S. Government Printing Office, 1980.

Creen, T. Presentation at "Not-In-My-Backyard Syndrome." Ontario, Canada, May 13–14, 1983.

Crouch, R., Eckert, R., and Rugg, D. *Monitoring Ground Water Quality: Economic Framework and Principles.* Springfield, VA: National Technical Information Service, 1976.

Cupitt, L. *Fate of Toxic and Hazardous Materials in the Air Environment.* Research Triangle Park, North Carolina: Environmental Sciences Research Lab, 1980.

Dandliker, W., Hicks, A., Levison, S., Brown, R. *Effects of Pesticides on the Immune Response*. Springfield, VA: National Technical Information Service, 1979.

Eichenberger, B., Edwards, J., Chen, K., Stephens, R. *A Case Study of Hazardous Wastes in Class I Landfills*. Springfield, VA: National Technical Information Service, 1978.

Eisler, R., Rossoll, R., Gaboury, G. *Annotated Bibliography on Biological Effects of Metals in the Aquatic Environments*. Springfield, VA: National Technical Information Service, 1979.

*Environmental Influences on Fertility, Pregnancy and Development: Directions for Future Research*. Conference, Cincinnati, Ohio, May 24–25, 1982.

*Environmental Science and Technology*. Vol. 14, 1980, p. 1412.

Epler, J., Larimer, F. Rao, T., Burnett, E., Griest, W. *Toxicity of Leachates*. Springfield, VA: National Technical Information Service, 1980.

Everett, L., et al. *Monitoring Ground Water Quality: Methods and Costs*. Springfield, VA: National Technical Information Service, 1976.

Florio, J. U.S. Congress. House Joint Hearing before the Subcommittee on Health and the Environment and the Subcommittee on Transportation and Commerce of the Committee on Interstate and Foreign Commerce, 96th Congress, 2nd Session, August 22, 1980, Serial 96219, Washington, D.C.: U.S. Government Printing Office, 1981.

Freudenthal, H., Rubenstein, J., Uzzo, A. *Effects of Pathogenic and Toxic Materials Transported Via Cooling Device Drift*. 2 Vols. Research Triangle Park, NC: U.S. Environmental Protection Agency, 1979.

Friedman, R. *Sensitive Populations and Environmental Standards*. Washington, D.C.: Conservation Foundation, 1981.

Fuller, W. *Movement of Selected Metals, Asbestos, and Cyanide in Soil, Applications to Waste Disposal Problem*. Springfield, VA: National Technical Information Service, 1977.

———. *Investigation of Landfill Leachate Pollutant Attenuation by Soils*. Springfield, VA: National Technical Information Service, 1978.

Fungaroli, A., Steiner, L. *Investigation of Sanitary Landfill Behavior*. 2 Vols. Springfield, VA: National Technical Information Service, 1979.

Ghassemi, M., Quinlivan, S. *A Study of Selected Landfills Designed as Pesticide Disposal Sites*. Springfield, VA: National Technical Information Service, 1975.

Gibbs, L. *The Love Canal: My Story*. Albany, NY: State University of New York Press, 1982.

Hampton, N. *Monitoring Ground Water Quality: Data Management*. Springfield, VA: National Technical Information Service, 1976.

Hatayama, H., Chen, J., de Vera, E., Stephens, R., Storm, D. *A Method for Determining the Compatability of Hazardous Wastes*. Springfield, VA: National Technical Information Service, 1978.

Haxo, H., Haxo, R., White, R. *Liner Materials Exposed to Hazardous and Toxic Sludges*. Springfield, VA: National Technical Information Service, 1977.

Holleman, J., Hummons, A. *Levels of Chemical Contaminants in Nonoccupationally Exposed U.S. Residents*. Springfield, VA: National Technical Information Service, 1980.

Janerich, D., Burnett, W., Feck, G., Hoff, M., Nasca, P., Polednak, A., Greenwald, P., Vianna, N. "Cancer Incidence in the Love Canal Area." *Science*, Vol. 212, 1981, pp. 1404–1407.

Jenkins, D. *Toxic Trace Metals in Mammalian Hair and Nails*. Springfield, VA: National Technical Information Service, 1979.

Josephson, J. "Monitoring Airborne Organics." *Environmental Science and Technology*, Vol. 15, 1981, pp. 731–733.

———. "Immobilization and Leachability of Hazardous Waste." *Environmental Science and Technology*. Vol. 16, 1982, pp. 219A–223A.

Jones, P., Leber, P., eds. *Polynuclear Aromatic Hydrocarbons*. 3 Vols. Woburn, MA: Ann Arbor Science, 1979.

Kushnir, J., Nagy, S. *Assessment of Industrial Hazardous Waste Practices, Rubber and Plastics Industry*. 4 Vols. Springfield, VA: National Technical Information Service, 1978.

Lassiter, R., Baughman, G., Burns, L. "Fate of Toxic Organic Substances in the Aquatic Environment." In Vol. 7, *State-of-the-Art in Ecological Modelling*, 1981, pp. 219–246.

Lee, S., Mudd, J., eds. *Assessing Toxic Effects of Environmental Pollutants*. Woburn, MA: Ann Arbor Science, 1980.

Leonard, R., Ziegler, R., Brown, W., Yang, J., Reif, H. *Assessment of Industrial Hazardous Waste Practices in the Metal Smelting and Refining Industry*. 4 Vols. Springfield, VA: National Technical Information Service, 1977.

Levine, A. *Love Canal: Science, Politics and People*. Lexington, MA: Lexington Books, 1982.

Lewis, R., Tatkin, R. *Registry of Toxic Effects of Chemical Substances, 1978 Edition*. Washington, D.C.: U.S. Government Printing Office, 1979.

Lowrance, W. *Assessment of Health Effects at Chemical Disposal Sites*. Los Altos, CA: Wm. Kaufmann, Inc., 1981.

Massey, D. *Attitudes of Nearby Residents Toward Establishing Sanitary Landfills*. Washington, D.C.: U.S. Environmental Protection Agency, 1978.

Miller, D., DeLuca, F., Tessier, T. *Ground Water Contamination in the Northeast States*. Washington, D.C.: U.S. Government Printing Office, 1974.

Miller, D., Braids, O., Walker, W. *The Prevalence of Subsurface Migration of Hazardous Chemical Substances at Selected Industrial Waste Land Disposal Sites*. Washington, D.C.: U.S. Environmental Protection Agency, 1977a.

Miller, J., Hackenberry, P., DeLuca, F. *Ground Water Pollution Problems in the Southeastern United States*. Washington, D.C.: U.S. Environmental Protection Agency, 1977b.

Miller, D., ed. *Waste Disposal Effects on Ground Water*. Berkeley, CA: Premier Press, 1980.

Montague, P. *New Jersey Hazardous Waste News*. Vol. 2, 1982, p. 1.

Moore, D., Ishler, A. *Pennsylvania: The Citizen's Viewpoint*. University Park, PA: Pennsylvania State Cooperative Extension Service, 1980.

*New Jersey Hazardous Waste News*. "Landfill Threatens Atlantic City Water." Vol. 1, 1981, p. 1.

Normandy, M., Reynolds, R. *Acute Toxicity Testing Criteria for New Chemical Substances*. Springfield, VA: National Technical Information Service, 1979.

Page, G. "Comparison of Groundwater and Surface Water for Patterns and Levels of Contamination by Toxic Substances." *Environmental Science and Technology*, Vol. 15, 1981, pp. 1475–1481.

Philipovich, P. "Coal Region Doesn't Want Garbage." *Compost Science*, Vol. 9, 1968, pp. 29–30.

Pollock, E. "Residents Against Landfill." *Solid Waste Management*, Vol. 16, 1974, pp. 80 and 88.

Popper F. "Sitting LULU's." *Planning*, Vol. 47, 1981, pp. 12–15.

Reese, C., Dodson, I., Ulrich, V., Becker, D., Kempter, C. *Pesticides in the Aquatic Environment*. Springfield, VA: National Technical Information Service, 1972.

Rizwanul, H., ed. *Dynamics, Exposure and Hazard Assessment of Toxic Chemicals*. Woburn, MA: Ann Arbor Science, 1980.

Safe Drinking Water Committee, National Research Council. *Drinking Water and Health*. 3 Vols. Washington, D.C.: National Academy Press, 1977, 1980.

Sax, I., ed. *Dangerous Properties of Industrial Materials*. New York: Van Nostrand Reinhold, 1978.

Scalf, M., Keeley, J., LaFevers, C. *Ground Water Pollution in the South Central States*. Springfield, VA: National Technical Information Service, 1973.

SCCOSH *News*, "Silicon Valley's 'Love Canal.'" Vol. 3, 1981.

Schimmel, S., Patrick, J., Faas, L., Oglesby, J., Wilson, A. "Kepone: Toxicity and Bio-accumulation in Blue Crabs." *Estuaries*, Vol. 2, 1979, pp. 9–15.

Schuetzle, D., ed. *Monitoring Toxic Substances*. Washington, D.C.: American Chemical Society, 1979.

Singer, G. ". . .Nor any Drop to Drink: Public Policies Toward Chemical Contamination of Drinking Water." Draft Paper, Princeton, NJ: Center for Energy and Environmental Studies, Princeton University, 1981.

Sittig, M. *Priority Toxic Pollutants — Health Impacts and Allowable Limits*. Park Ridge, N.J.: Noyes Data Corp., 1980.

Smith, R. "Love Canal Reviewed." *Science*, Vol. 210, 1980, p. 513.

Stevens, B. *Criteria for Regional Solid Waste Management Planning*. Cincinnati, OH: U.S. Environmental Protection Agency, 1974.

Suta, B. *Assessment of Human Exposure to Atmospheric Acrylonitrile*. Springfield, VA: National Technical Information Service, 1982.

*Time*. "The Poisoning of America." September 22, 1980.

U.S. Comptroller General. *Waste Disposal Practices — A Threat to Health and the Nation's Water Supply, Report to Congress*. Washington, D.C.: U.S. General Accounting Office, 1978.

U.S. Environmental Protection Agency. *Hazardous Wastes*. Washington, D.C.: U.S. Government Printing Office, 1975.

———. *Pharmaceutical Industry: Hazardous Waste Generation, Treatment, and Disposal*. Springfield, VA: National Technical Information Service, 1976.

———. *The Report to Congress: Waste Disposal Practices and Their Effects on Ground Water*. Washington. D.C.: U.S. Government Printing Office, 1977.

———. *Damages and Threats Caused by Hazardous Material Spills*. Washington, D.C.: The Agency, 1980a, p. 1.

———. *Everybody's Problem: Hazardous Waste*. Washington, D.C.: U.S. Government Printing Office, 1980b.

———. *Environmental Monitoring at Love Canal*. 3 Vols. Springfield, VA: National Technical Information Service, 1982a.

———. *Test Guidelines: Health Effects*. Springfield, VA: National Technical Information Service, 1982b.

———. U.S. Federal Register, 40 CFR, parts 122, 260, 264, 265, 1982c, pp. 32247–32388.

van der Leeden, F., Cerrillo, L., Miller, D. *Ground Water Pollution Problems in the Northwestern United States*. Springfield, VA: National Technical Information Service, 1975.

Vianna, N. "Adverse Pregnancy Outcomes — Potential Endpoints of Human Toxicity in the Love Canal, Preliminary Results." In Porter, I. and Hook, E., eds., *Human Embryonic and Fetal Death*. New York: Academic Press, 1980, pp. 165–168.

Wang, H., Anderson, M. *Introduction to Groundwater Modeling*. San Francisco: W.H. Freeman and Co., 1981.

Warren, J. "Water, Water Everywhere." *The American Journal*, Vol. 3, 1981, pp. 17–21.

Wehran Engineering Corporation and Geraghty and Miller, Inc. *Procedures Manual for Monitoring Solid Waste Disposal Sites*. Washington, D.C.: U.S. Environmental Protection Agency, 1976.

Weinberg, D. "We Almost Lost Elizabeth." *New Jersey Monthly*, Vol. 4, August 1980, pp. 35–39, 97–113.

Wilkinson, R., Kelso, G., Hopkins, F. *State-of-the-Art Report: Pesticide Disposal Research*. Springfield, VA: National Technical Information Service, 1978.

*4*

# The Orphans: Abandoned Hazardous Waste Sites In The United States

Some people are impatient with those who would review early efforts to determine the scope of the chemical hazardous waste problem in the United States. There are good reasons for their impatience: namely, the efforts reveal how little was known; the material is tedious; and it is not particularly helpful for future planning. It might therefore be politic to skip quietly over initial efforts to estimate the scope of the problem. But there are two very strong counterarguments which led us to write this chapter. Uncertainty and its impact on credibility and decisionmaking are major themes that run throughout this volume. To be consistent to this theme, the saga of efforts to find abandoned sites is presented. Second, as will be explained in this chapter, we are not sanguine about the final list of abandoned sites, the list of priority sites, nor about the absence of a comprehensive list of sites which would include active chemical sites, lagoons, and ponds on industrial properties and on military and mining sites.

## INITIAL ESTIMATES

Love Canal raised the public consciousness and motivated the United States government through the Office of Management and Budget (OMB) and the U.S.EPA to determine the scope and potential damage caused by hazardous waste sites. The U.S.EPA regions and Fred C. Hart Associates provided the first estimates of the number of sites and estimates of the worst sites.

106

## U.S. EPA Region Estimates

In late 1978, Thomas Jorling, then Assistant Administrator for Water and Waste Management of the U.S.EPA, addressing the concern that the government might be called upon to fund other Love-Canal type claims, sent a memo to all regional administrators requesting the following:

1. A rough estimate of the total number of landfill, storage and other sites that may contain hazardous wastes in any quantity which now or potentially could cause adverse impact on public health or the environment;
2. A rough estimate of the number of these sites that may contain significant quantities of hazardous wastes which could cause significant imminent hazard to public health (this is a subset of above estimate);
3. An inventory and description of those sites for which EPA has information in its files (this is a further subset of the above estimates); and
4. An estimate of the costs of (a) assessing the public health and environmental hazard, (b) engineering studies to determine remedial measures and (c) remedial measures for a dozen or more sites which typify various types of incidents.

The response from the ten U.S. EPA regions was that there were 32,000 sites which may contain hazardous wastes and 838 which may contain significant quantities of hazardous wastes. The estimates were, however, inconsistent and imprecise. Many of the regions made qualitative estimates and four of the ten regions did not state the method they used. Sites were not included because of insufficient information; some regions included all municipal landfills, others did not; and two regions did not estimate the worst sites.

Some of the results were hard to believe. Region 7 (Iowa, Missouri, Kansas, Nebraska), a relatively rural region, was estimated to have the second highest number of sites, indeed sixteen times as many sites as the urban-industrial New Jersey-New York region (Region 2), and more than twenty times as many sites as Region 9 (which includes California) and Region 6 (which includes Texas) (Table 4-1 column 1, Figure 4-1). This estimate implied that rural regions of the United States were bearing a greater share of the hazardous waste burden than would be expected by their economies.

## Fred C. Hart Associates

Fred C. Hart Associates was retained by the EPA to provide an alternative estimate of the number of sites and to provide cleanup costs. Their method had four steps:

## TABLE 4-1

### Hazardous Waste Sites By U.S. EPA Region: U.S. EPA, Fred C. Hart, Quick-Look, And Emergency Remedial Response System

| Region number | Center | Number of Sites U.S.EPA[1] | Hart[2] | EPA Quick Look[3] | ERRS[4] |
|---|---|---|---|---|---|
| 1 | Boston | 1,200 | 1,560 | 760 | 657 |
| 2 | New York City | 509 | 2,243 | 1,508 | 1,796 |
| 3 | Philadelphia | 5,000 | 1,850 | 822 | 1,117 |
| 4 | Atlanta | 14,000 | 2,711 | 1,402 | 2,965 |
| 5 | Chicago | 1,800 | 4,665 | 2,519 | 2,148 |
| 6 | Dallas | 320 | 1,956 | 2,140 | 1,578 |
| 7 | Kansas City | 8,000 | 1,180 | 414 | 970 |
| 8 | Denver | 25 | 613 | 266 | 533 |
| 9 | San Francisco | 400 | 1,949 | 819 | 1,059 |
| 10 | Seattle | 1,000 | 638 | 616 | 569 |
| Total | U.S.A. | 32,254 | 19,365 | 11,266 | 13,392 |

Notes: [1]Data gathered by U.S.EPA from each region. Method varied in every region.
[2]Estimated from 16-industry study and census materials. They also estimate 31,299 inactive sites for a total of 50,664.
[3]A running total of potential sites kept by the EPA.
[4]The U.S. EPA Emergency Remedial Response System gathered under Superfund as of January 1983. The number is now estimated to be more than 16,000.
Sources: Fred C. Hart, 1979 and U.S.EPA Quick Look system as of September 1981.

1. Identify Active Sites. Those treatment, storage and disposal facilities presently handling various types and volumes of hazardous wastes must be estimated, including such factors as (a) waste type(s); (b) technology used (e.g., landfill, lagooning, incineration, etc.); and (c) condition of the site, including whether it is in an environmentally sensitive area (e.g., wetlands, floodplain, etc.).

2. Identify Inactive Sites. The number of sites formerly used as hazardous waste facilities must be estimated, along with the range of information identified in Step 1 above.

3. Assess Environmental Adequacy of Site. Based on site data and treatment, storage and disposal facility guidelines as mandated under RCRA, the adequacy of both active and inactive sites must be determined.

4. Assign Required Level of Clean-up. The necessity of Level I measures (e.g.,

## FIGURE 4-1

## U.S. EPA REGIONS
### (48 contiguous states)

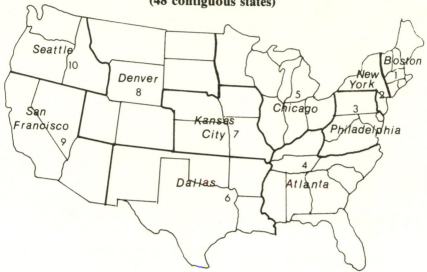

emergency mitigative measures), Level II step (e.g., extensive clean-up procedures, removal of wastes, etc.) or some phased combination of the two must be assessed.

The first step combined two data sources: studies of hazardous waste management practices of sixteen major hazardous waste producers (see Chapter 1), and U.S. Department of Commerce sources of the economies of different parts of the United States. The result was an estimate of 19,365 active hazardous waste sites (Table 4-1, column 2).

The second step in the Fred C. Hart project was to estimate inactive sites. It was assumed that a site would be used for a decade and that an improperly operated site could require post-closure monitoring and maintenance for 40 years. Production data were inadequate for the task of estimating the prevalence of sites during earlier decades. Accordingly, a rough estimating equation was prepared from examing historical data:

$$AE = (.80 - n(.05)) \times AG_{1970-1980}$$

where AE is the average number of generators during a decade before 1970–1980; n is the number of decades away from 1970–1980; and AG is the number of active generators during 1970–1980 (19,365).

Solving for the period 1960–1970, we get

AG = (.80-1(.05)(19,365)) = .75(19,365) = 14,524

Applying this equation back to 1930–1940 yielded an estimate of over 50,000 active and inactive sites in the United States compared to the EPA survey estimate of 32,000. Suffice it to say, these were rough extrapolations that may not resemble reality.

The third step taken by Fred C. Hart Associates was to estimate the number of sites posing a significant threat. Two approaches were taken. The simpler was applying the 4 percent rule: multiplying the percentage of problem sites reported in the initial EPA survey by the total number of sites estimated by Fred C. Hart Associates. The second approach was to apply two coefficients to the estimate of the total number of sites. One was a widely quoted EPA estimate that 90 percent of hazardous waste volume is improperly disposed. The second coefficient comes from Fred C. Hart Associates research in which it was found that 75 percent of landfill sites were located on major aquifers, floodplains, and wetlands. Combining the two coefficients leads to the conclusion that two-thirds (.75 x .90 = .675) of the wastes were disposed of on significant sites that could lead to serious water pollution.

Applying these two approaches to the estimated total number of hazardous waste sites yielded estimates ranging from 1.2 to 34.5 thousand significant problem sites (Table 4-2).

### TABLE 4-2

#### Comparison of Initial Estimates of Total And of Priority Sites

| Source of Estimate of Total Sites | Total Sites | Priority Sites | |
|---|---|---|---|
| | | 4 % rule[1] | Alternative[2] |
| U.S.EPA | 32,254 | 1,204 | 21,933 |
| Fred C. Hart | 50,664 | 2,027 | 34,452 |

Notes: [1].04 × total number of hazardous waste sites.
       [2](.75 × .90) × total number of hazardous waste sites.
Source: Fred C. Hart, 1979, p. 25.

## SECOND SET OF ESTIMATES

The numbers 30,000–50,000 for total sites and 2,000 sites posing imminent hazards continue to be widely quoted. However, these intitial estimates
were supplanted within two years of their publication.

### Number of Sites: EPA Quick-Look Report

The EPA regional offices compiled lists of sites, excluding gasoline stations, dry cleaning establishments, and other less dangerous activities. The
list of more than 11,000 sites, called the Quick-Look Site Tracking System,
was the first systematic attempt to determine the potential for hazardous
waste contamination. Sites were identified as potentially dangerous because
of reported incidents or knowledge of materials handled at the site.

When examined by EPA region, the Quick-Look results were similar to
the Fred C. Hart estimates (Table 4-1 column 3). Regions 5 (Chicago), 6
(Dallas), 2 (New York) and 4 (Atlanta) had the greatest number of sites in
both lists, and Regions 8 (Denver), 7 (Kansas City), 10 (Seattle), and 1
(Boston) had the smallest number of sites. Neither the Fred C. Hart nor the
Quick-Look list bears a systematic relationship to the initial EPA list.

Both the Fred C. Hart study and the Quick-Look system give the general
impression of a strong relationship between the location of sites and industrialization. This is not surprising in light of the fact that industry is the
direct source of most of the waste included in the U.S. EPA studies. This
impression is strengthened by examining state data. Eighteen states are
estimated to generate 80 percent of the hazardous waste (see Chapter 1).
These 18 states contained 63 percent of the Quick-Look sites. According to
the Quick-Look report, 11 states had 59 percent of the sites (see Table 4-3).
With one exception, Oklahoma, all are populous, urbanized, and industrialized states. Most of the remaining sites reported by the Quick-Look
system were in the Southeast.

A less impressionistic view of the correlates of the location of sites was
gained by some simple statistical tests. The 50 states were divided into three
groups based on their number of Quick-Look sites:

1. > 350 sites = 11 states
2. 150–349 sites = 12 states
3. < 150 sites = 27 states.

Cross tabulations were made between this trichotomy measuring the
number of potential waste sites and the location of activities associated with
production and use of hazardous materials. Contingency coefficients and
significance tests measure the strength of the relationships (Table 4-4).

**TABLE 4-3**

### Location of Quick-Look Sites by State

| State | Number of Quick-Look Sites |
|---|---|
| 1. Texas | 922 |
| 2. New York | 881 |
| 3. Ohio | 686 |
| 4. Michigan | 622 |
| 5. Illinois | 618 |
| 6. New Jersey | 539 |
| 7. Oklahoma | 530 |
| 8. California | 497 |
| 9. Massachusetts | 475 |
| 10. Pennsylvania | 403 |
| 11. Indiana | 386 |
| Total | 6,559 |
| % of Total | 59 |

As expected, there were strong associations between the number of Quick-Look sites and the number of chemical, ferrous and non-ferrous metal workers, total manufacturing workers, and population distribution. Associations with indicators of mineral and farm production were weaker than they were with the manufacturing industries and population distribution.

There are some interesting exceptions to the general association between where the waste was dumped and sources. Oklahoma was a clear exception because it was not among the most populous or industrialized states. Unlike the case in many of the other states, the number of Quick-Look sites in Oklahoma was probably due to mineral-producing activities. Conspicuous by their absence from states with the greatest numbers of potential sites were four states which are populous and/or have a large manufacturing base: Florida, Tennessee, North Carolina, and Louisiana.

Summarizing, the EPA Quick-Look list of potential sites provided the first detailed list of potential sites in the United States and produced the expected association between sources of and sinks for hazardous chemical wastes.

## TABLE 4-4

### Contingency Coefficients Between Number of Potential Hazardous Waste Sites from the Quick-Look Report and Potential Sources of Hazardous Waste: State Scale

| Indicator | Contingency Coefficient[1] | Significance[2] |
|---|---|---|
| 1. Chemical production workers, 1972 (SIC 28)[3] | .85 | .001 |
| 2. Total manufacturing production workers, 1972 (SIC 19–39) | .80 | .001 |
| 3. Total population, 1975 | .80 | .001 |
| 4. Non-ferrous metal production workers, 1972 (SIC 34) | .78 | .001 |
| 5. Ferrous metal production workers, 1972 (SIC 33) | .76 | .001 |
| 6. Mineral production workers, 1972 | .56 | .02 |
| 7. Farm population, 1970 | .45 | — |

Notes: [1]Maximum coefficent value for a 3 by 3 table is .8165. Therefore, the contingency coefficent is divided by .8165 to obtain a range of -1 to 1.
[2]Significance shown if .05 or higher.
[3]SIC is the standard industrial code used by the U.S. Bureau of the Census to classify industrial groups. For example, SIC 28 is chemicals.
Source: U.S. Bureau of the Census, 1973a, 1973b, 1977.

## Worst Sites: U.S. EPA and the Congress

The Congress and EPA began to accumulate data about the types of sites and the problems they created, and to identify particularly dangerous sites. In 1980, the U.S. House of Representatives Subcommittee on Environment, Energy and National Resources working from a list of 2,100 sites, named 250 sites where hazardous wastes were identified as a threat to drinking water supplies. Nine states had 73 percent of the sites (see Table 4-5).

Florida is among the most populous states and is as dependent upon groundwater as is Mississippi. Ohio, Pennsylvania, and Michigan are urban-industrial states with many disposal sites. The reasons for the large number of sites in Connecticut, Missouri, South Carolina, and Tennessee

## TABLE 4-5

### Initial Worst Sites, By State

| State | House of Rep. List | EPA Quick Look | % of Pop. Served by Groundwater[1] |
|-------|--------------------|----------------|-------------------------------------|
| | | Number of Sites | |
| 1. Florida | 54 | 166 | 88 |
| 2. South Carolina | 23 | 154 | 18 |
| 3. Ohio | 21 | 686 | 32 |
| 4. Pennsylvania | 20 | 403 | 20 |
| 5. Connecticut | 16 | 185 | 12 |
| 6. Mississippi | 14 | 59 | 86 |
| 7. Missouri | 13 | 210 | 21 |
| 8. Michigan | 11 | 622 | 20 |
| 9. Tennessee | 10 | 308 | 39 |
| Total | 182 | 2,793 | — |
| % of total | 73 | 25 | — |

Source: [1]Murray and Reeves, 1977.

were not intuitively obvious, and the reasons were not available at the time of the publication of the list. Subsequent analysis suggests that rather than releasing a list of worst sites which had been scientifically selected, the list was released because the subcommittee felt the need to attract attention to pending legislation. In the words of Congressman Moffett, (D-Connecticut), chairman of the subcommittee, the list was "a piece of cake politically. Nothing comes close to rivaling the issue of contaminated water. Every member, from conservative Republicans to liberal Democrats, will support this effort to pass legislation that would clean up the sites" (*New York Times* 1980).

In 1981, as part of the EPA implementation of Superfund, 20 sites were chosen for engineering design studies. This list of 20 is very important because 18 of the 20 sites appeared in the later list of the 115 worst sites in the U.S. and 11 of the 20 were the highest priority sites in their states. Accordingly, a verbal synopsis of each of these "pre-Superfund" engineering study sites is provided along with a characterization of the type of facility, type of waste and type of problem (Tables 4-6 and 4-7).

There is a good deal of variation among the sites. Some were spread over more than one hundred acres (Woburn, Kin-Buc, Burnt Fly Bog, North Hollywood); others were small sites of less than 20 acres (Bridgeport,

## TABLE 4-6

## Brief Description of Sites Selected for Pre-Superfund Engineering Studies, 1981

1. Arkansas City Dump; Arkansas City, Kansas
   15- to 20-acre former refinery in early 1900s; refinery products contained in dikes, ponds and pits; ground- and surface water contamination.

2. Bridgeport Rental & Oil Service; Logan, New Jersey
   12-acre lagoon; waste oil recovery and disposal 1969–1980; serious ground- and surface water pollution.

3. Bruin Lagoon; Bruin, Pennsylvania
   3-acre lagoon; former petroleum refinery, 1930–1960s; sludge and liquids containing wastes from oil production and reclamation; dike collapse could contaminate surface water; dike breach already killed 4 million fish.

4. Burnt Fly Bog; Marlboro, New Jersey
   160-acre former landfill 1950–1976; contaminated soil and groundwater; major drinking water aquifer nearby.

5. BWS-Tate Cove; Ville Platte, Louisiana
   Temporary storage site for 5,000 drums of industrial waste; ground- and surface water pollution.

6. Caron Chemical; Monmouth, Oregon
   Former waste collection and distillation facility; left 1,700 barrels on site; insecure site, accessible to children; air and water pollution possible.

7. Cordova Chemical; Dalton, Michigan
   Poor water management practices cause ground- and surface water contamination; local population switched to bottled water.

8. Denver Radium Sites; Denver, Colorado
   35 areas where radium was processed, refined or fabricated 1914–1920; on vacant land, in buildings, under streets.

9. Gratiot County Landfill; near St. Louis, Michigan
   40-acre abandoned landfill; hundreds of thousands of pounds of polybrominated biphenyls dumped 1971–1973; groundwater contamination documented.

10. Kin-Buc Landfill; Edison, New Jersey
    220-acre former landfill; enormous amount of chemical wastes accepted during 1971–1976; leachate from site contaminating ground- and surface water; explosions and fires occurred; worker killed.

11. Lipari Landfill; Pitman, New Jersey
    6 to 7 acre former gravel pit and landfill 1958–1971; received liquid wastes from nearby chemical plants; leaching into ground- and surface water; air pollution, amidst orchards.

12. Love Canal; Niagara Falls, New York
    dumpsite for industrial and perhaps military wastes 1942–1953; surface and ground-water contamination; evacuation of hundreds of people and closing of homes built on the land.

## TABLE 4-6 (Continued)

## Brief Description of Sites Selected for Pre-Superfund
## Engineering Studies, 1981

13. Motco; La Marque, Texas
    11-acre burrow pit 3 miles from Galveston Bay; easily flooded; probable groundwater and air pollution as well.

14. North Hollywood Dump; Memphis, Tennessee
    130-acre dump 1930–1967, operated in the floodplain of a river; adjacent to a school and residential area; migration of wastes from petroleum refining and chemical manufacturing into surface and groundwater.

15. PAS; Oswego, New York
    Former Pollution Abatement Services, 1970–1976, operated incinerator for liquid wastes; over 15,000 drums left; serious ground- and surface water pollution.

16. Reilly-Tar and Chemical Corporation; St. Louis Park, Minnesota
    80-acre site, 1917–1972 used for creosote and wood preserving chemicals; serious ground- and surface water contamination.

17. Seymour Recycling Corporation; Seymour, Indiana
    Former waste recycling and incineration site; 10,000 drums and 500,000 gallons of liquid waste left in large tanks; fire, explosion hazard, groundwater threat.

18. Stringfellow Landfill; near Glen Avon, California
    17-acre former landfill operated 1956–1972; chemicals dumped into open, unlined ponds; ground- and surface water contamination.

19. Valley of the Drums; near Brooks, Kentucky
    23-acre site tens of thousands of drums left or spilled into pits; ground- and surface water contamination.

20. Woburn; Woburn, Massachusetts
    800-acre highly industrialized area in city; waste disposal for many years on ground and into lagoons; air, water and soil pollution.

---

Lipari, Bruin, Motco, Stringfellow). Some had probably been receiving large quantities of wastes, including hazardous wastes, before 1940 (Woburn, Bruin, North Hollywood, Reilly Tar); others began receiving hazardous wastes only during the 1970s (Kin-Buc, PAS). The typical site had above-ground storage and disposal of organics and inorganics, potentially threatening the groundwater.

**TABLE 4-7**

**Summary of Type of Facility, Wastes, and Problems at Twenty
Hazardous Waste Sites Selected for Pre-Superfund
Engineering Studies, 1981[1]**

| | |
|---|---|
| A. FACILITY TYPE | % |
|    1. Above-ground storage/disposal | 60 |
|    2. Uncovered pits, ponds, lagoons-below grade | 35 |
|    3. Covered pits, landfills | 35 |
| B. WASTE TYPE | % |
|    1. Pesticides and highly toxic organics | 70 |
|    2. Other organics | 70 |
|    3. Inorganics | 60 |
|    4. Radioactive substances | 5 |
|    5. Explosives and flammables | 15 |
| C. PROBLEM TYPE | % |
|    1. Explosion | 5 |
|    2. Fire | 20 |
|    3. Air pollution | 25 |
|    4. Groundwater contamination—potential potable supply | 75 |
|    5. Surface water contamination—potential potable supply | 60 |
|    6. Ecological impacts | 30 |

Note: [1]Column totals exceed 100 because many sites had more than one facility type, waste type and problem type.

Source: Author analysis of U.S.EPA pre-Superfund list, released in February, 1981.

## MOST RECENT ESTIMATES OF NUMBER OF
## INACTIVE AND WORST SITES

### Emergency Remedial Response System

The initial U.S. EPA, Fred C. Hart, and Quick-Look lists included active as well as inactive sites, although most of the sites were inactive. The most recent list of inactive sites, the Emergency Remedial Response System, was developed by EPA by selecting inactive sites from the Quick-Look list and adding inactive sites from two other lists. About one-fourth of the sites on the list came from Quick-Look. Another one-fourth came from the list of 8,755 sites gathered under section 103(c) of Superfund. The 103(c) requirement (U.S. EPA 1982) was any person who

> owns or operates or who owned or operated, or who accepted hazardous substances for transport and selected, a facility at which hazardous substances are or have been stored, treated, or disposed of shall, unless such facility has a permit issued under or has been accorded interim status under Subtitle C of the Solid Waste Disposal Act, notify the Environmental Protection Agency of the existence of such facility.

The third component of the Emergency Remedial Response System list, also contributing about one-fourth of the sites, was firms that EPA identified (under RCRA legislation) as inactive sites while searching for active sites. Specifically, EPA identified about 400,000 firms that could be handling hazardous waste because of the nature of their business. Approximately 67,000 firms responded. A small number had inactive sites on their properties. The Quick-Look, 103(c), and RCRA lists along with sites mentioned on two or three of the lists were joined, yielding a list of 13–14,000 inactive sites (Table 4-1, column 4), now raised to more than 16,000 sites.

It can be seen that most of the sites are located in the urbanized and industrialized EPA regions (Table 4-1, column 4). At the state scale, the states that produced 60 percent of the waste (California, Illinois, Indiana, Michigan, New Jersey, New York, Ohio, Pennsylvania, Tennessee, Texas) had 52 percent of the Quick-Look and 46 percent of the Emergency Remedial Response sites. The 18 states that produced 80 percent of the waste had 63 percent of the Quick-Look and 66 percent of the Emergency Remedial Response sites.

According to the EPA, the Emergency Remedial Response System list is an imperfect indicator of the spatial distribution of inactive sites. EPA officials estimate that the list includes too many RCRA sites for Regions 4, 6, 7 and 8. These lists are being scrutinized to achieve uniformity in reporting among the EPA regions. As of early 1984, because of differences in the data provided by the states and regional offices of the EPA, the Emergency Remedial Response list can be used to paint only a general portrait of the distribution of inactive sites.

## Worst Sites: The Mitre Model and Its Application by the U.S. EPA

Section 105(8) of the Comprehensive Environmental Response, Compensation, and Liability Act (Superfund) requires the establishment of priorities for remedial action. A comprehensive and quantitative method was needed because the abandoned dumpsites varied in size, by type of hazardous materials, and in danger to people and ecosystems.

The Mitre Corporation (1981) developed a hazard ranking score model which in their words uses the "best engineering judgment and does not consider socio-economic factors." The ranking reflects the "relative potential to inflict damage, the likelihood and rate at which they (abandoned sites) would reach the potential human and environmental targets, and the magnitude of the potential impacts."

Because it was used to choose the initial priority sites and because planners with whom we have spoken about the model have been very interested in learning about it, the site ranking model is described and illustrated in the following section. The model has three interdependent segments:

1. routes or pathways
2. impact categories
3. rating factors

There are five routes or pathways:

1.1 groundwater
1.2 surface water
1.3 air
1.4 fire and explosion
1.5 direct contact

The severity of the impacts through each of the five routes is measured by four impact categories:

2.1 release
2.2 waste characteristics
2.3 hazardous waste quantity
2.4 targets

Release may be either observed or estimated. If releases have not been observed or monitored, they are estimated by considering route characteristics and containments. The route characteristics include, for example, depth to aquifer, net precipitation, permeability of the unsaturated zone, slope, flood potential, and the presence of ignition sources. Dirt covers and diversion systems are considered containments of some releases.

Waste characteristics include physical state of substances, persistence, toxicity, reactivity, and compatibility with other substances. The targets are people and valuable ecosystems and are measured by such indicators as drinking water supplies, fishing and boating.

The rating factors are the keys to the method. At this point, an example will be introduced to illustrate the operation of the model, particularly the complex set of rating weights. Let us assume that excavations have found an old dumpsite with about 100 drums buried within 1,000 feet of a water body. We will focus on the second route (surface water). Keep in mind that each of the five routes is considered of equal importance and is assigned a final score ranging from 0 (no danger) to 97.2 (most dangerous).

If a release from the site has been observed or monitored, then 45 points (the maximum) are assigned. If a release has not been observed, then the potential for release is calculated. Let us assume that a release has not been observed so that we must calculate the potential for a release. Four factors are considered under route characteristics: site slope and terrain; one-year, 24-hour rainfall; distance to nearest surface water body; and site flood potential. As the numbers in table 4-8 indicate, the route characteristics at the site are unfavorable. The slope exceeds 8 percent (the worst case); a one-year, 24-hour rainfall exceeds 3 inches (the worst case); and the distance to the nearest surface water body is less than 1,000 feet (the worst case). Each of the first three site characteristics places the site in the worst possible category, 3. The flood potential of the site is rated 1 (in the 100-year floodplain, but not qualified for the worst categories which are annual flooding or flooding every decade). The site ratings are multiplied by a weight and then added. The final score in the illustrations is 11 out of a possible 15.

The first set of calculations illustrates two characteristics of the Mitre model. One is that site rating scores and multipliers are used to weight some

## TABLE 4-8

### Example of Application of Mitre Model:
### Estimate of Release Potential

| Rating Factor | Site Rating | Multiplier | Site Score | Maximum Score |
|---|---|---|---|---|
| 1. site slope and terrain | 0,1,2,3* | 1 | 3 | 3 |
| 2. 1-yr., 24-hr. rainfall | 0,1,2,3* | 1 | 3 | 3 |
| 3. distance to surface water body | 0,1,2,3* | 1 | 3 | 3 |
| 4. flood potential | 0,1*,2,3 | 2 | 2 | 6 |
| | | subtotal | 11 | 15 |

rating factors higher than others. Second, the effects of rating factors within each impact category are aggregated by adding.

The next step is to estimate the degree of containment at the site. In this case, it is assumed that the site is neither adequately covered nor is waste migration controlled by diversion systems. Accordingly, the worst containment value, 3, is assigned and multiplied by the potential route characteristic value calculated above, 11, to yield the potential for release value, 33 (the maximum value is 45).

Having estimated the release impact category, three characteristics of the waste are examined. It is assumed that the physical state of the material uncovered at the site is a sludge, slurry, and fine powder which rates a value of 2 out of a maximum of 3 (liquid, gas). The material found is heavy metals which have the maximum toxicity value, 3; and these heavy metals are extremely persistent, another maximum value of 3. As shown in Table 4-9, these waste characteristics imply a severe threat (14 out of a possible 15).

The third impact category is waste quantity. About 100 drums were found at the site. The site ranking model considers 100 drums to be in the second lowest category, a value of 1. The highest quantity, 5 points, is given for more than 3,500 drums. The total waste quantity score is 1 out of a maximum of 5.

The final category is targets. Drinking water is considered to be the use most incompatible with hazardous waste. The site drains into a water body used for drinking water and therefore receives the maximum value, 3. The site is within the 100-year floodplain which is considered a value of 2, out of a possible 3. Finally, the population that gets its water from the potentially

## TABLE 4-9

### Example of Application of Mitre Model: Estimate of Waste Characteristics Impact

| Rating Factor | Site Rating | Multiplier | Site Score | Maximum Score |
|---|---|---|---|---|
| 1. physical state | 0,1,2*,3 | 1 | 2 | 3 |
| 2. toxicity/ infectiousness | 0,1,2,3* | 2 | 6 | 6 |
| 3. persistence | 0,1,2,3* | 2 | 6 | 6 |
| | | subtotal | 14 | 15 |

contaminated site is 100,000, a value of 5, the maximum value (> 10,000 is assigned a value of 5). The total target values are 43 out of a possible 45:

**TABLE 4-10**

**Example of Application of Mitre Model:
Estimate of Impacts on Targets**

| Rating Factor | Site Rating | Multiplier | Site Score | Maximum Value |
|---|---|---|---|---|
| 1. surface water | 0,1,2,3* | 3 | 9 | 9 |
| 2. critical habitats | 0,1,2*,3 | 2 | 4 | 6 |
| 3. population served by water intake within 3 miles of the site | 0,1,2,3,4,5* | 6 | 30 | 30 |
| | | subtotal | 43 | 45 |

Next, the values of each of the four impact categories are multiplied to derive the surface water subtotal:

(1) surface water subtotal score = potential release score × waste characteristic score × waste quantity score × targets

for the illustration: 33 × 14 × 1 × 43 = 19,866

for maximum possible: 45 × 15 × 5 × 45 = 151, 875

The final score, 19,866, is multiplied by a normalization factor, 0.64 and divided by 1,000. The normalization factor is used so that the maximum value for each of the five routes is 97.2. The value for the illustration is 12.7. Overall, the sample had serious release, waste characteristic, and target values, but since it had only 100 drums, the overall score is low for the surface water route. Had 5,000 drums rather than 100 drums been uncovered, the score would have been close to the maximum.

Scores would also be computed for the other routes and then a combined score would be derived. This has not been done here because the illustration, as it stands, identifies some of the strengths and weaknesses of the Mitre model. The main strengths of the model are that it accounts for the different media, it provides quantitative results, and the data are not expensive to gather or to estimate.

Some of the questions about the model concern its many value judgments. For example, some multipliers are 1, others are 6; addition is used in some places, multiplication in others. Second, the method favors sites with large volumes of different types of wastes while considering sites with a small amount of only one type of waste to be less important, even if the wastes at the latter sites are very toxic. Third, the method tends to ignore sites removed from large numbers of people, and, thus, implicitly favors the protection of urban areas over rural areas. Fourth, the model ignores the varying capability of communities to respond to emergencies at sites. In short, a good deal of criticism has been aimed at the model and is summarized elsewhere (*Environmental Science and Technology*, 1982, Maugh 1982).

Whatever its shortcomings, the U.S. EPA used the Mitre model with some minor changes to create the first official list of priority sites in the United States and its overseas possessions. The list of 115 sites was developed from a list of 282 sites prepared by the states and the EPA's regional offices (U.S. EPA 1981). Another 45 sites were added to the initial list in July 1982. After subtracting a few sites from the list of 160, new sites were added in December 1982 to reach a total of 418. Additional sites were added in September of 1983 to bring the total to 546. The geographical distribution of the initial 115 and 418 sites and final list of 546 sites is similar.

Since the initial 115 sites were considered to be the most dangerous, the following analyses that focus on characteristics of the worst sites use the 115 sites as the data base; the analyses that are concerned with location use the full list of 546. As expected, most of the sites are in urban areas. Almost 30 percent of the counties that contain priority sites were more than 90 percent urban in 1970. Only 25 percent of the sites were in counties that were more rural than urban in 1970. The median percentage of urban population in 1970 in the counties containing these sites was 83 compared to 73.5 percent of the United States population as a whole.

Although the sites are largely in urban areas, they are found throughout the United States. For example, 44 states and territories had at least one site on the initial list of 115. Indeed, it was the intent that each state would have at least one site, if they could identify a priority site. The following eight states, however, did not have a priority site in the initial list: Louisiana—a state with many sites and a large chemical industry, Idaho, Montana, Nebraska, Nevada, Oregon, Wisconsin, and Wyoming. The list of 418 had at least one site in every state but Alaska, Hawaii, Nevada, and Wisconsin. The list of 546 includes 20 sites from Wisconsin, an intriguing jump from none in the prior lists.

Most of the sites were in northeastern, Great Lakes, and southern states as shown in Table 4-11 which lists the 10 states with the most sites.

**TABLE 4-11**

**U.S. EPA List of Priority Sites:**
**Ten States with Greatest Number of Sites**

| State | Number of Priority Sites |
|---|---|
| 1. New Jersey | 85 |
| 2. Michigan | 48 |
| 3. Pennsylvania | 39 |
| 4. New York | 29 |
| 5. Florida | 29 |
| 6. Minnesota | 23 |
| 7. Ohio | 22 |
| 8. Wisconsin | 20 |
| 9. California | 19 |
| 10. Massachusetts | 16 |
| Total | 330 |
| % of total in the U.S. | 60 |

The geographical distribution of sites closely resembles what was known as the American Manufacturing Belt. From east to west, urban-industrial Massachusetts, New York, New Jersey, Pennsylvania, Ohio, Indiana, Illinois, Michigan, Wisconsin, and Minnesota had 57 percent of the sites (311 of 546). In contrast, the Plains and Mountain states have few priority sites (Figure 4-2). Nine of the 10 states that in aggregate produce 60 percent of the hazardous waste in the United States are among the states with at least 10 sites: California, Illinois, Indiana, Michigan, New Jersey, New York, Ohio, Pennsylvania and Texas. Tennessee, the other major hazardous waste producing state, had 6 sites. The presence of populous Florida and populous and industrialized Massachusetts is not surprising. But Minnesota, New Hampshire, and Wisconsin are not among the most populous nor the most industrialized states and are therefore conspicuous by their presence on the list of states with 10 or more sites.

A set of indices was prepared to try to find the best set of correlates with the overall spatial distribution of priority sites by states. The intent of the index was to find deviants from a general pattern. One of the simplest was the best: an index derived by multiplying the number of total sites in the state times the number of people served by groundwater in the state and

**FIGURE 4-2**

**Location of 546 Priority Hazardous Waste Sites
by State, 1984 (48 contiguous states)**

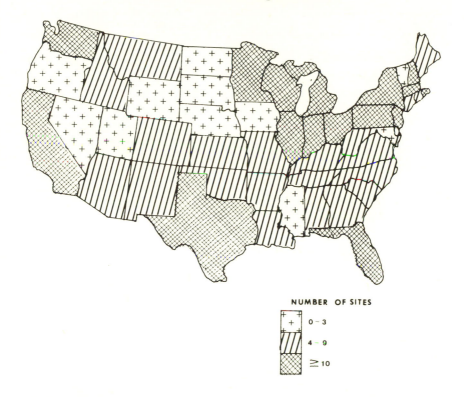

NUMBER OF SITES

0 - 3

4 - 9

≥ 10

dividing the result by the land area. The resulting numbers were ranked 1 through 50, with 1 representing the state with the highest index value (total number of sites × number of people served by groundwater/land area). The ranks for the 10 states with the greatest number of priority sites are displayed in Table 4-12.

Among the 10 states, Minnesota and Wisconsin seem conspicuous by being on the list. The relatively few sites in Georgia (index rank 20) and absence of any sites in Wisconsin (index rank 24) until the most recent addition to the list are very interesting. Finally, Louisiana, Tennessee, and North Carolina should have had more priority sites based on their industrial structures and population sizes.

Do states like New Jersey, Michigan, and Minnesota have more serious hazardous wastes management problems than states like Texas and Loui-

## TABLE 4-12

### Ranking of States with Greatest Number of Priority Sites and Index of Potential Groundwater Contamination

| State | Total Number of Priority Sites: 546 | Rank in number of hazardous waste sites × number of people served by groundwater/land area |
|---|---|---|
| 1. New Jersey | 85 | 1 |
| 2. Michigan | 48 | 11 |
| 3. Pennsylvania | 39 | 9 |
| 4. New York | 29 | 3 |
| 5. Florida | 29 | 7 |
| 6. Minnesota | 23 | 31 |
| 7. Ohio | 22 | 4 |
| 8. Wisconsin | 20 | 24 |
| 9. California | 19 | 6 |
| 10. Massachusetts | 16 | 2 |

siana? Or is there another explanation? Perhaps the first group of states worked harder to get sites on the priority list. If this institutional effort explanation is even partially correct, then the final list of over 500 priority sites is misleading, and the strong, negative publicity about states like New Jersey and Michigan as the hazardous waste capitals of the United States is misleading. The evidence to support the institutional effort explanation of the priority site list is anecdotal, based largely on off-the-record conversations with waste managers and insurance underwriters. A formal analysis of the institutional effort explanation is warranted.

Since almost every one of the pre-Superfund sites was on the final list of 115 priority sites, it is not surprising that the types of facilities, waste, and problems found at the 115 sites are similar to those found at the 20 pre-Superfund sites (Table 4-6). Above-ground storage/disposal which usually consisted of laying materials or drums on the ground is the most widespread disposal practice at the priority sites (56 percent). Covered landfills and pits are mentioned for about one-third of the sites, and uncovered pits, ponds and lagoons (below grade) for almost 30 percent of the sites. Some of the sites have all three practices.

## TABLE 4-13

### Summary of Type of Facility, Wastes and Problems at Initial Set of 115 Priority Sites[1]

| | % |
|---|---|
| **A. FACILITY TYPE** | % |
| 1. Above ground storage/disposal | 56 |
| 2. Uncovered pits, ponds, lagoons, mines—below grade | 29 |
| 3. Covered pits, landfills, pipelines | 33 |
| 4. Underground injection | 3 |
| 5. Direct dumping into surface water | 5 |
| **B. WASTE TYPE** | % |
| 1. Pesticides and highly toxic organics | 65 |
| 2. Other organics | 52 |
| 3. Inorganics | 56 |
| 4. Radioactive substances | 4 |
| 5. Explosives and flammables | 9 |
| **C. PROBLEM TYPE** | % |
| 1. Explosion | 6 |
| 2. Fire | 8 |
| 3. Air pollution, including direct contact | 22 |
| 4. Groundwater contamination—potential potable supply | 70 |
| 5. Surface water contamination—potential potable supply | 49 |
| 6. Ecological impacts | 21 |
| **D. DATE OPERATIONS STARTED** | % |
| 1. Prior to or during the 1940s | 24 |
| 2. 1950s | 17 |
| 3. 1960s | 17 |
| 4. 1970s | 26 |
| 5. Not known | 30 |

Note: [1]Column totals exceed 100 because many sites had more than one facility type, waste type and problem type.

Source: Author analysis of U.S. EPA reports. Some descriptions were very detailed, others were brief. Accordingly, the data should be regarded as rough estimates.

Pesticides and other organics and inorganics are each mentioned in more than half of the cases. Explosives, flammables, and radioactive substances were reported far less frequently.

Serious groundwater contamination already or potentially affecting water supplies was reported in the vast majority of the cases, followed closely by surface water contamination. A final point is that almost one-fourth of the sites may have been receiving hazardous wastes prior to 1950 and almost half were probably receiving some quantities of hazardous wastes by 1960. This is important because it implies that environmental effects could be widespread at these sites.

While, as stressed in Chapter 3, each hazardous waste site is unique in some ways, the following composite of a priority site emerges: a 5 to 15% acre site used for 10-20 years for manufacturing, storing, or dumping of organic and inorganic wastes on the ground, with ground and surface water contamination as its usual effects.

## SITES BY OTHER NAMES

Abandoned chemical waste sites, probably the most dangerous hazardous waste sites, have been widely publicized. But we should not be lulled into focusing all our attention on them. Planners and other local officials must also take cognizance of other types of sites because they could be more dangerous in many locations than abandoned chemical waste sites. These are active chemical waste sites; military chemical and nuclear waste sites; above and below ground mines; commercial nuclear waste facilities; municipal landfills, and pits, ponds, and lagoons on industrial properties that contain toxic and hazardous substances not classified as hazardous wastes by the EPA; and finally, wastes from sources that are too small to be caught in the EPA regulatory net. These will be considered in chapter 8 because they are or should be part of the same political process that will determine the course of action on chemical waste sites.

## SUMMARY

This chapter has shown that during the period 1979-1982 the U.S. EPA and its consultants initially estimated the number of active and inactive hazardous waste sites at between 30,000-50,000 and the number of extremely dangerous sites at 2,000. Detailed field surveys and mathematical analyses reduced the list to more than 16,000 inactive sites and 546 priority sites. Nearly all the states with many high priority sites are densely-populated, urban-industrial states and rely heavily on ground water for their drinking water. The priority sites are primarily located in urbanized areas, are aboveground storage and disposal sites for toxic organic and inorganic chemicals, and have potentially or already contaminated water supplies.

Yet, the data about sites is deficient. The list of total sites is by no means complete. The list of priority sites was based on a widely criticized mathematical model, the data provided to choose the sites may be of unequal quality, and we believe that some states made a much greater effort than others to get sites included on the priority list. Finally, the list of hazardous waste sites under Superfund does not include many types of hazardous waste sites.

## REFERENCES

*Environmental Science and Technology.* "Currents." Vol. 16, 1982, p. 9A.

Hart, Fred C., Associates. *Preliminary Assessment of Cleanup Costs for National Hazardous Waste Problems.* Washington, D.C.: U.S. Environmental Protection Agency, 1979.

Jorling, T. "Information Needed on Disposal Sites Where Hazardous Waste Threatens Public Health." Memorandum to regional administrators, Environmental Protection Agency, Washington, D.C., October, 1978.

Maugh, T. "Just How Hazardous Are Dumps?" *Science*, Vol. 215, 1982, pp. 490–493.

Mitre Corporation. "Site Ranking Model for Determining Remedial Action Priorities Among Uncontrolled Hazardous Substances Facilities." Working Paper for Environmental Protection Agency, Washington, D.C., 1981.

Murray, C. and Reeves, E. "Estimated Water Use in the United States in 1975." Geological Survey Circular 765, U.S. Geological Survey, Arlington, Virginia, 1977.

*New York Times.* "House Panel Lists Toxic Sites Threatening Water Supplies in U.S.," September 28, 1980, p. 45.

U.S. Bureau of the Census. *Census of Manufactures, 1972, Area Statistics.* Washington, D.C.: U.S. Government Printing Office, 1973a.

———. *Census of Mineral Industries, 1972, Area Statistics.* Washington, D.C.: U.S. Government Printing Office, 1973b.

———. *County and City Data Book: 1977.* Washington, D.C.: U.S. Government Printing Office, 1977.

U.S. Environmental Protection Agency. *Damages and Threats Caused by Hazardous Material Sites.* Washington, D.C.: U.S. Government Printing Office, 1980.

———. "EPA Announces First 114 Top-Priority Superfund Sites." Memorandum, U.S. Environmental Protection Agency, Washington, D.C. October 23, 1981.

———. "Notification of Hazardous Waste Sites Required Under Section 103(3) of the Comprehensive Environmental Response, Compensation and Liability Act (CERCLA) of 1980, PL 96–510." Springfield, VA: National Technical Information Service, 1982.

# 5

# Abandoned Hazardous Waste Dumpsites in New Jersey: Where and What Effects

Municipal garbage was mixed with toxic wastes (Stringfellow, California site) in a fashion that would have been considered remarkable even in New Jersey.

The environmental ravaging here (Louisiana) was more blatant than anywhere else except New Jersey.

Michael Brown, 1979

There are numerous existing and proposed hazardous chemical waste sites, but a dearth of money and scientific knowledge to investigate the effects of all of these sites. An important short-term research goal is thus to determine if available medical, environmental, land use, and demographic data can provide clues about the effects of hazardous waste sites. This research is more important to planners than to most people because planners and elected officials will bear the brunt of dealing with a hostile public about the effects of sites at the local government scale. Furthermore, planners are likely to be involved in such research because they control or have access to much of the data.

This chapter examines the effect of sites on health, demographic change, and property values; and it studies the association between economic, demographic, political, and physical attributes of communities and the location of abandoned sites in order to assess distributional effects. Few would question exploring health effects and impacts on property values and demographic structure, although most people consider health effects to be more important than demographic and economic change. Frankly, there have been mixed reactions to our efforts at studying whether some types of communities have borne an unusually high share of the hazardous waste burden. Many scientists and engineers think that answers are intuitively obvious. And even if they were not obvious, these distributional effects should not have a bearing on priorities for the cleanup of abandoned sites or the location of new sites. The main arguments for studying existing distributional effects are that what may seem intuitively obvious is not always so, and that siting new facilities is ultimately a political decision, one in which decisionmakers should be cognizant of *all* past mistakes, not just physical siting mistakes, so as not to repeat them, if possible.

One limitation about the research presented in this chapter is that we do not know the extent to which the results can contribute to an understanding of conditions in other states. Viewed from the perspectives of economy, demography, hydrology, and geology, the urbanized New England, Mid-Atlantic, Gulf Coast, Great Lakes and West Coast states should most closely resemble the New Jersey case. But this is only an educated guess, one awaiting verification by replicate studies. A second limitation is that most of the data are at the community scale, so it is possible that we could commit the ecological fallacy of attributing results observed at the community scale to specific individuals living in the community.

## LOCATION OF ABANDONED SITES IN NEW JERSEY

As part of their submission to acquire Superfund money, the Department of Environmental Protection of the State of New Jersey compiled a list of more than 350 abandoned hazardous waste dumpsites in New Jersey and developed a priority list of 22 sites (as of spring 1983 there were more than 700 sites, 85 of which were priority sites under Superfund).

The majority of the sites are found in urban industrial areas of New Jersey. As of late 1981, 28 percent of New Jersey's 567 communities (160) had at least one abandoned dumpsite. Twenty-one had at least four. Newark, the most populous city in New Jersey, had more than 30. The geographical distribution of the communities with many sites is not random (Figure 5-1). At one extreme, 9 of urban-industrial Hudson County's 12 communities had at least one site; at the other extreme, only 1 of rural Cumberland County's 14 had a site. Almost every community along the urban-industrial spine of New Jersey between New York City and Philadelphia had at least one site. The northwestern, relatively rural counties (Sussex, Warren, and Hunterdon) and southern counties (Cape May, Cumberland, Salem, and Atlantic) had few abandoned dumpsites.

Most of the priority sites are located in communities with many sites. The 22 highest priority sites, 12 of which were considered to be among the initial

**FIGURE 5-1**

**Abandoned Hazardous Waste Dumpsites, 1981**

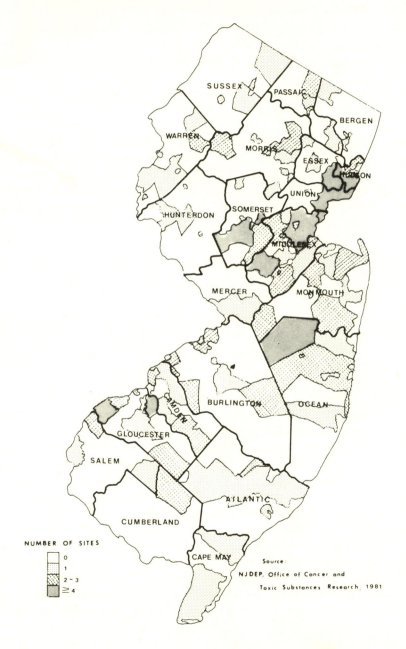

list of worst 115 in the United States (see Chapter 4), are found in 18 communities in 11 counties.

Thirty-one of New Jersey's 567 communities were classified as dumpsite communities (Figure 5-2). They are as follows:

1. 8 that have at least 4 dumpsites and at least 1 of the worst sites (hereafter called WORMOST);
2. 13 that have at least 4 sites, but none of the worst sites (called the MOST);
3. 10 that have at least 1 of the worst sites, but less than 4 sites (called the WORST) (Table 5-1).

The remaining 536 communities were called NONDUMPS. They were aggregated into 21 areas (Table 5-1), eight of which are entire counties because the counties have no dumpsite towns. The areas representing the 13 counties that have at least one dumpsite town are aggregates of the nondumpsite towns. The 21 non-dumpsite areas and the 31 dumpsite communities cover the entire state. These groups are used in this chapter to test hypotheses.

## HEALTH EFFECTS OF DUMPSITES IN NEW JERSEY: STUDIES OF ECOLOGICAL DATA

Many indicators of potential effects have been considered to study the relationships between hazardous waste sites and health. Urine and serum samples can be used, but tests must be done soon after exposure. Adipose tissue, hair, and nails serve as personal monitors, but only for a limited number of substances. The major types of endpoints are effects on the reproductive process, carcinogenesis, and toxicity to specific parts of the body (Lowrance 1981; Bloom 1981; Environmental Influences on Fertility, Pregnancy and Development, 1982).

The percentage of low birthweight babies is the best indicator of reproductive effects for an ecological study. It is routinely collected with a high degree of accuracy; it is a continuous variable which is an advantage for statistical analysis; and it correlates well with other reproductive outcomes. The main disadvantages of low birthweight as an indicator are that it does not incorporate infertility, very early losses, and late fetal deaths, and it is affected by other factors such as maternal age, parity, and exposure to substances through personal habits such as smoking, diet, and occupation.

Alternative indicators are even more limited. Sperm samples are difficult to obtain. Spontaneous abortions, congenital malformations, fetal deaths, and transplacental cancers are rare events, a fact which limits the number of

## FIGURE 5-2

### Communities With Worst and Most Dumpsites
### in New Jersey, 1981

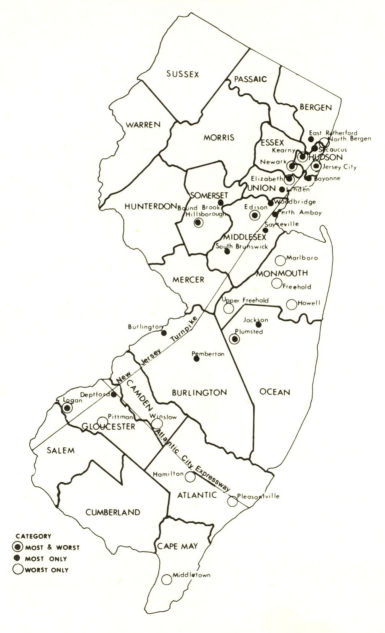

## TABLE 5-1

### Dumpsite and Nondumpsite Areas

| *Dumpsite Communities* | *Nondumpsite Counties (NONDUMPS)* |
|---|---|
| 1. Worst and Most (WORMOST) | |
|   1. Edison | 1. Atlantic (a) |
|   2. Elizabeth | 2. Bergen (a) |
|   3. Hillsborough | 3. Burlington (a) |
|   4. Jersey City | 4. Camden (a) |
|   5. Kearny | 5. Cape May (a) |
|   6. Logan | 6. Cumberland (b) |
|   7. Newark | 7. Essex (a) |
|   8. Plumsted | 8. Gloucester (a) |
| 2. Most (MOST) | 9. Hudson (a) |
|   9. Bayonne | 10. Hunterdon (b) |
|   10. Bound Brook | 11. Mercer (b) |
|   11. Burlington Boro | 12. Middlesex (a) |
|   12. Deptford Boro | 13. Monmouth (a) |
|   13. East Rutherford | 14. Morris (b) |
|   14. Jackson | 15. Ocean (a) |
|   15. Linden | 16. Passaic (b) |
|   16. Pemberton Boro | 17. Salem (b) |
|   17. Perth Amboy | 18. Somerset (a) |
|   18. Sayreville | 19. Sussex (b) |
|   19. Secaucus | 20. Union (a) |
|   20. South Brunswick | 21. Warren (b) |
|   21. Woodbridge | |
| 3. Worst (WORST) | |
|   22. Freehold Boro | |
|   23. Hamilton | |
|   24. Howell | |
|   25. Marlboro | |
|   26. Middletown | |
|   27. North Bergen | |
|   28. Pittman | |
|   29. Pleasantville | |
|   30. Upper Freehold | |
|   31. Winslow | |

Notes: (a) Nondumpsite communities in the county.
      (b) Entire county.

cases; and recollections and official records of these events are often affected by subsequent publicity. Chromosomal abnormality tests are expensive, difficult to interpret, and confounded by numerous other causes of chromosome damage including smoking, coffee, medical x-rays, and viruses. In short, if one is to do an ecological study using readily available and reliable data, the percentage of low birthweight babies is chosen by default. If an ecological study of communities discloses some with high percentages of low birthweight babies, and these percentages cannot be readily explained by other factors, then an individual-site, case-control study of other negative outcomes would be done.

Similarly, cancer is the only widely available indicator for an ecological study of chronic effects. There are clear disadvantages of using cancer to represent chronic diseases. The most troublesome of these is the mismatch between a group of diseases which often takes 20–40 years to appear and a practice (land disposal of hazardous wastes) which has been in widespread use at the majority of sites for less than 20 years. Furthermore, given that contaminated water is likely to be the main path of public exposure, exposure at many sites is limited by the fact that many people obtain their water from supplies located far away from hazardous waste sites. Next, numerous personal habits (e.g., smoking, alcohol consumption, diet), and many occupations expose people to carcinogens or cocarcinogens. Finally, migration of exposed people away from the dumpsite area during the lengthy latency period for cancer limits the reliability of cancer records.

Frankly, because of these limitations, the authors would feel more confident about using selected individual-site studies of the few sites used for dumping for decades (e.g., Woburn), where the contaminants can be determined and for which there is proof that the wastes have come into contact with people. Alternatively, the approach of studying workers exposed to high concentrations at existing sites and extrapolating these to the public could be followed at sites which have had a large and stable labor force.

Despite the preference to go directly to individual-site case-control and environmental studies, a preference which the authors share with many others, ecological studies of cancer will undoubtedly be done because of public pressure. Two types of ecological cancer studies are feasible. One is to compare cancer rates of specific organs (e.g., bladder, liver, lung, colon) in communities that are similar, except that one group of communities has one or more waste sites and the other group does not. If control communities are difficult to find, which is likely if the study is being done for a specific state or region, then surrounding communities or the state will have to serve as the control areas.

A second type of cancer study, one we have even less faith in at this time, is to estimate the number of people who could get cancer by coming into contact with substances escaping from the site. Such a study requires two data sets: concentrations of chemicals in groundwater and surface water; and dose-response models for those chemicals. The method is to estimate the risk of cancer that might result from lifetime ingestion of contaminated water. For example, the senior author and a colleague (Greenberg and Page 1981) estimated additional cancer cases due to the consumption of toxic chemicals in the ground- and surface waters of New Jersey. It was estimated that less than 4 additional cancers would be produced per 100,000 people if the 80 percent least-contaminated groundwater sources were consumed over a lifetime. However, the 3 percent most-polluted sources, several of which were contaminated by hazardous waste disposal practices, were estimated to produce 500 additional cancers per 100,000.

The method is not without logic, but it presently requires too many unrealistic assumptions. First, a linear dose-response model is usually assumed. When available linear dose-response models were examined, it was found that many of the models produced results that were clearly too high (Greenberg and Page 1981). Second, the models are almost always calibrated for average-sized, middle-aged males, not the most sensitive people. Third, dose-response models do not exist for the mixtures so commonly found at hazardous waste sites, so the results of applying the models are additive, ignoring interactive effects of different substances. Finally, it is difficult to accept the lifetime exposure assumption because few people remain in the same neighborhood for a lifetime. Although we do not have faith in the approach at this time, it should become more reasonable to apply the approach to hazardous waste disposal sites, if and when dose-response models can be calculated for the most sensitive populations and for shorter-term, low-dose exposures, and as good sets of monitoring data become available.

With the above caveats noted, two ecological studies in New Jersey examined off-the-shelf cancer mortality and birthweight data. Frankly, our expectations of the reliability of the results were not high because of the problems noted above. One goal was to determine if there was a consistent association between the presence of the worst abandoned dumpsites and high cancer rates and high percentages of low birthweight babies. Positive associations do not imply cause-and-effect; but after considering other explanations, a finding that some communities with priority abandoned sites had higher percentages of low birthweight babies and higher cancer rates than those without them implies that an individual-site study is clearly more warranted in these communities than in others. Negative results do not imply that there are no effects, only that they may not have been detected by crude community-scale data or that the impacts have not yet occurred.

## Cancer

During 1976–1981, the senior author investigated the spatial distribution of cancer mortality rates in New Jersey for the State Department of Environmental Protection (1980a, 1980b, 1980c, 1981a, 1981b, 1983). The research had been prompted by the fact that during the period 1950–1969, New Jersey was found to have the highest white male and second-highest white female cancer mortality rates in the United States. The following is one of the questions most often asked of the author: Is there a relationship between New Jersey's high cancer rates and abandoned dumpsites?

At this time, the question cannot be answered with any certainty. Cancer has a long latency period. If the majority of dumpsites are the products of dumping in the 1970s, cancers associated with dumpsites are not likely to be observed until the 1990s.

Scale is a second data problem. The neighborhood scale is the most appropriate for measuring local effects, but off-the-shelf data were not available at the neighborhood scale. The type of cancer data was a third problem. Incidence data are preferred in order to minimize the problem of population migration. Incidence data have been collected in New Jersey for two years, but are not yet available.

Cancer mortality data were available at the county scale for 1950–1975 and at the community scale for 1967–1976 (Greenberg, et al. 1981a; New Jersey State Department of Health 1981a). The county scale is inappropriate because the effects of most of the dumpsites should be localized, except for those that have affected major drinking supplies. In short, community scale mortality data for 1967–1976 were the only data set available.

Controlling for other etiological factors and differences among the dumpsites are additional problems. The effects of carcinogens from dumpsites are likely to be felt in the respiratory, digestive, and urinary systems. A definitive study of the effects of dumpsites on cancer would have to control for such factors as cigarette smoking, alcohol use, diet, occupational exposures, and other sources of air and water pollution. In addition, no one is sure how far contamination has spread from each dumpsite; some sites may be bigger problems than others. Until the extent and content of the pollution plumes are traced, we will not know the extent of threat posed by each of the dumpsites.

Finally, the potential for ecological fallacy is present. Even if one finds that the dumpsite towns have consistently higher rates than the NON-DUMPS, the investigator cannot be sure that those people who have died from cancer came in contact with dumpsite effluent.

In short, limited to community-scale cancer mortality data for 1967–

1976, lacking information about control factors, and absent information about the migratory patterns of cancer victims, the following analysis is not an answer to the often asked question about the relationship between dumpsites and cancer; it was an effort to find some clues from readily available data.

With the above caveats in mind, a limited comparison between the non-dumpsite and dumpsite communities of the mortality rates of selected types of cancer is presented. The data were white male and female age-adjusted cancer mortality rates for 1967–1976 standardized to the 1960 population of the United States. The New Jersey Department of Health prepared these cancer mortality rates for 546 of the state's 567 communities. The rates of the 21 remaining communities were joined to others.

The results are presented for those communities that have significantly higher rates than the state as a whole ($p < .05$) and communities in the upper decile of rates among the 546 communities. If the dumpsite communities have a serious cancer problem, then they should be found to be disproportionately represented in the group of communities with excessive rates. A difference-of-proportions statistic is used as the testing device. For example, 7 of the 31 dumpsite communities (22.6 percent) have high rates of male stomach cancer compared to 81 of the 515 nondumpsite communities (15.7 percent). The test determines the confidence one can have in the conclusion that the dumpsite and nondumpsite towns are drawn from the same population of towns.

The results are inconclusive. The dumpsite towns had higher proportions of excessive cancer rates than the nondumpsite towns in 11 of the 14 comparisons (Table 5-2). Four of the proportions are significantly higher at $p < .20$. However, most of the communities in the excessive rate group among the dumpsite communities are located along the northeast urban corridor (Newark, Bayonne, Jersey City, Kearny) and do not drink local ground- or surface water sources, presumably the most widespread source of contamination from dumps. It is therefore difficult to attribute high digestive and urinary tract cancers in these towns to local abandoned dumpsites. Among the dumpsite communities, only Pemberton and Plumsted drink local water supplies and have relatively high cancer mortality rates for many of the types of cancer thought to be associated with water pollution.

It is also difficult to make a case for a respiratory-dumpsite link because as noted above, many of the communities with high cancer rates also have industrial activities which could cause occupational as well as air pollution exposures. Moreover, smoking data were not available. Among the dumpsite towns with high respiratory cancer mortality rates, only Jackson and Pemberton do not have large industrial bases.

## TABLE 5-2

### Comparison of White Population Cancer Mortality Rates in Dumpsite and Nondumpsite Communities, 1967–1976

| Type | Proportion of Communities with High Rates[1] | | (1)/(2) | Signif. if < .2 |
| | Dumpsite (1) | Nondumpsite (2) | | |
| --- | --- | --- | --- | --- |
| 1. stomach | | | | |
| male | .226 | .157 | 1.44 | — |
| female | .290 | .134 | 2.16 | .02 |
| 2. colon | | | | |
| male | .161 | .144 | 1.12 | — |
| female | .161 | .146 | 1.10 | — |
| 3. rectum | | | | |
| male | .226 | .142 | 1.59 | .20 |
| female | .194 | .126 | 1.54 | — |
| 4. pancreas | | | | |
| male | .161 | .146 | 1.10 | — |
| female | .129 | .138 | .93 | — |
| 5. trachea, bronchus, lung | | | | |
| male | .290 | .138 | 2.10 | .03 |
| female | .194 | .132 | 1.47 | — |
| 6. bladder | | | | |
| male | .065 | .109 | .60 | — |
| female | .065 | .109 | .60 | — |
| 7. all sites | | | | |
| male | .355 | .235 | 1.51 | .15 |
| female | .226 | .208 | 1.09 | — |

Note: [1]Rates in the upper decile and/or significantly higher than the state rate at .05.

## Low Birthweight

The desire to avoid a lengthy lag between exposure and effect suggests that low birthweight should be better than cancer for a study of the relationships between hazardous waste sites and health. A birthweight of less than 2500 grams (5 pounds, 8 ounces) is considered to be underweight.

It is hypothesized that a population exposed to toxic substances would have a higher percentage of low birthweights than a population not exposed. Earlier it was reported that differences in birthweights are due to prenatal care, the age of the mother, the number of previous births, and when the child was born during the birth cycle. These factors are thought to be associated with socioeconomic status and race. Communities with a large proportion of poor people and blacks are expected to have relatively high proportions of low birthweight babies. Accordingly, the results were tested for relationships with these two characteristics.

The statistical test is a difference-of-proportions, where the proportion of low birthweights in the dumpsite communities is compared to the remainder of the state. The best set of birthweight data were available for 1980 (New Jersey State Department of Health 1981b).

The results are once again inconclusive. Some of the dumpsite communities have higher proportions of low birthweight babies than the remainder of the state. Most of these are communities with a relatively large proportion of low socioeconomic status and black people.

There were almost 100,000 births in the State of New Jersey in 1980. About 7,000 of the infants (7.24 percent) had birthweights of less than 2500 grams. As a whole, the proportion for the 31 dumpsite communities is 9.10 percent compared to 6.74 percent for the remainder of the state ($p < .05$). Twelve of the 31 dumpsite communities have rates higher than the remainder of the state and three of these are significantly higher ($p < .05$): Newark, Jersey City, and Elizabeth (Table 5-3).

Aggregate dumpsite versus non-dumpsite birth weights were calculated for the 13 counties with dumpsite towns (Table 5-4).

The dumpsite communities have rates higher than the remaining portions of their counties in 9 of the 13 comparisons and significantly so in 4 of the 13.

Upon taking into account socioeconomic status and race, the case for a dumpsite-birthweight link becomes much weaker. Among the 12 dumpsite communities with proportion of low birthweight infants higher than the remainder of the state, 10 (83 percent) had a percentage of black citizens of at least 7 percent in 1970 and 8 (66.7 percent) had less than 10.7 percent of professional and managerial workers. The analogous figures for the 19 dumpsite communities that had a percentage of birthweights less than the remainder of the state are clearly different: only 4 of 19 (21 percent) had a black percentage higher than 7 percent and 3 of 19 (16 percent) had less than 10.7 percent of their working population employed as professionals and managers.

The case for an effect due to the presence of dumpsites is also weaker at the county scale. While it is true that dumpsite communities had a higher proportion of low birthweights than the nondumpsite communities in 9 of the 13 counties, in 8 of these 9 counties the dumpsite communities had a

## TABLE 5-3

### Dumpsite Communities with Higher Proportions of Underweight Babies than the Remainder of the State, 1980

| Community | % of Births 2500 Grams or Less | Black Pop.> 7%, 1970 1 = yes, 0 = no | % Prof., Manag.< 10.7%, 1970 1 = yes, 0 = no |
|---|---|---|---|
| 1. Newark | 12.36 | 1 | 1 |
| 2. Logan | 11.76 | 1 | 1 |
| 3. Burlington Boro | 10.61 | 1 | 1 |
| 4. Jersey City | 10.21 | 1 | 1 |
| 5. Perth Amboy | 10.14 | 1 | 1 |
| 6. Pleasantville | 10.14 | 1 | 1 |
| 7. Linden | 8.84 | 1 | 1 |
| 8. Bound Brook | 8.54 | 0 | 0 |
| 9. Deptford Boro | 8.36 | 1 | 1 |
| 10. Elizabeth | 8.02 | 1 | 0 |
| 11. Freehold Boro | 7.44 | 1 | 0 |
| 12. Howell | 7.09 | 0 | 0 |

higher proportion of blacks and lower proportion of professionals and managers than the remainder of the county.

In short, 12 of the 31 dumpsite communities had a higher proportion of low birthweight babies than the remainder of the State of New Jersey in 1980. But factors related to socioeconomic status and ethnicity, which in turn are related to the mother's condition during pregnancy, may explain these findings rather than exposure to toxic substances from abandoned dumpsites. In conclusion, these studies of cancer and low birthweights suggest some communities for further study. But only an epidemiological study controlling for other explanations can clearly test the hypothesis that there is a unique relationship between dumpsites and health effects among infants and adults. As we expected, there do not seem to be any shortcuts to reach conclusions, at least in New Jersey.

## TABLE 5-4

### Comparison of Low Birthweight Proportions in Dumpsite and Nondumpsite Communities by County, 1980

| County | DUMPSITE Number | COMMUNITIES % Low Birthweight (1) | NONDUMPS % Low Birthweight (2) | Signif. if (1) > (2) at < .20 |
|---|---|---|---|---|
| 1. Atlantic | 2 | 8.50 | 8.22 | — |
| 2. Bergen | 1 | 6.36 | 5.67 | — |
| 3. Burlington | 2 | 9.06 | 6.18 | .05 |
| 4. Camden | 1 | 5.54 | 7.77 | — |
| 5. Cape May | 1 | 6.70 | 5.82 | — |
| 6. Essex | 1 | 12.36 | 7.85 | .01 |
| 7. Gloucester | 3 | 7.91 | 6.34 | — |
| 8. Hudson | 5 | 8.94 | 6.74 | .01 |
| 9. Middlesex | 5 | 6.32 | 6.36 | — |
| 10. Monmouth | 4 | 6.44 | 6.11 | — |
| 11. Ocean | 2 | 4.69 | 5.24 | — |
| 12. Somerset | 2 | 5.39 | 5.40 | — |
| 13. Union | 2 | 8.18 | 6.24 | .01 |

## EFFECTS ON POPULATION CHANGE, PROPERTY VALUES, AND LAND USE

Cooper (1972) says that the body and the home are the two most important symbols of self. We looked to see if dumpsites had left a psychological mark that was manifested by relative changes in population, property values, and land uses. Towns and neighborhoods that have many and the worst dumpsites should be less attractive than towns and neighborhoods that do not.

### Population Change at the Community Scale

Communities with priority sites should have experienced less population growth during the 1970s than the 1960s and less population growth than their neighbors in the 1970s. The caveats for this study were many. First, not every dumpsite has engendered the same amount of publicity. While they are all priority sites, some may be higher priority sites in the eyes of the public than others. Second, some sites may be many miles from the nearest settlement in a community and therefore may not be perceived as an immediate threat, while others may be highly visible. Third, given that groundwater contamination is the most common problem, those communities containing priority sites that do not rely on local groundwater supplies may not perceive a threat.

The data are far from perfect. The test uses 1960-1970 as a control period and assumes that the impact was felt during 1970-1980. Although much of the dumping occurred during the 1970s, dumpsites and related industrial activities must have stereotyped some communities prior to 1970, thus undermining the use of 1960-1970 as the control period. The period 1970-1980 may be too short to measure the impact on population change, particularly in light of the weakened status of the home building segment of the American economy during the latter part of the decade.

Population change, which is used as the indicator, is an imperfect indicator of the willingness of people to live in a community. Birth and death rates as well as migration govern population change. Migration has been the dominant factor at the community scale, but the combination of the three components of population change varies by community. Lastly, there are potential problems of ecological fallacy (generalizing to individuals from aggregate data) and spurious correlation. Without interviewing migrants, it is not possible to know if other important forces guided population change in communities with priority sites. In this regard, small, relatively unpopulated, rural communities would be expected to be more sensitive to a priority site than large, populous cities that face numerous economic, social, political and environmental problems.

Data were available to test this hypothesis for the initial set of 115 priority abandoned hazardous waste sites in the United States. So this part of the analysis is not limited to New Jersey.

The test was made on 85 of the initial 115 sites. The priority sites in American Samoa, Guam and Saipan were excluded because it was assumed that the populations living near them are probably not comparable to continental Americans in attitude toward hazardous substances and ability of the people to migrate. In three cases there were no control areas because the city and the county were the same. Lastly, 26 sites were excluded because the boundaries of the communities were sufficiently different in 1960 and 1980 that the comparisons could not be made.

Population change was examined in the 78 communities. Next, because it was assumed that the negative effect would be more pronounced in less populated communities than in large, populous cities with many positive and negative attributes, a subset of 33 communities with populations less than 10,000 in 1960 was studied. The results did not show that places with priority hazardous waste sites have *so far* acquired such negative images that they experienced population changes that are markedly different than those of their neighbors. But clearly, because of the imperfect data that were used to make the test and the fact that, like many chronic diseases, the effects of the dumpsites may take more than a decade to become apparent, the hypothesis must not be abandoned.

**Property Value Change at the Community Scale**

It was hypothesized that communities with priority sites should be viewed as poor places to purchase residential property and that property values in the dumpsite communities should not have kept pace with rates of housing appreciation in the remainder of the county. The same trend should also hold for rental properties, albeit perhaps less so than for houses because tenants are less stable than homeowners.

Residential property values and rents of eighteen dumpsite communities in New Jersey with populations of less than 15,000 in 1970 were chosen for the analysis from among the 31 dumpsite communities in New Jersey. Communities with more than 15,000 people were excluded because changes in property values in populous communities would be difficult to attribute to a single factor.

The median housing values and median contract rents were obtained for the years 1960, 1970, and 1980 for each of these communities from the U.S. Census (U.S. Department of Commerce 1961a, 1961b, 1961c, 1963, 1972, and 1982).

The property values and contract rents for each of the 18 communities were compared to those of the remainder of the host county for the three sample years. For example, community A had a median housing value of $40,000 in 1980 compared to $50,000 in the remainder of the county. The ratio of the community and remainder of the county numbers is 0.8. If there were negative effects from the sites, the community/rest of county ratios should have been higher in 1960 and 1970 than in 1980.

The results do not support the hypothesis. As a group the property values and rents in the 18 dumpsite communities have appreciated more than those of the remainder of their counties. The dumpsite communities had lower housing values and contract rents than their counties in 1960. The ratios decreased between 1960 and 1970 prior to widespread publicity about dumpsites, and they increased during the 1970s when we hypothesized that they would decrease. Eleven of the 18 housing value ratios and 13 of the 18 rental value ratios increased during the 1970s. It cannot be concluded that dumpsites have *so far* had a consistent, detrimental impact on property values in the communities in New Jersey with the worst dumpsites.

It is possible that the period 1970–1980 is a poor benchmark period. The early part was one of substantial growth in many communities. The appreciation of land values recorded in the 1980 census may have occurred during the early part of the decade and before most of the hazardous waste sites were widely publicized.

## Population, Land Use and Property Values at the Neighborhood Scale

Neighborhoods containing the worst sites should have grown less rapidly than surrounding neighborhoods, and properties in neighborhoods with sites should have less value than properties in adjacent areas. These effects of the worst dumpsites should be most pronounced in affluent neighborhoods that are located in larger communities that are not dependent on industrial and commercial rateables.

Case studies were required to test these hypotheses. After studying all 22 communities considered to have priority sites by the state of New Jersey, three were chosen. Each had been widely publicized so that the public would be aware of the potential danger of living near the site. Plumsted represents a relatively poor rural community. Hillsborough was selected as a relatively affluent, suburban community with valuable residential properties near the site, and with a knowledgeable health and planning staff. A third community, Edison, was chosen to represent a suburban community, but an urban community with a large industrial tax base.

Before presenting the case studies, some warnings are in order. It would be a mistake to generalize from the dumpsite neighborhoods in these three communities to all the neighborhoods with dumpsites. The "individualistic fallacy," the counterpart of the "ecological fallacy," can lead to erroneous generalizations, as much as can its more well-known counterpart. Furthermore, each of these cases has prompted legal actions, and as a result it was not possible to get a complete picture of what has happened and what may occur. Information was obtained from interviews, newspapers, and site visits.

*Plumsted*

Labelled as a "sprawling toxic dump" by the largest selling newspaper in New Jersey (*Newark Star Ledger* July 3, 1980), the Plumsted area sites consist of seven sites in a 21-square-mile area in central New Jersey. Five of the 7 were in Plumsted, the others in nearby Jackson and Upper Freehold. Five of the 7 sites made the priority list of 22 prepared by the State of New Jersey, and the three in Plumsted made the initial list of 115 priority sites in the United States. Thus, Plumsted had the unenviable distinction of being one of only three communities in the United States with as many as three priority sites.

It is highly doubtful that the hazardous waste came from Plumsted, a small agricultural community with fewer than 5,000 residents. Plumsted's local manufacturing base consists of an egg packing plant. Its agricultural base could have produced some of the metals and heavy organic chemicals found at the sites, but not the light chlorinated hydrocarbons. It is alleged that the source was the Thiokol Corporation, a Pennsylvania-based manufacturer of chemicals and rocket fuels (Varrelmann 1982). Thiokol's link to Plumsted is alleged to be Edward Wilson, a worker at Thiokol, who also had a farm in Plumsted. It is claimed that between 1945 and 1970 Wilson and another local resident hauled waste from Thiokol's Trenton plant and dumped it on the Goose, Pijac, Spence, and Wilson farms. It is alleged that the dumpers were aware of what they were doing but did not realize the potential damage. In 1980, a local resident led county officials to the site. Infrared photography and excavation found thousands of buried drums.

Nearly all of Plumsted's population is in two areas located 1.5 to 2 miles from the sites (Figure 5-3). In comparison to Ocean County, the county in which it is located, Plumsted grew far less rapidly in population and jobs in 1960–1980. Its population is younger and less affluent than that of the county as a whole. Housing values and rents increased more rapidly than the county's during the period 1960–1980, but were below the county's in 1980.

We thought that the combination of a relatively poor population and a site which is far removed from population concentrations would result in little local and state concern with the site. We were wrong.

The state government has strongly responded to what it perceived as a potentially serious health threat. Spence farm was rated as the third worst hazardous waste site in the state, Goose farm as the fourth worst and Pijack as the fifth worst. Five million dollars were spent on cleaning up Goose farm where approximately 5,000 drums and contaminated soils were removed. Wilson farm was also cleaned up at a much lesser cost. The others await cleanup dollars from Superfund (Varrelmann 1982).

**FIGURE 5-3**
**Three Worst Plumsted Sites and Vicinity**

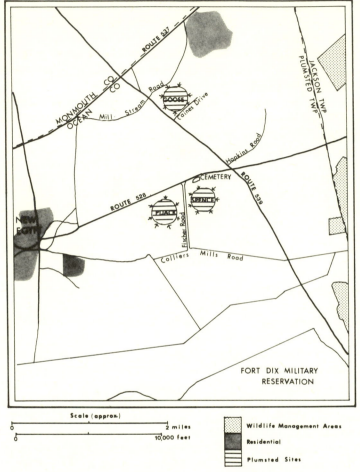

The State of New Jersey feared that the local groundwater supply was contaminated and that other waste sites might be found. As a result, they initially urged a building moratorium in Plumsted (Burke 1982). Once all the sites were delineated, building restrictions were placed on the sites and adjacent lands. No building is allowed on the sites. Severe restrictions were placed on development within 1,000 feet of the sites, with more lenient restrictions from 1,000 out to 1,500 feet. The following conditions must be met before a building permit is granted (Onsdorff 1980):

1. Site inspection by a consultant must be made to confirm the absence of drums and other hazardous debris.

2. Wells must be drilled to make sure that a contaminated plume is not moving toward the property.
3. Groundwater samples must be taken and tested for over 100 chemicals prior to occupancy and during occupancy to confirm that groundwater is potable.
4. Building contractors consult with the state on what to look for during excavation and report any unusual observations made during construction to the state.
5. The developer assumes all risks of developing the site and the community of Plumsted, County of Ocean, and State of New Jersey are not held responsible for any injuries, illnesses, and any other injuries that might occur.

There has been little development or in-migration in Plumsted since these steps were taken through early 1984. Some of this is undoubtedly due to the weaknesses of the housing market. In an interview with the Apple Real Estate Agency (Varrelmann 1982), it was learned that this agency had sold no more than two or three homes during the year since the sites were discovered. Studies have so far shown that groundwater contamination has been confined to the uppermost aquifer. No water supply wells have been contaminated. Nevertheless, people appear to be afraid to move into a town that was labelled a "mini Love Canal" by the media. It remains to be seen how long development in Plumsted will be retarded by the combination of the economy and the dumpsites.

In conclusion, the strong media and state reactions to Plumsted's sites seem to have at least temporarily stigmatized this rural town, located 50 miles from New York City and Philadelphia, as an undesirable place to move to. There are both economic and distributional effects in Plumsted. Discussions with Barbara Greer of the New Jersey Department of Environmental Protection (1982) lead us to conclude that Plumsted has engendered the strongest state reaction. However, Plumsted is not a unique case; New Jersey officials are involved in actions in three other dumpsite towns. The communities as well as the U.S. Department of Housing and Urban Development want advice on what policies should be formed for neighborhoods surrounding these sites.

## Hillsborough

Hillsborough is a growing and well-to-do community of almost 20,000 people in an affluent county with rapidly appreciating housing values and a small industrial economic base (less than 10 percent of property value). The Krysowaty farm is tucked into the northwest corner of Hillsborough Township, immediately adjacent to three other communities and far removed from the developing portion of suburban and rural Hillsborough (Figure 5-4). The site is surrounded by farms, unused grain fields, dairy land, and has few people. Roughly 200 drums and assorted debris were buried at the site, a small fraction of the amount discarded at Plumsted and Edison. Frankly, after a visit to the site, the senior author was left with the impression that this site would have easily been ignored by state and federal authorities. The site did not give the manifest appearance of the industrial potpourri so frequently portrayed by the media as a dumpsite. Yet, it has not been ignored. Krysowaty was included among the list of national priority sites during the second screening in July 1982. In the authors' opinion, the designation of this site as a priority was primarily due to the unprecedented (as best as we can tell) action taken by the township. Since learning about the site in late 1980, Hillsborough has vigorously pushed for action and backed its words with its own funds.

Eyewitnesses report that about 200 drums were crushed and buried in a

## FIGURE 5-4

### Krysowaty Site and Vicinity

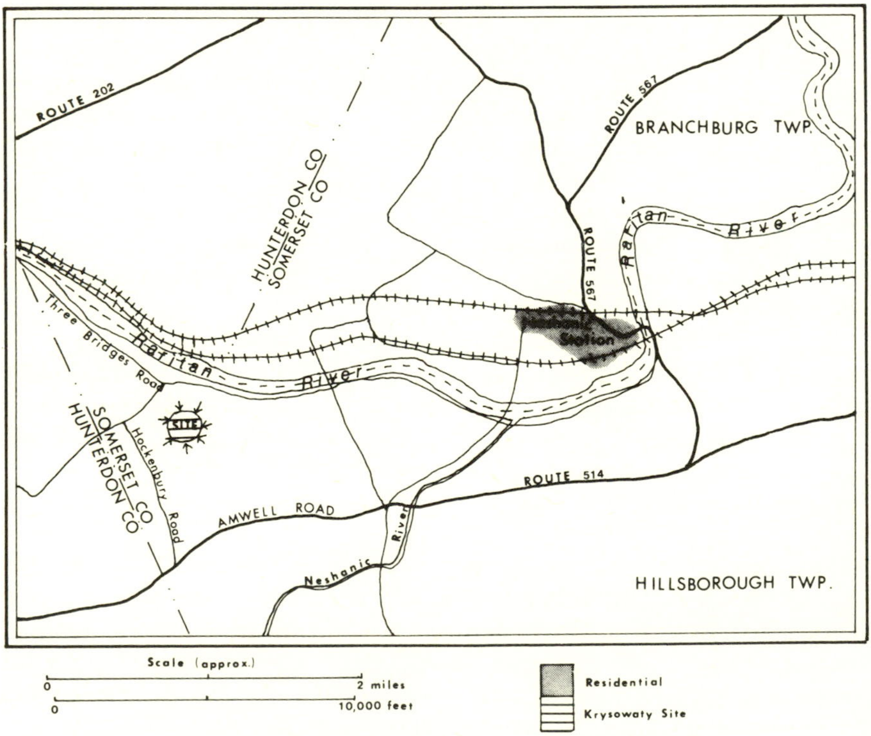

ravine at the farm between 1965 and 1975 (Betz, Converse and Murdoch 1982). Hillsborough hired a consulting firm to conduct a backhoe excavation at the site on July 1, 1981. Benzene, xylene, and benzidine, along with 20–30 crushed drums and fragments, were found. Shallow-depth monitoring wells installed by the state of New Jersey found a variety of synthetic organic chemicals.

Next, and again with its own money, the town hired the firm of Betz, Converse and Murdoch to determine the extent of the contamination and if and where contaminants were moving. Samples were taken of groundwater and surface water, of composite solids, and of twelve nearby residential wells downgrade of the site. The samples disclosed the presence of hazardous substances, and these substances were moving in the fractured red shale (Triassic) rock in the direction of the nearest settlement along Three Bridges Road (Figure 5-4). For example, one of the three monitoring wells downgradient of the site reported 42 parts per billion of the carcinogen benzidine (Betz, Converse and Murdoch 1982). The people living in this settlement rely on individual wells. They had reported unexplained illnesses, dizziness, nausea, irritability, and skin rashes in 1977, long before a site had been identified. These reactions are commonly reported once a site has been identified, so some regard the symptoms as a psychological reaction. The symptoms may have been psychological in this case; however, it should be reported that members of the Betz, Converse and Murdoch sampling team reported dermatitis-like skin reactions on their hands and ankles despite the use of protective clothing. Moreover, the public reports occurred before the site was identified, so perhaps they were real. The consulting firm also reported that the plume of pollution was moving in the direction of the South Branch of the Raritan River, the major source of drinking water for more than one million people in New Jersey. However, this report has been disputed and is being reanalyzed.

Betz, Converse and Murdoch had strong recommendations for Hillsborough: a new potable source of water for the residents of Three Bridges Road; excavation and removal of wastes and contaminated media, including perhaps solids and low-lying marsh deposits; a security system for the site; interception and treatment of the contaminated groundwater; covering with impermeable materials and trenching; and on-site waste treatment of the substances.

The town is pursuing all of the recommendations. The initial priority is to get a new water supply for the local residents. To this end, negotiations on a $500,000 connection to the Elizabethtown Water Supply Company satellite water system are underway to be funded from Superfund (Belnay, personal communication, 1982). As of early 1984, the U.S. EPA had concluded that a new water supply was not justified. Even if the EPA is correct, the impact of its decision is to damage badly its local credibility because the decision is perceived as motivated by EPA's desire to save money.

The state and federal governments along, undoubtedly, with input in the form of money, political pressure, and lawsuits from the township, will determine if and how much money will be spent on other remedial actions at the Krysowaty farm. Hillsborough, in short, did not wait for the federal and state governments to initiate work at its site; its financial investment and political pressures have made what might have been an overlooked site into a priority site.

In this climate of strong local government action, it is highly unlikely that development will be permitted near the site. Glen Belnay, the township health officer and acting director of planning, says that he would strongly discourage development and try to prevent development, unless he could be convinced that no harm would result. There clearly are economic effects in Hillsborough in the form of expenditures to study the site and restrictions on development.

## Edison

The Edison site is very different from the Plumsted and Hillsborough sites. The Krysowaty and Plumsted sites were remote, were apparently the result of a few misinformed individuals, and did not receive notoriety until the 1980s. The Kin-Buc landfill in Edison is certainly not hidden; Kin-Buc is a 90-foot high, 20-acre mound, about 3,500 feet from the New Jersey Turnpike, a twelve-lane artery between New York City and Philadelphia (Figure 5-5). During the early 1970s, there were frequent fires, not infrequent explosions, and a death at Kin-Buc. The authors can recall looking out of the windows at their offices at Rutgers University and seeing plumes of smoke and fire rising from Kin-Buc about four miles away. The media were filled with Kin-Buc stories, which can best be described as outstanding tales of horror prior to Love Canal. We believe that the thousands of people living within five miles of Kin-Buc knew what was occurring at the site.

If they have forgotten, the 90-foot mound now covered by a plastic liner and vegetation serves as a reminder along with the Kin-Buc stories that are still appearing in the media more than six years after Kin-Buc was closed. For example, in January 1982, the newspapers reported that the 1,500 drums of PCB-contaminated leachate that had oozed from the landfill were being stored on the site due to a lack of funds to ship them to Arkansas for destruction (*Newark Star Ledger* January 10, 1982). In April 1982, Aravest International, Inc. was reported to have proposed a regional resource-recovery plant and a toxic waste treatment facility next to Kin-Buc which

## FIGURE 5-5

### The Kin-Buc Landfill and Vicinity

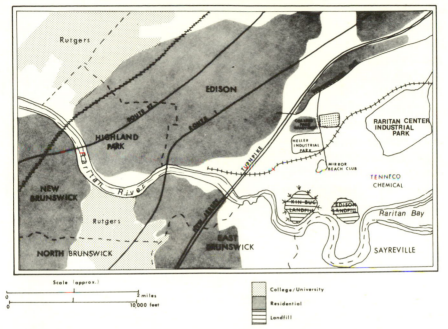

would treat local and out-of-state waste. Township officials were quoted as voicing strong opposition to the proposed project on the grounds that the community already had its share of facilities (*Home News* April 28, 1982).

Kin-Buc was opened in 1959 as a municipal sanitary landfill with the eventual aim of reclamation of the meadowlands along the Raritan River (Figure 5-5). In the early 1970s it began to accept hazardous waste and experience the most unsightly and obvious ramifications of this activity.

Kin-Buc's sources were not a few, local industries; they came from the entire East Coast of the United States. It was reported that during 1973–1976, Kin-Buc received 70 million gallons of hazardous waste (Lautenberg 1982). Drums were buried along with municipal solid waste dumped at the site, and chemicals were poured into pools of garbage.

Over one million dollars were spent at Kin-Buc to close it, to cover it with plastic, to erect a dike, and to build a trench around it. In April 1982, the U.S. Environmental Protection Agency was reported to have released $2.8 million to clean up wastes at Kin-Buc. Most of the money is for a collection-and-separation system (*Home News* April 28, 1982).

Logically, the publicity about Kin-Buc should have discouraged, if not halted, development near the site. But development was not halted; instead, it continued while Kin-Buc was open and while Kin-Buc II was being debated. Furthermore, we found no evidence that existing land use was changed or that planned development was modified while Kin-Buc was open and accepting hazardous waste. The Mirror Lake Beach Club, about one-half mile from Kin-Buc, remained open; Middlesex County College, about one-mile away, expanded; and Heller Industrial Park, a little more than one-half mile away, was constructed after its owner had an environmental assessment made of Kin-Buc and the proposed Kin-Buc II (Lautenberg 1982).

Finally and most surprising, was the construction of new housing within one mile of the site and the appreciation of housing values in the area. The new housing consisted of a few single-family homes in the limited areas zoned for such land use between the heavily used New Jersey Turnpike and Woodbridge Avenue less than one mile from Kin-Buc (Figure 5-5; Terziani, 1982). The closest residential construction was the College Park Apartments, 156 units opened in 1975, less than one mile and easily visible from Kin-Buc (Lautenberg 1982). These new garden apartments have few, if any, vacancies, and their rents are higher than rents in almost every other major apartment complex in Edison (Middlesex County Planning Board 1981).

Furthermore, the census tract that includes Kin-Buc (18.01, see Figure 5-6) seems to have been the most attractive site for major, new developments in Edison Township during the 1970s. The population of Edison Township increased less than 5 percent in 1970–1980; but the increase in census tract 18.01 was 93 percent (from 2,588 to 5,002). The median value of housing in the Kin-Buc census tract rose from 82 percent of the town median in 1970 to 89 percent in 1980, and the median contract rent increased from 65 percent to 114 percent of the town median. The area surrounding Kin-Buc, in short, has become a mix of heavy and light industry, higher education facilities, municipal solid waste disposal sites, and residential housing clearly separated from the larger towns and neighboring communities by major highways and the Raritan River. There is no obvious evidence that Kin-Buc thwarted development in this area. New residential units and industrial parks were constructed, and residential property values substantially increased.

In light of what was observed in Hillsborough and Plumsted, the Edison case is certainly different. Yet, what has occurred in Edison is not that surprising. Unlike rural Plumsted and suburban/rural Hillsborough, there are few spaces left for development in urban Edison. The township was in the process of constructing a $7.6 million trunk sewer through the Kin-Buc area which encouraged development (Lautenberg 1982). Edison's citizens are much more dependent upon industrial ratables than residents of the vast

## FIGURE 5-6

### Edison Township and Vicinity

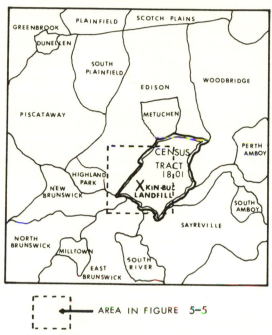

majority of New Jersey communities (25 percent of property value for taxation). The developments near Kin-Buc were a response to the land uses permitted by the zoning ordinances. Finally, those already living in the Kin-Buc area or those who would consider moving into the area would have to be tolerant of the noises, smells, and visual affront associated with dense automobile traffic, industry, and landfills. From the perspective of the 1980s, Kin-Buc may no longer be the most serious environmental insult to the area.

## DISTRIBUTIONAL EFFECTS

This category of social effects (Chapter 3) can occur for a variety of reasons. One is deliberate siting in towns with relatively powerless people. Another is that both abandoned sites and relatively powerless people are located in the same areas, but the former were not deliberately sited and then abandoned to take advantage of the latter. Indeed, the abandoned factory, the pariah of 1984, may once have brought jobs, revenue, and power to the town. At the community scale of analysis, the best that can be hoped for in the way of an explanation is to measure the extent to which the distribution of abandoned sites and relatively powerless people covary along with the traditional location factors of economic efficiency and physical suitability.

As described earlier in the chapter, the geography of dumpsites in New Jersey is not random. The 31 communities with at least 4 abandoned sites and/or 1 of the worst sites are clustered, especially in the northeastern part of the state. Five types of hypotheses were set forth to help explain the distribution. To test these hypotheses, a comparison was made between the 31 dumpsite communities and the 21 NONDUMPS. To conserve space, the data and the result are only briefly summarized. Persons desiring the full list of 45 variables and statistical results should contact the authors. The first sentence in each of the following sections is a statement of the hypothesis.

### Minimize Cost of Waste Disposal

It was hypothesized that dumpsites are close to hazardous waste producers, transporters and users; existing waste disposal sites; and major transportation routes in order to minimize the cost of disposal.

The data were the locations of permitted waste handling facilities, the major sources of hazardous waste, and the road networks. The location of each of the 31 dumpsite towns and the 21 NONDUMPS was indexed to the above sources of waste and the road network. The assumption was that the 31 dumpsite towns would be relatively closer to the waste sources than would the 21 NONDUMPS, thereby encouraging dumping to save transportation costs.

The source hypotheses were important discriminating factors between the communities that have at least 4 dumpsites (WORMOST and MOST) and the 21 NONDUMPS. Twelve of the 21 (57 percent) of the first two groups had at least 15 sources within a 10-mile radius compared to only 3 of the 21 (14 percent) NONDUMPS.

Communities with the most dumpsites have the greatest number of nearby sources of waste and existing landfills and the best access to the major transportation routes. However, the source variables do not help explain the differences between the WORST and NONDUMPS. Communities like Pleasantville, Freehold Boro, and Howell have one of the worst sites, but have neither many sources nearby nor particularly good transportation access to these sources.

## Political Strength

It was hypothesized that dumpsites are not likely to be found in populous communities with a strong, mayor-council form of government, planning boards and environmental commissions; with voters who demonstrate strong support for environmental issues; and in communities that are near to important seats of political power. Underlying the hypothesis is the belief that relatively powerless communities are disproportionately bearing the burden of such sites.

There were 8 political variables. They measured the distance from the center of the community to the center of the county seat; the existence of a planning board, planning staff, and an environmental commission; the type of government; and the vote of the community on environmental bond issues in New Jersey. The distance variable assumes that the further away a community is from the county seat, the more likely it is to suffer from political weaknesses that might lead to a dumpsite. The existence of a planning board, environmental commission, and a strong vote on environmental bond issues implies a political climate which would militate against the presence of a disposal site. The mayor-council form of government was assumed to be the strongest form of government.

None of the political hypotheses were supported by the statistical tests. Indeed, the dumpsite communities were more likely than the NONDUMPS to have the political attributes that should have prevented dumpsites. Dumpsite towns are not consistently at the periphery of their counties, far removed from the seat of county political power. Four of the 31 dumpsite communities (Elizabeth, Freehold, Jersey City, Newark) are county seats. The mayor-council form of government certainly did not consistently prevent dumpsites. Less than 9 percent of the communities in New Jersey have a mayor-council form of government compared to 42 percent of the dumpsite communities. Forty-eight percent of the dumpsite communities had environmental commissions compared to 42 percent in the remainder of the state. Virtually every community has a planning board, and a larger percentage of the dumpsite towns have planning staffs than do the remaining communities in New Jersey.

The bond issue votes show greater support in the WORMOST and MOST communities than in the NONDUMPS. However, there is surprisingly little difference between the WORST and NONDUMPS even though many of the priority dumpsites are located in the WORST communities which have had a great deal of negative publicity about the sites.

## Economic and Land Use Compatibility

It was hypothesized that dumpsites are likely to be found in towns with a large industrial economic base and land uses compatible with industrial activities. These variables are a second indicator of possible community attributes affecting distribution of sites because they measure the extent to which dumpsites are found in communities which directly benefit from ratables. They indicate the size of the economic base and the relative strength of industrial, residential, and agricultural economic bases. Towns with economic bases dependent upon industry were expected to be more vulnerable to the placing of dumpsites. The data were gathered from State of New Jersey Department of Community Affairs Reports.

It was found that towns with economic bases oriented toward industry were far more likely to have many dumpsites. Fourteen of the 21 WORMOST and MOST communities (66.7 percent) had at least 15 percent of their property value from industry compared to only 4 of the 21 (19 percent) of the NONDUMPS. However, an economic base with an important industrial component does not help distinguish between the WORST and the NONDUMPS.

## Demographic Strength

It was hypothesized that dumpsites are unlikely to be found in populous communities whose population has a high socioeconomic status and contains few young, few elderly, and few minorities, and whose population has substantially increased due to migration. These demographic variables are a third type of community attributes which may affect distribution of hazardous waste sites. A positive finding implies that some groups are disproportionately bearing the burden. All of the demographic variables were taken from census reports.

The findings showed that the NONDUMPS have a more affluent population, a population that has increased more, and smaller proportions of younger, older, blacks, and foreign-born people than the 31 dumpsite communities. The demographic variables are the only set that suggest a consistent pattern of difference between the WORST and NONDUMPS. The WORST had a greater proportion of children, elderly, and blacks; and a smaller proportion of persons aged 35–54, families with incomes exceeding $15,000 in 1969, and residents engaged in professional occupations than the NONDUMPS.

The most consistent difference between the dumpsite communities and NONDUMPS is socioeconomic status. This difference is true even among those communities for which the SOURCE variables failed in the tests that were previously reported. Specifically, 11 of the 31 dumpsite communities have few local sources and a small industrial base. Seven of these 11 were in the WORST group. Dumpsite/NONDUMP ratios by county were calculated for each of these 11 communities. For example, the percentage of professionals in Plumsted in 1970 was 9.0 compared to 14.7 percent in the NONDUMP portion of Ocean County, a ratio of .612. Ten of the 11 comparisons for the socioeconomic status variables showed that the dumpsite communities had lower socioeconomic status than the NONDUMPS in their counties. The only exception is Jackson Township which had slightly higher socioeconomic status than the NONDUMP portion of Ocean County, but lower socioeconomic status than Monmouth County which it borders.

These differences in socioeconomic status are statistically significant. The average dumpsite/NONDUMP ratio for the 11 communities for the $15,000 income variable was .77 (p < .01), and it was .75 for the professional worker variable (p < .01). Differences by race, foreign born and age were not nearly as marked.

In conclusion, dumpsite communities that do not have nearby sources do have a significantly lower socioeconomic status profile than their neighbors, implying that the lack of political power derived from high socioeconomic status may have made these communities vulnerable to dumping and abandonment. Suffice it to say that this conclusion, while plausible, has been drawn from an inferential analysis and must be interpreted with caution.

## Physical Compatibility

Lastly, it was hypothesized that dumpsites are located in communities with the most favorable geological formations removed from population centers and water supplies. A strong association between physical compatibility and site locations implies fewer health and environmental effects than would have occurred if siting was dictated by other factors.

The New Jersey Department of Environmental Protection and the Delaware River Basin Commission retained Environmental Resources Management (1981) to study the suitability of their overlapping regions for the siting of hazardous waste treatment, storage, and disposal facilities (see Chapter 6 for additional detail). Separate criteria were prepared for two categories of facilities: (1) land emplacement (secure landfills, solidification, landfarming), and (2) storage/treatment (recovery, thermal treatment, biological treatment, chemical treatment, physical treatment, storage).

Three levels of analysis were conducted, each at smaller scales. The Level

I criteria included: coastal flood hazard areas; coastal wetlands; diabase or basalt bedrock areas; anthracite mining areas; public water supply watersheds; aquifer (well yield; critical recharge areas); aquicludes (geologic formations consisting of significant clay beds); seismic risk zones; and natural areas of significance. The Level I criteria were used to eliminate broad areas with one exception. Aquicludes are preferred sites because they absorb water slowly and transport water so slowly that they usually do not supply groundwater.

Maps roughly displaying the general location of unsuitable, neutral and promising areas were prepared at a scale of 1 inch = 5 miles. The land emplacement map is used in this study because the siting criteria are more strictly applied for land emplacement than for storage and treatment.

Each of the 567 communities in New Jersey was classified as unsuitable, neutral, or promising by overlaying a political map on the Level I criteria land emplacement map. Unsuitable communities have no promising or neutral areas. A community was classified as promising if it had any promising areas and as neutral if it had any neutral, but no promising areas. The method, in short, is conservative because a dumpsite may be located in a town that has a promising or neutral area, but the dumpsite may not be in the section of the town that has the promising area.

The most promising area for land emplacement of hazardous waste in New Jersey runs through the central and southern portion of the urban-industrial corridor (eastern Middlesex, western Monmouth, western Burlington, western Camden, and western Gloucester Counties). As a result, the dumpsite communities have a higher probability of containing promising and neutral areas. But the probabilities are not statistically significant at $p < .20$.

On the basis of empirical findings as well as observation, the hypothesis that the dumpsites were placed in the best areas for hazardous waste management is rejected.

## SUMMARY

New Jersey ranks first in population density, first in chemical production, first in the number of priority dumpsites, and during 1950–1969, first in the rate of white male cancer mortality. Because of these dubious attributes and despite relatively strong state programs, New Jersey may also rank first in the hazardous waste management credibility gap. New Jersey, therefore, should be an excellent place to analyze the health, economic, and distributional effects of hazardous waste sites.

Most of the abandoned dumpsites in New Jersey are located along the urban-industrial corridor between New York City and Philadelphia. Some sites, however, are found in rural areas.

The health effects of dumpsites are difficult to measure because of gaps in theory and data. Many of the communities in New Jersey with the most and worst dumpsites have higher cancer mortality rates than the state. It would be mistaken to jump to a causal conclusion for the following reasons: There is insufficient information to control for confounding factors (e.g., occupation, smoking); the cancer data and water quality data are too general to allow a conclusion that there is a causal association between water source and urinary and digestive tract cancers; and the latency period between exposure to carcinogens and development of cancer further undermines the search for an association because most of the sites were not heavily used for dumping until the early 1970s. At this time all of these factors make cancer a difficult group of diseases to try to associate with the dumping of chemicals. Nevertheless, our personal experiences tell us that laymen frequently do not believe those who make this statement.

Low birthweight data overcome some of the disadvantages of the cancer data (e.g., latency), but many problems of theory and data remain. Furthermore, in examining this data, when confounding factors were taken into account, they seemed to explain the pattern of low birthweights.

Population, land use, and property value changes served as indicators of the psychological impact of dumpsites on communities. No consistent effect was observed at the community scale. Communities in New Jersey with the worst and most dumpsites did not exhibit marked or even relative population or property value declines during 1970–1980. However, the last year, 1980, is probably an inadequate baseline on which to measure effects. Case studies of three communities suggest that socioeconomic impacts do occur, and they depend upon the citizens in the neighborhood; the demographic composition, political strength, and economic base of the community; and the reaction of the state government.

Intuitively, it is reasonable to expect that many of the abandoned sites and perhaps many proposed sites will be in communities that are weak because they do not have the political power that comes with being populous, do not have a strong form of government, are located in geographically isolated areas away from seats of political power and contain many poor, minority, elderly and young people. Furthemore, dump communities should be expected to be more dependent on industrial ratables than NONDUMPS.

As expected, it was found that communities with the greatest number of inactive hazardous waste sites tend to be near potential sources of hazardous waste and themselves have important industrial economic bases. These communities also tend to have more poor, elderly, young, and black residents than their neighbors. Communities with the worst inactive sites and that also have many sites fit the above profile. However, those that have only 1 or 2 sites, but among the most hazardous sites, are not markedly different from their neighbors when measured by distance to waste sources and by industrial economic base. They are, however, lower socioeconomically than their neighbors and to a lesser extent have more younger and black people than their neighbors. The political and physical hypotheses did not help explain the statistical differences between communities with many and the worst sites and the remaining communities of New Jersey. In short, this study implies that relatively poor communities are bearing a disproportional share of the burden of inactive hazardous waste sites in New Jersey. This finding will not make poor communities feel hospitable to those proposing new sites, nor will it be likely to make middle income communities feel guilty and therefore less hostile to proposals which they fear can lead their communities down the path of disinvestment.

## REFERENCES

Belnay, G. Personal communications with Michael Greenberg, 1982.

Betz, Converse, Murdoch, Inc., Consulting Engineers, Planners and Scientists, Township of Hillsborough, Somerset County, New Jersey. "Phase I Investigation Hydrology, Groundwater and Surfacewater Contamination at the Krysowaty Farms, Abandoned Hazardous Waste Disposal Site." Plymouth Meeting, PA, 1982.

Bloom, A., ed. *Guidelines for Studies of Human Populations Exposed to Mutagenic and Reproductive Hazards*. White Plains, NY: March of Dimes Birth Defects Foundation, 1981.

Brown, M. *Laying Waste: The Poisoning of America by Toxic Chemicals*. New York: Pantheon Books, 1979.

Burke, J. Personal communications with Michael Greenberg, 1982.

Cooper, C. "The House as Symbol." *Design and Environment*, Vol. 3, 1972.

Environmental Influences on Fertility, Pregnancy and Development: Directions for Future Research. Conference in Cincinnati. Ohio, May 24–25, 1982.

Environmental Resources Management, Inc. for the Delaware River Basin Commission and the New Jersey Department of Environmental Protection. "Technical Criteria for Identification and Screening of Sites for Hazardous Waste Facilities." Trenton, NJ: New Jersey Department of Environmental Protection, 1981.

Greenberg, M. *The Spatial Distribution of Cancer Mortality and of High and Low Risk Factors in the New Jersey-New York-Philadelphia Metropolitan Regions, 1950-1969, Part I*. Trenton, NJ: New Jersey Department of Environmental Protection and Springfield, VA: National Technical Information Service, 1980a.

Greenberg, M., McKay, F., and White, P. "A Time Series Comparison of Cancer Mortality Rates in the New Jersey-New York-Philadelphia Metropolitan Region and the Remainder of the United States, 1950-1969." *American Journal of Epidemiology*, Vol. 111, 1980b, pp. 166–174.

Greenberg, M., Caruana, J., Holcomb, B., Greenberg, G., Parker, R., Louis, J., and White, P. "High Cancer Mortality Rates from Childhood Leukemia and Young Adult Hodgkin's

Disease and Lymphoma in the New Jersey–New York–Philadelphia Metropolitan Corridor, 1950–1969." *Cancer Research*, Vol. 40, 1980c, pp. 439–443.

Greenberg, M., Caruana, J., Louis, J., and Streenland, K. *Trends in Cancer Mortality in the New Jersey–New York–Philadelphia Region, 1950–1975*. 2 Vols. Trenton, NJ: New Jersey Department of Environmental Protection, 1981a.

Greenberg, M. "A Note on the Changing Geography of Cancer Mortality Within Metropolitan Regions of the United States." *Demography*, Vol. 18, 1981b, pp. 411–420.

Greenberg, M. and Page, G. "Planning With Great Uncertainty: A Review and Case Study of the Safe Drinking Water Controversy." *Socio-Economic Planning Sciences*, Vol. 15, 1981, pp. 65–74.

Greenberg, M. *Urbanization and Cancer Mortality: The United States Experience, 1950–1975*. New York: Oxford University Press, 1983.

Greer, B. Personal communications with Michael Greenberg, 1982.

*Home News*. April 28, 1982, p. 1.

Lautenberg, S. "The Effect of Abandoned Hazardous Waste Dump Sites on Land Use and Values in Edison, New Jersey." Unpublished paper, Department of Urban Planning and Policy Development, New Brunswick, NJ, 1982, and interview of S. Lautenberg with Paul Petto, Middlesex County Department of Solid Waste, 1982.

Lowrance, W. *Assessment of Health Effects at Chemical Disposal Sites*, Los Altos, CA: Wm. Kaufmann, 1981.

Middlesex County Planning Board, Housing Section. Mimeograph of Telephone Survey of Privately Owned Apartment Complexes, March 5, 1981.

New Jersey Department of Health, Cancer Epidemiology Program. *Descriptive Epidemiology of Cancer Mortality in New Jersey: 1949–1976*. Vol. 1, *Discussion and Analysis*. Vol. 2, *Statistical Appendix*. Trenton, NJ: The Department, 1981a.

New Jersey State Department of Health, Health Planning and Resources Development. *Health Data Services, Birth 1980*. VS20–8102, Trenton: The Department, 1981b.

*Newark Star Ledger*. July 3, 1980, p. 1.

———. January 10, 1982, pp. 1 and 30.

Onsdorff, K. Chief, Office of Enforcement, New Jersey State Department of Environmental Protection. Letter to Angela Seeds, Clerk, Town of Plumsted, July 2, 1980.

Terziani, P. Interview with Mr. McWhorton, Building Inspector, Edison Township, May 18, 1982.

United States Department of Commerce, Bureau of the Census. *United States Census of Population and Housing: 1960 Census Tracts: Middlesex County, New Jersey*. Washington, D.C.: U.S. Government Printing Office, 1961a.

———. *United States Census of Population and Housing: 1960 Census Tracts: Philadelphia SMSA*. Washington, D.C.: U.S. Government Printing Office, 1961b.

———. *United States Census of Population and Housing: 1960 Census Tracts: Somerset County, New Jersey*. Washington, D.C.: U.S. Government Printing Office, 1961c.

———. *United States Census of Metropolitan Housing. Vol. 1, States and Small Areas. Part 6: New Jersey–Ohio*. Washington, D.C.: U.S. Government Printing Office, 1963.

———. *Housing Characteristics for States, Cities and Communities. Vol. 1, Part 2, New Jersey*. Washington, D.C.: U.S. Government Printing Office, 1972.

———. Unpublished census data for New Jersey for 1980, 1982.

Varrelmann, C. "The Impact of Abandoned Dumpsites on Plumsted Township." Unpublished paper, Department of Urban Studies, Rutgers University, New Brunswick, New Jersey, 1982 and interviews with William Gollnick, Treasurer, Township of Plumsted; Angela Seeds, Municipal Clerk of Plumsted; Joseph Przywara, Ocean County Health Department; John DeMeo, Councilman of Plumsted Township; Apple Real Estate Agency, 1982.

# 6

# The Unwanted: Finding New Hazardous Waste Sites in the United States

The purpose of this chapter is to review efforts to find new hazardous waste sites in the United States. We start with a brief analysis of public opposition to allowing new facilities in a community. While opposition is formidable, it is not unconditional. Next, we review the legislative charge to the EPA under the authority of RCRA and CERCLA to examine the need for new management facilities, and we discuss the need for facilities and institutional mechanisms to aid facility siting. This is followed by an examination of selected regional and state programs which may serve as models for establishing a legal framework for siting procedures and for developing a siting protocol to aid location decisions.

It is not our intent to present a complete inventory of siting effort. Others have written entire treatises focused solely on the siting issue. (The most comprehensive treatments of the topic are Centaur Associates 1979; Morell and Magorian 1982; and Swift 1973). The objective here is to examine some salient factors related to the success and failure of siting efforts, and to discuss how different states have approached the issue. The urban northeast is selected for studying state programs because the authors have access to decision makers in the area and because the Northeast has the most severe problem caused by the high density of population, a long history of chemical dumping, and strong environmental groups.

## PUBLIC OPPOSITION TO NEW HAZARDOUS WASTE FACILITIES

Efforts to site nonpolluting facilities, such as neighborhood health clinics, and day care centers, have sparked serious locational conflicts between citizens, developers, and government (Reynolds and Honey 1978;

Seley 1983; O'Hare et al. 1983). Locational decisions concerning noxious industries, new hazardous waste facilities included, have become extremely controversial. Popper (1981) aptly describes hazardous waste facilities as locally unwanted land uses (LULUs). It has become conventional wisdom that hazardous waste sites impose serious localized distributional effects and offer regionally diffuse benefits. In this section we characterize the key factors associated with the few successful efforts to site facilities. Chapter 8 presents a broader perspective on the origins of public opposition to hazardous waste facilities.

Citizen opposition to new hazardous waste facilities is formidable and is based on a convergence of real, potential, and imagined local impacts. The distributional effects discussed in Chapters 4 and 5 with respect to existing and abandoned waste sites are both serious and important. Morell and Magorian (1982) persuasively argue that community residents resent not only the psychological and physical threat of a damage incident related to a waste site, but also the specter of state preemption of local land use decisions. The fear and uncertainty concerning the inequitable distribution of local impacts that accompany new facilities has been the rallying point of organized community resistance. Drawing on experience from the civil rights movement, the anti-Viet Nam War protests, the multifarious examples of neighborhood opposition to urban renewal projects, and civil disobedience with respect to blocking construction of nuclear power plants, the organized and increasingly militant opposition to new waste facilities will not easily be brushed aside (see Chapter 8).

Most people suffer from the so-called not-in-my-backyard syndrome (NIMBY) (Cornwall 1983). Having attended a good number of conferences, committee and commission meetings and public hearings, the authors have found that the public is eager to discuss siting but does not believe what the so-called "experts" tell them. Scientists, engineers, government officials, and industrial representatives have little credibility when it comes to siting hazardous waste facilities.

Much of the public is unwilling to accept the conclusion that we really need few facilities. Some argue that federal and state hazardous waste management programs should be solely devoted to cleaning up troublesome and abandoned existing waste sites. Others argue that priority should be given to upgrading existing facilities (increase TSDF capacity) on existing sites. Much of the public rejects arguments made by industrial and government officials that RCRA is technology-forcing legislation that will usher in a new, technically efficient, and less polluting hazardous waste management industry, and that efforts to site new facilities should be supported.

The public does not want new sites near them because they do not believe that they will be safe. The uncertainty involved with contaminant migration from waste sites (discussed at length in Chapter 3) is a strong argument against accepting new facilities. This uncertainty is confounded by the conflicting messages emanating from the RCRA regulations and EPA personnel. RCRA regulations concerning landfills recognize the inevitable probability of contaminant migration. While the regulations presume to remedy this situation by groundwater monitoring and performance standards, this remedy is seen by people we have spoken with as inadequate and as the result of political and bureaucratic compromises that favor the economic interests of industry by allowing them to continue to use land disposal. The fact that today's land disposal methods are better than those used formerly does little to reassure the public that waste sites are safe. Questions concerning the integrity of design standards widens the uncertainty over the level of risks involved with accepting a new facility. (See Chapter 8 for a further discussion.)

Nevertheless, there appear to be certain instances where public opposition is not unconditional. Centaur Associates (1979) documented the chronology of events with respect to 21 separate facility siting efforts. The conclusions from this report list 10 specific recommendations that could reduce the level of public opposition. In general, these include provision of information, assurances, and economic incentives to the public. The report suggests that community residents be fully informed about how and what waste streams will be managed, and the level of risk to health and the environment. It further recommends that assurances be made with respect to the integrity of the owner or operator; a substantive role for the public and local officials in the siting process; a genuine enforcement/compliance monitoring program; post-closure maintenance; the ability of government to judge competently and independently the merits of the site design and technical site suitability. Other recommendations include that the site be chosen in an area of compatible land use and that benefits be offered to offset risks.

The Centaur Associates report reveals other useful information about the conditional character of public opposition. For example, the Gulf Coast Waste Disposal Authority, a public corporation with jurisdiction over a three-county area around Houston-Galveston, Texas, was granted a permit for a 200-acre landfill and landfarming operation in Texas City (Centaur Associates 1979, pp. 54–60). The Authority kept a low profile during the siting process and this may account, in part, for the lack of substantial public opposition. The Authority followed all procedural requirements to obtain a RCRA permit, and even held the necessary public hearings. On the other hand, the Authority did not widely publicize its intentions via the media, and there was no effort made to educate the public about the proposed facility and issues concerning environmental protection and the safety of public health.

Other factors that may have been of equal, if not greater, importance included the fact that the facility was proposed for an area that had land uses compatible with a hazardous waste facility. The location suggested by local officials was in an industrial zone near various refineries and a commercial deep-well injection disposal site. Service was intended to be limited to industrial wastes generated within the three-county jurisdiction of the Authority. These factors suggest that community residents either did not know, or if they did know, did not care about the facility or felt that it did not constitute any greater threat to health and environment than existing activities in the area.

Another successful siting effort involved a proposal by Monsanto for an on-site, 18-acre, secure landfill facility situated in Logan Township, New Jersey. The proposal did not generate local opposition. The success of this effort is attributable to the on-site nature of the facility and the limiting of service to on-site generated wastes; the image of Monsanto as a trusted, responsible corporation (Monsanto is a major employer in the area); a demanding state government review of design and performance standards; and support by the local elected officials and environmental commission (Centaur Associates 1979; Morell and Magorian 1982). Since the facility was on-site, it was a compatible land use. Another ingredient of the successful siting was that Bridgeport, the Logan Township area where Monsanto is located, had a population of less than 1,000 people. Third, a legitimate siting process was conducted which included both technical and public review components and attempts to secure support from local officials.

Although the siting efforts in both of these cases were successful, sharp contrast between the two may be seen in the proponents' attitudes about public knowledge of their proposals. Monsanto submitted an application for construction and operation of its proposed facility and entered a highly visible period of discussion and negotiation with the New Jersey Department of Environmental Protection, local officials, and environmentalists. The Gulf Coast Waste Disposal Authority maintained a low profile during the siting process. Perhaps the difference between the two cases may be explained by the need to deal directly with environmental organizations living in the highly-industrialized Northeast.

A third successful siting attempt took place in East Liverpool, Ohio. This effort involved the proposal of Waste Technologies Industries (WTI) to construct and operate an incinerator requiring 21.5 acres of land. WTI made early attempts to generate local support by opening an office in East Liverpool and staffing it with local residents. The firm developed and circulated a "white paper" which explained most of the facts about the proposed facility. Public opposition appeared strong at first, but diminished over a two-year period (1981 to 1983). John Payne, the Mayor of East

Liverpool and who described the successful nature of the siting effort (1982), placed great emphasis on the forthright willingness of WTI to account publicly for the character of the proposal and the scope of operations. The Mayor also emphasized that the site was located on Columbiana County Port Authority land. Local support and the fact that the proposed site was a compatible land use were both important in this third case. The WTI facility has been issued a RCRA Subtitle C permit, but is experiencing difficulty with obtaining the necessary state permit.

The successful siting efforts are the exceptions rather than the rule. The failures have been conspicuous, and current siting efforts are facing a remarkable level of public accountability. The Centaur report and Morell and Magorian's book offer a thorough account of Earthline's 1978 attempt to operate a 5-acre secure hazardous waste landfill in Bordentown, New Jersey. Public opposition to Earthline's use of the site was aroused by three concerns: (1) concern with the company's credibility (and that of its parent corporation—SCA); (2) the deep concern over the ability of the state's Solid Waste Authority to perform an adequate technical review; and, (3) the township's fear of becoming the state "dumping ground." Two other extremely important objections in the siting conflict dealt with long-range impacts. First, the fact that the site would have been compatible with the surrounding 100-acre sanitary landfill was of little consolation to residents whose children would be attending high school across the street from the facility. And second, although the technical design of the landfill cells, the clay-hypalon-sand-clay liner, the protective clay berm, the segregated cell areas, and the post-closure maintenance were fairly close to the yet unwritten RCRA standards (Parts 264 and 265), residents were deeply concerned about the potential contamination of a major local groundwater source, the Magothy-Raritan aquifer.

In contrasting the experiences of Earthline and Monsanto in siting waste facilities, it is interesting to note that the Earthline-Bordentown siting failure was partially due to local opposition based on technical environmental and public health concerns. In the case of the Monsanto siting, a similar publicly visible environmental concern was not manifest, despite the fact that the landfill was within 150 feet of a stream and, like Bordentown, is located in southern New Jersey. The Monsanto and Earthline siting experiences illustrate the unpredictability of waste site selection in New Jersey and elsewhere in the United States.

Another interesting difference between the Bordentown and Monsanto cases was the level of local opposition. The opposition in Bordentown became more solidified during the period of permit review. Organizers promised continued opposition even when the Solid Waste Authority granted the permit to Earthline, and ultimately, Earthline-SCA decided not to construct the facility. By contrast, Monsanto's proposal raised relatively little opposition.

Upgrading the management options allowable for hazardous waste will encourage technological innovation and reduce the need for disposal facilities. But industry continues to press for increases to current hazardous waste treatment capacity and new sites because it perceives a real market for such services in light of RCRA regulations. Government officials, especially the EPA and its state equivalents, have been placed between the hazardous waste management industry and local opponents, as reluctant mediators of locational conflict. Their position is not to be envied as they try to carry out a congressional mandate widely supported by a national public and almost always vehemently opposed by the local public.

## FEDERAL EPA ACTIVITIES RELATED TO FACILITY SITING

A series of reports and studies initiated by the EPA, mandated by Congress (RCRA and CERCLA), and charged via Executive Order provide the basic information which EPA has used to develop hazardous waste policy. In this section we are primarily interested in the need for new facilities, the development of a siting protocol, and the importance of siting criteria.

Perhaps the earliest serious attempt at assessing the equilibrium between supply of capacity and demand for it was Swift's report on the feasibility of a national hazardous waste disposal system (1973), written in response to a mandate specified in Section 212 of the Solid Waste Disposal Act (P.L. 89–272). This report proposed a National Disposal Site Concept, based on a comparison of industrial hazardous waste generation. Some 36 waste treatment regions were identified which were roughly 200–250 miles in area. The two main criteria for region delineation were the amount of industrial hazardous waste generated and the location of the waste generators.

Seventy-four counties were identified as the best potential sites for either treatment facilities or long-term storage and disposal facilities. These were selected based on a ranking of all counties (3,050) of the continental United States according to four general criteria: (1) geology, hydrology, climatology; (2) transportation risks and costs; (3) ecological factors; and (4) characteristics of the human environment. Included among the characteristics of the human environment were demographic considerations, level of industrialization, and assumptions regarding public acceptance. Many of the 74 counties (e.g., Dooly, Georgia; Inyo, California; Sumter, Alabama; etc.) are rural, with very low population density (less than one-fourth of the population was urban). Although this was not explicitly stated as a measure of public acceptance, a rural population of low density is often assumed to be associated with less local political activity and less likelihood of organized opposition (see Chapter 5).

The 74 counties also included a few highly urbanized areas such as Hartford, Connecticut, and Ventura, California. These areas are also highly industrialized with a high level of manufacturing. Because manufacturing employment is substantial, a relationship may have been assumed between jobs and willingness to accept new facilities, although this was not explicitly stated, nor is it likely to be the case when the object to be sited is perceived with great fear.

The National Disposal System (NDS) approach was abandoned by EPA as a feasible planning approach. The major problem with the NDS was its reliance on estimated hazardous waste volume data. It did not clearly distinguish between the fraction of on-site and off-site waste streams; and it did not include the array of wastes regulated under the RCRA Subtitle C definition. This shows the importance of accurate generation data (Chapter 1).

More recently, EPA has undertaken, or contracted out, a number of efforts to describe more accurately the relationship between supply and demand for hazardous waste management capacity. Three reports are relevant here. First, Straus (1977) developed the first usable national list of commercial firms involved with incineration, land disposal, treatment, reclamation, reprocessing, and petroleum re-refining. Although it was an incomplete list of firms, roughly 109 facilities involved with the waste management options mentioned above were identified. The Straus report elaborates on the types of wastes handled, the method of handling, the waste streams which were excluded, and the final disposal method.

The Straus report was intended to provide an initial list of operating commercial facilities and their scope of services. The report was not intended to make specific measurements of the volume of hazardous waste handled at these facilities.

Booz-Allen & Hamilton and Putnam, Hayes and Bartlett (1980) were contracted by EPA to assess the demand for and supply of commercial hazardous waste management. The first section of this assessment has been reviewed in Chapter 1 with respect to the 42 million metric tons of hazardous waste volume estimated to be generated in the United States in 1980. The remaining sections of the Booz-Allen & Hamilton et al. study reported that roughly 9 million metric tons of hazardous waste in 1980 were destined for commercial, off-site hazardous waste facilities. The study also estimated, based on a survey of 90 out of 127[1] operating facilities, that 1980 hazardous waste management capacity was slightly over 18 million metric tons. Thus, at the national scale, according to this report, there appeared to be no pressing need for increasing capacity, and consequently, there was no pressing need to locate new facilities.

The report is based on an assumption of only 42 million metric tons of hazardous waste generated per year, a figure that is probably much too low. Moreover, it did recognize the fact that there are mismatches between demand and supply. Indeed, there was roughly 8.7 million metric tons of hazardous waste capacity that was not utilized. However, excess capacity was found in some EPA regions (II [New York City], III [Philadelphia], IV [Atlanta], VI [Dallas], IX [San Francisco] while other EPA regions (I [Boston], V [Chicago], VII [Kansas City], VIII [Denver], and X [Seattle] experienced a shortage in capacity. It is in the latter regions where siting efforts are especially needed to create an additional management capacity of about 1.4 million metric tons based on deficits suggested in the study. This translates the siting question into more of a regional problem than a national problem.

The report estimated commercial off-site facility capacity shortfalls by region. These shortfalls range from a low of 154,000 metric tons in Region VIII (Denver) to a high of 489,000 metric tons in Region V (Chicago). The potential capacity shortfalls and surpluses among the 10 regions beyond 1981 depend on a number of factors: (1) those which increase demand for off-site TSDFs; (2) those which decrease demand for off-site TSDFs; and (3) those which determine off-site supply (see Table 6-1). The Booz-Allen & Hamilton report recognized these factors as contributing much uncertainty in efforts to forecast supply and demand levels. Factors affecting demand for off-site capacity appear related to industry adjustment to Congressional legislation and EPA regulatory policy. The report explicitly identifies three major factors which determine the supply of off-site hazardous waste management capacity. They are as follows: (1) the potential for private sector profit; (2) regulatory requirements which favor more costly new facilities and which may have the effect of shutting down inadequate existing facilities; and (3) recognition of public opposition to new facilities as a major obstacle.

The Booz-Allen et al. report did not offer a bold national approach such as the NDS. On the contrary, it revealed an appreciation of the regional aspects of commercial off-site facility supply and demand in the United States. Site selection criteria were not focused on in this report, and there was no attempt to identify facility locations. The scope of the report was limited to commercial off-site facilities and did not include a discussion of on-site facilities.

Both the Straus (1977) report and the Booz-Allen et al. (1980) report reveal that the commercial off-site hazardous waste management industry is

## TABLE 6-1

### Factors Affecting Demand for Off-Site Hazardous Waste Management: Capacity and Factors Determining Off-Site Capacity Supply

Factors Increasing Demand for Off-Site TSDFs

Broader hazardous waste listing under RCRA
Additional wastes accumulated via removal efforts initiated under CERCLA
Existing facilities forced to close because of noncompliance with RCRA

Factors Decreasing Demand

Industry inertia related to uncertainty over the RCRA regulations
Incentives incorporated in RCRA regulations for waste reduction
The shift from off-site to on-site waste management

Factors Determining Off-Site Supply

Potential for large profits from operating a hazardous waste facility
Regulatory actions could reduce the number of existing facilities and encourage/discourage
  the incentive to develop new facilities
The level of public opposition to new facility proposals

Source: Adapted from Booz-Allen and Hamilton (1982), see References

small and concentrated among a few industry leaders. The second report identifies a considerable regional demand for additional capacity. Booz-Allen & Hamilton (1982) updated information in the 1980 report on the plans of the nine leading hazardous waste management firms to increase capacity. The planned capacity increases were moderate in scope, but did add both revenues and market share to the nine leading firms (which now control 60 percent of the off-site market).[2]

The Booz-Allen & Hamilton (1982) *Update* further reported that the nine industry leaders operated 46 facilities in 1981, 10 more than in 1980. Only three of the 10 additional facilities were new and added to total capacity. The other seven facilities represented acquisition of existing facilities. Capacity increases through expansion of existing facilities were also made by other commercial facilities not surveyed in the update report. However, curiously, much of the additional landfill capacity occurred in regions which did not experience a capacity shortfall in 1980 (Booz-Allen & Hamilton 1982).

The supply and demand question with respect to commercial off-site facilities may be beyond accurate measurement for some time into the future. The three studies discussed above point out the difficulty attending efforts to be extremely precise (see Table 6-1). The update study published in 1982 reports that off-site demand dropped slightly between 1980 and 1981. The report explains this drop in demand as a result of the 1981 industrial recession, waste reduction measures taken by hazardous waste generators who are responsive to TSDF costs, and delisting of waste streams (certain pickle liquor and paint sludges). Another interesting feature influencing demand identified in the report involves an aggressive shifting of off-site waste streams to on-site management. This is due partially to the fact that self-sufficiency is easier to manage at this time, and partially to the high costs of liability protection and TSDF price schedules.

The large majority of hazardous wastes are controlled on site. A working estimate of on-site and off-site fractions could be determined if all states used a universal manifest form which would standardize the data. Curtis Haymore (1983) of the EPA Office of Solid Waste cites the Booz-Allen et al. (1980) study and other estimates that the off-site portion may really lie within the 5 to 20 percent range. Haymore further observes that while demand has decreased slightly, the concentration and complexity of the chemical waste stream has increased tremendously. There are no data available about the adequacy of on-site hazardous waste control. This gains special importance as the Part B TSDF applications are being called in for EPA review. The Part B applications include the performance, operation, and design standards with which owners and operators of facilities must be in compliance to obtain a RCRA Subtitle C facility permit.

The most ambitious effort by EPA to determine on-site and off-site fractions of hazardous waste management was a survey conducted by Westat Incorporated (EPA 1983).[3] Westat used existing lists of EPA generator notifications and Part A applications for TSDFs from which to construct a sample. There were three purposes for this national survey of generators and TSDFs regulated under RCRA. One was the need to characterize the types of waste. The second purpose was to meet the requirements of Executive Order 12291 which charges EPA to assess the impacts of regulatory policy on the regulated community. This is part of the continuing RCRA Regulatory Impact Analysis. Finally, the survey was intended to provide a baseline of computerized data concerning the volume of hazardous waste generation and the scope of TSDF activities.

The generator sample of 11,220 was chosen from the roughly 60,000 notifiers. EPA (1983) reports that only 2,016 of the returned responses offered useful information. From these responses EPA estimated that there are roughly 14,100 generators producing 1,000 kilograms or more of regulated hazardous waste per month. The 14,100 generators are estimated to have produced 150 million metric tons in 1981. This is nearly four times greater than the Booz-Allen et al. estimate of about 42 million metric tons.

Curtis Haymore (1983) pointed out that the 150 million metric ton estimate is accurate within plus or minus 40 percent, at the 67 percent confidence level (one standard deviation above or below the estimated volume total, or from 90 to 210 million metric tons). Furthermore, the sample included one firm (DuPont at Deepwater, New Jersey) that disposed of a large volume of hazardous wastes via underground injection. The most recent study (Westat 1984) estimates national volume to be around 250 million metric tons. The conflicting volume estimates remain a serious problem because planning is very difficult without reasonable estimates of waste type by region of generation.

Roughly 8,500 Part A applications were filed by those who treat, store or dispose of hazardous waste or intend to do so. The survey included 2,599 Part A applicants. Of these 1,462 respondents formed the basis for extrapolating to the universe of TSDFs.[4] The TSDFs which were surveyed included on-site as well as off-site facilities. The preliminary results suggest that there are 4,820 active facilities which control the estimated 250 million tons of hazardous waste generated. The survey also suggests that only 5 percent of these wastes (12.5 million metric tons) are transported to commercial off-site facilities. A very clear conclusion may be drawn from the survey: nearly all wastes are handled on site.

The EPA has taken other actions beyond these research studies relevant to the facility siting issue. CERCLA Title III — Section 301 reports are addressing the supply and demand question and the issue of public opposition. The EPA is also consulting with President Reagan's Cabinet Council which was established to investigate the use of federal lands for new hazardous waste sites. EPA is reviewing the first two sites being considered (Rainbow Valley, Arizona; Hanover, Washington) (Haymore 1983).

The states have been encouraged to develop individual hazardous waste programs. A model statute was suggested by EPA (1977) for state decision-makers to copy. The statute would establish state authority to control hazardous wastes within the state. State hazardous waste legislation provided the legal framework necessary to develop a facility siting protocol.

Overall, the numerous facility siting protocols which have emerged vary by region or state. The activities follow a logical sequence. First, RCRA was enacted in order to define the regulators, the regulated community, and the regulated objects. Second, a survey was conducted by the federal and selected state and regional governments to determine if new facilities are needed, and what type. The third sequence of activity (the current sequence) requires the initiation of a facility siting proposal by public authorities (probably state) or private interest or some combination of the two. A fourth activity includes the technical and political review of the proposal. Obviously there is some overlap between the third and fourth activities. The fifth activity involves the active life of the facility and its safe operation. The final step is site maintenance in perpetuity.

The EPA has focused attention on the technical and political review of siting proposals in order to underscore factors which lead to successful siting efforts. A series of four handbooks was planned by the EPA to address siting issues directly. Two of these have been published (McMahon et al. 1982; Bellman et al. 1982). McMahon et al. (1982) discusses ways to compensate communities for allowing new facilities to be constructed and operated. The handbook outlines the roles played by state and local governments, facility owners, and the local resident. The compensation techniques identified include monetary payments, land value guarantees, contingency funds and special insurance, and in-kind replacements (such as providing firefighting equipment). See Chapter 8 for a further discussion.

Bellman et al. (1982) outlines procedures for mediating disputes over hazardous waste facility siting proposals. Calling on past successes with mediating proposals to site sanitary landfills, this handbook describes how local opposition may be confronted through an "outside party." Mediation is different from arbitration in the sense that mediation efforts do not begin with the understanding that a binding agreement must be met. Rather, it relies on the efforts of mediators to defuse the emotional arguments and identify the technical and political aspects of opposition. By focusing on these issues, it is the intent of mediation to arrive at rational, and consensual agreements that can be monitored over time.

The remaining two handbooks are in process. However, the message is clear with regard to siting new facilities. The EPA has decided to encourage regional and state solutions rather than to impose a federal program at this time.

## REGIONAL AND STATE FACILITY SITING ACTIVITIES IN THE NORTHEAST

### Approaches at the Regional Level

There have been two noteworthy attempts at the regional level to establish a siting protocol to aid facility location decisions. One was conducted by the New England Regional Commission (NERCOM), and another by the Delaware River Basin Commission (DRBC) and the New Jersey Department of Environmental Protection (NJDEP). Both of these efforts were based on sound land use planning practices, considered the requirements of a rational siting protocol, and placed great emphasis on siting criteria and impact minimization. However, neither of these approaches has been vested with legislative authority and therefore has had little success.

An ambitious program undertaken by NERCOM (1980a, 1980b, 1980c, 1980d) to establish a facility siting protocol has been described in a series of publications. The *Decision Guide* (1980c) outlines a three-phase decision process. The first phase is restricted to orientation, whereby the developer notifies the public and a dialogue begins to establish basic information. The second phase involves consultation through an institutionalized network involving the developer, government authorities at the local and state levels, and community residents. The end of this phase is marked by an understanding of the differences among these actors, and the beginning of talks about trade-offs. The final phase entails the negotiation period where the trade-offs are settled and the facility specifications are redesigned.

The NERCOM model resembles an adapted form of the environmental impact statement requirements of the National Environmental Policy Act (NEPA). It considers alternative projects, comprehensive assessment of impacts, and risk assessment. The NERCOM approach also includes provision for public hearing. The objective of the protocol is to open the decision-making process to those who will live near the facility. An advantage of this protocol is the emphasis it places on identifying impacts and weighing their importance in terms of risks to public health and the environment.

The NERCOM siting approach identifies the following six categories of siting criteria relevant to hazardous waste facility location decisions (NERCOM 1980b): (1) surface and groundwater, (2) air, (3) transportation systems, (4) land use, (5) economics, and (6) other. Each of the categories includes component criteria. For example, under the surface and groundwater category, the component criteria include estimated contaminant migration, predictability of contaminant pathways, and potential effect on public water supplies. The land use category includes consideration of the impact of a facility on environmentally sensitive lands, its proximity to residential areas, and its compatability with existing and planned future land uses. There are 19 criteria in all.

The 19 NERCOM siting criteria are accompanied by a rating scheme designed to aid decisionmakers rank a proposal vis-à-vis each siting factor in a checklist fashion. For example, under the air category, one siting criterion is the potential for human exposure to hazardous air pollutants. The rating scheme allows three rankings: low, moderate, and high. The ranking should be based on factors such as climatic conditions and neighboring populations. Under transportation systems, another criterion is safety of transportation route which is rated as very low risk, low risk, moderate risk, and high risk. The appropriate ranking is determined by review of the site-specific proposal and consideration of roadway designs and natural hazards.

The NERCOM siting criteria process has been designed as an iterative procedure. After reviewing a proposal according to the listed criteria, an affected community should negotiate for corrective or mitigative measures where individual criterion are flagged as problematic. The method allows for reviewers to modify the rating scheme and weight the criteria differently. While the number of criteria presented by NERCOM are somewhat limited, the siting approach in general appears to be a sound method that is sensitive to land use constraints.

Another attempt to develop siting criteria was jointly sponsored by the DRBC and NJDEP as part of a regional hazardous waste management program. This approach outlines a protocol for siting facilities in the four basin states (Delaware, New Jersey, New York and Pennsylvania). It is not a regulatory program with statutory authority; however, it serves as an interesting planning tool.

The DRBC–NJDEP (1979) developed a facility siting procedure based on three levels of screening. Each level considered different siting criteria at varying geographic scales. The first level of screening focused on the entire basin region with an emphasis on areas of roughly 5 square miles or greater. At this scale, 11 criteria almost exclusively related to the physical environment were examined: (1) coastal flood hazard areas, (2) coastal wetlands, (3) anthracite mining areas, (4) diabase or basalt bedrock areas, (5) public water supply watersheds, (6) aquifer/well yield, (7) critical recharge areas, (8) aquicludes, (9) seismic risk zones, (10) zones of contaminated ground water, and (11) natural areas of significance. These criteria were reviewed to determine what type(s) of facilities would or would not be suitable in the region. Evaluation of the criteria depended upon a ranking system similar to the Battelle (Dee et al. 1973) environmental evaluation system that utilized expert judgment to divide the study area into three categories of suitability (i.e., "red," "yellow," or "green" interpreted similar to a traffic light.) The DRBC–NJDEP criteria evaluation also relied on expert judgment to review technical information sources and to categorize the basin into "unsuitable," "neutral," or "promising" areas. At the first level of analysis, broad areas were eliminated from consideration as a facility location if a technical review of the criteria revealed natural limitations. The results of the first level of analysis were used in Chapter 5.

The second level of evaluation focused on the "neutral" and "promising" areas identified from level one screening. The purpose of this level of evaluation was to identify existing facility sites and candidate areas for new facilities. Again, relying on technical information and expert judgment, four criteria were reviewed for areas at a scale of approximately 1 square mile. The first three criteria concern compatible land uses appropriate for hazardous waste facility operations. They were as follows: (1) lands designated for industrial use, (2) sites of existing facilities, and (3) lands in public trust. The third criterion divides public lands into incompatible uses (i.e., parks, recreation areas, registered historic sites, game lands), and compatible uses (i.e., military reservations). The fourth criterion concerns transportation access routes in relation to traffic volume, congestion, and type of highway (i.e., federal, Class I or Class II state highway).

The third and final level of evaluation was to be applied only to the specific sites identified from the second level screening. The amount of detail required was substantial since it focused on criteria for these sites at a scale of about 2,000 square feet. Criteria reviewed at this level were of two types. The first type considered the following: (1) flood hazard areas, (2) aquifer use, (3) groundwater flow systems, (4) geologic faults, (5) bedrock, (6) soil permeability, and (7) freshwater wetlands. These were similar to the level one criteria, but were examined at the site-specific scale for this level of analysis. These criteria were used to exclude an area outright from further consideration. The second type of criteria at this level concerned variables related to air and water quality, soil characteristics, and socioeconomic factors (i.e., labor supply, economic activities, surrounding structures, and transportation access routes). These criteria were evaluated to determine general suitability. However, the precise evaluation procedure was not very clear.

The DRBC–NJDEP approach had two major advantages. First, it was the only approach that began at a regional scale and worked down to local areas. Most approaches are based on an advocacy procedure in which developers propose a specific site without serious consideration of whether a generally more suitable area exists. A second advantage of the DRBC–NJDEP model was the wide array of appropriate criteria identified for evaluation. The major drawback of this approach has been the absence of political support to follow the results of the research.

The two regional approaches discussed above have not been used to finalize facility location decisions at the time of this writing. In fact, there appears to be some retrenchment from the regional approach. A memorandum submitted by Massachusetts environmental officials to the EPA requested that the Commonwealth of Massachusetts decide where a facility should be sited within its borders.[5] The DRBC study, likewise, did not arrive at a specific location decision. It is likely that the four states in the basin will have to make individual decisions for their states.

A similar situation is currently emerging with respect to siting low-level radioactive waste disposal facilities. The Low-Level Radioactive Policy Act of 1980[6] encourages regional facilities, referring to their economic efficiency as a primary factor. A number of multiple state-regional compacts have been formed which are currently investigating the feasibility of selecting a site(s). A proposed compact (named CONEG) of states in the northeastern United States has begun negotiations to identify acceptable sites. Each state in the compact would supposedly have an equal chance of being selected to host a facility. However, in November of 1982, Massachusetts voters overwhelmingly passed Question #3, a referendum which requires legislative and voter approval before any low-level radioactive waste storage or disposal facility can be built in Massachusetts. As in the regional hazardous waste facility siting efforts, most states will be likely to opt to "go it alone."

The NERCOM and DRBC approaches are far from failures. Indeed, they go a long way in setting the stage for debate at the state level to examine siting protocol and to identify and evaluate siting criteria. The critical flaw in these regional approaches is the lack of legislative authority, and the fear that one state will become the regional dumping ground for other states.

## Approaches at the State Level in the Northeast

State approaches to finding new hazardous waste facilities are widely divergent. For example, some states do not have an active program for locating new facilities. At the other extreme, Kentucky, New Jersey, New York, and a handful of other states have passed legislation requiring that facility sites be selected. Other states fall somewhere between these extremes.

Curiously enough, there have been abundant studies characterizing state hazardous waste legislation, but there has been very little systematic work done on state facility siting efforts. Steeler and Bulanowski (1982) have compiled summary abstracts of 25 state laws that establish a legal protocol for hazardous waste facility siting. The summary considers the following: the legal approach, the use of eminent domain, public participation, financial/non-financial assurances, and incentives and compensation techniques.

Another compilation, produced by the National Governors' Association (1982), summarizes 13 state facility siting laws. This study focuses on establishing siting boards, a needs survey, the use of siting criteria and an inventory of candidate sites, compensation and incentives, feasibility of state ownership, public participation, and interstate cooperative agreements. Both the Steeler and Bulanowski and the National Governors' Association compilations offer interesting case study information.

In this section, we discuss siting policies developed in eight states situated in the Northeast as an illustration of the similarity in basic approach and differences in specific implementation procedures that can occur in one region of the United States. By limiting the presentation to these states, we control to some extent differences in climate and geology. The primary focus of this review of state programs is on the presence or absence of siting boards, councils or commissions; their membership; and their scope of activity. We also briefly review the types of siting criteria or location standards established by these states to facilitate site suitability evaluations.

### Connecticut

The state of Connecticut has enacted legislation specifically designed to regulate the siting of hazardous waste facilities.[7] The law provides for the establishment of a facility siting council called the Connecticut Siting Council which is in the Department of Public Utility Control. The Council is comprised of 9 members: 5 members representing the public and appointed by the governor; the Commissioner of Environmental Protection; the Chairman of the Public Utilities Control Authority; and one designee each of the Speaker of the House and the President Pro Tempore of the Senate (for a total of 2 members). The Council is directed by the Act to adopt, promulgate, amend, or rescind regulations designed to protect public safety and present and future water supplies (Wood 1981). The Council is also charged with balancing a concern about environmental impacts with a need for economic development.

The state has adopted a procedure called a global review for evaluating permit applications for new facilities.[8] The types of information reviewed include: air quality and movement, ground and surface water conditions, vegetation, wildlife, seismology, hydrogeology, flood plains, access routes, surrounding land uses, population density, traffic volume and patterns, and institutional buildings, among others. The only strict location standards actually spelled out are that a minimum distance of 400 feet from other land uses be maintained for land-based facilities, and 150 feet for non land-based facilities (i.e., incineration, treatment, etc.).[9] There is also provision for examining effects on neighboring communities.

Decisions by the Council to grant or deny permits must consider risk of impacts with supporting review information from the Connecticut Department of Environmental Protection. The actual permitting process allows for enlarging the Council to include the commissioners of Health Services and Public Safety, and four ad hoc members (three of whom are electors from the proposed host municipality and one of whom is from the neighboring municipality most affected).

The law is not intended to empower the Siting Council with the use of eminent domain. However, after environmental review of hazardous waste facility proposals by the Connecticut Department of Environmental Protection and the Siting Council, if local communities refuse to grant a zoning variance for an otherwise acceptable proposal, the Council could intervene and override home rule (Wood 1981).

## Maine

The state of Maine enacted Title 38—Waste Management Laws: Solid Waste, Hazardous Waste, Hazardous Matter, Hazardous Waste Fund in September of 1981.[10] Under various chapters, this law is intended to serve as Maine's counterpart to RCRA and provide for protection of public safety and environmental resources. The laws do not provide specifically for the siting of new facilities, nor do they provide for the establishment of a siting oversight council. The state has no demonstrated need for new facilities at the present time (Task Force of Hazardous Waste 1980). However, with the closure of some upstate New York landfills to out-of-state hazardous wastes that have been utilized by Maine, the need for a new facility in the state may soon be realized. The Maine Board of Environmental Protection has directed the state Department of Environmental Protection to begin drafting specific hazardous waste management facility siting criteria (Kaplan 1981). The Maine Task Force on Hazardous Waste (1980) anticipated the need for siting criteria and recommended "a broad geographic analysis of the State. . .based on specific criteria (e.g., geological, hydrological, meteorological) in order to generate site alternatives."

## Massachusetts

The Massachusetts legislature enacted Chapter 704—An Act Regulating the Generation, Transportation, Storage, Treatment and Disposal of Hazardous Waste in 1979.[11] Chapter 21C of the act establishes a Division of Hazardous Waste in the Department of Environmental Management, and a 9-member Hazardous Waste Advisory Committee appointed by the governor, to make recommendations concerning hazardous waste management practices to the Department of Environmental Quality Engineering (DEQE). The Hazardous Waste Advisory Committee is also charged with aiding administrative decisions for siting new facilities. DEQE is empowered to utilize the authority of eminent domain to acquire sites for new hazardous waste facilities. However, there appears to be no current intention of using such authority (Sanderson 1981). One intent of Chapter 704 is to establish an advocacy process of regulatory review of construction proposals for new facilities. The DEQE may require developers to submit information concerning topography, geological and soil conditions, climate, surface and groundwater hydrology including run-off and run-on characteristics, wetland and flooding conditions, drinking water supplies, and protection of air and land resources, as they are related to the proposed facility location. Chapter 21D of the act establishes on oversight body, the Site Safety Council, which has set forth generalized location standards for new facilities (Ozonoff 1981). The act also provides for potential host communities to receive grants of $15,000 (not limited to a single grant) to conduct proposal reviews by hiring technical experts and legal counsel.

## New Hampshire

The New Hampshire legislature enacted Chapter 567—An Act Relative to Hazardous Waste Facility Review and Waste Management in 1981. Like that of Massachusetts, the New Hampshire law is based on an advocacy process.[12] A developer proposes construction and must demonstrate that public safety and environmental resources will not be adversely affected. The primary intent of the legislation is to preserve and protect natural resources, especially water resources. When a proposal involves land disposal, either for a new facility or for an existing facility requiring a permit, the legislation provides for the establishment of a Municipal Hazardous Waste Facility Review Committee. The Committee is comprised of 5 to 9 members representing the local planning board, the board of adjustment, and the conservation committee, and including one or more selectmen. The Committee has the right of access to the permit application filed by the developer, and the Bureau of Solid Waste Management is authorized to offer the potential host community funds to conduct a review of the proposal. The Bureau also conducts its own review including a waste analysis and an analysis of hydrogeologic conditions around the proposed facility location (Ray 1981). The legislation does not provide for the development of specific facility siting criteria other than the criteria promulgated by the U.S. EPA under authority of RCRA. The Committee makes a final recommendation to the Bureau based on local regulations (e.g., zoning) and physical factors. However, the Bureau does not have to abide by the Committee recommendation, and the Commissioner of Public Health has the final administrative authority to approve or deny a facility permit.

*New Jersey*

The State of New Jersey has enacted the Major Hazardous Waste Facilities Siting Act which establishes a Hazardous Waste Facilities Siting Commission in the executive branch of the state government.[13] The Commission is comprised of nine gubernatorial appointees with three members representing each of the following three groups: county and municipal elected officials, industry, and environmental and public interest groups. The Commission is charged with preparing a plan for developing new major hazardous waste facilities in the state as needed. While the Commission is vested with the authority to approve or disapprove a facility proposal, there are provisions for at least three other stages of proposal review by state and local authorities and by an advisory council described below.

The Act also establishes in the Department of Environmental Protection the Hazardous Waste Advisory Council, consisting of 13 members appointed by the Governor with the advice and consent of the Senate. The Council is designed to be broadly representative by including members from public interest and environmental groups, county and municipal officials, community organizations, fire-fighters, industries using on-site management, waste generating industries, hazardous waste transporters, and the hazardous waste handling industry. The Council is charged with reviewing and commenting on proposal applications and advising the Commission on the preparation and adoption of a major facilities plan. The Council is also charged with advising the Department of Environmental Protection (DEP) on the development of facility siting criteria. The criteria are to be adopted by the DEP within one year of passage of the act.

DEP reviews proposal applications as part of the normal permit procedure. Under Section 9 of the Act, the department must establish facility siting criteria. The Act directs DEP to adopt five criteria designated in the Act. These include prohibitions against locating a facility within 2,000 yards of a routinely occupied structure, on wetlands, or on floodlands, where the seasonal high water table is within one foot of the surface, and within a 20-mile radius of a nuclear fission power plant that stores spent fuel rods. These location standards are to be fully complemented by a more comprehensive set of siting criteria to be jointly developed by DEP and the Council and reviewed by the Commission (Bennett 1981).

The Commission is mandated to designate appropriate major facility sites within 6 months of adoption of the criteria. The Commission has powers of eminent domain to expedite the major facilities siting plan. In order to designate sites, the Commission will depend on regional suitability studies (Bennett 1981). This is a substantially different approach than that taken by other states which rely on the developer–advocacy procedure.

*New York*

The state of New York has adopted legislation to regulate the siting of industrial hazardous waste management facilities.[14] The New York law and its associated regulations set stringent requirements for siting new facilities. This detailed regulatory approach has developed out of a genuine need for safe facilities given the diverse economic base of the state and the multitude of waste generators. It was also influenced by the widespread ignominy of the Love Canal contamination event.

Section 1105 of the law provides for the constitution of a facility siting board within 15 days of the receipt of an application for construction of a facility. The board is comprised of eight members, including the commissioners of transportation, environmental conservation, health, and commerce; the secretary of state; and three ad hoc members appointed by the governor (two of whom must be residents of the proposed host community). The governor appoints the chairman of the board, and the commissioner of environmental conservation provides technical staff to support the board in its responsibilities. The board has the power of final approval or denial of site acceptance and can exercise powers of eminent domain to override local opposition (Murphy 1982). The Department of Environmental Conservation, however, may set conditions for construction and operating permits based on discharges and environmental regulation.

Pursuant to the siting law, the Department of Environmental Conservation has promulgated a fairly comprehensive set of siting criteria.[15] Part 361.7 of the regulations lists siting criteria and sets forth an evaluation scheme based on three scenario situations: (1) most favorable, (2) less favorable, and (3) least favorable. Fourteen criteria are listed below:

1. Population density
2. Population adjacent to transport route
3. Risk of accident in transportation
4. Proximity to incompatible structures
5. Utility lines
6. Municipal effects
7. Contamination of ground and surface waters
8. Water supply sources
9. Fire and explosions
10. Air quality
11. Areas of mineral exploitation
12. Preservation of endangered species
13. Conservation of historic and cultural resources
14. Open space, recreational, and visual impacts

The siting board, with aid from the N.Y. Department of Environmental Conservation staff, evaluates specific proposals to locate facilities by assessing probable impacts as defined by the siting criteria. Impact assessments are estimated with the aid of expert judgment, since hard scientific rules for estimation are not available (Anderson and Wilson 1981). The assessment procedure is complex but very useful. For example, evaluating the potential impact on water supply sources varies as the proposed facility gets closer or farther away from the source. Assuming impacts attenuate with distance, a proposed location 10 miles from a potable source is probably most favorable. A proposed location within one-quarter mile is probably least favorable. The judgment exercise becomes difficult when attempting to distinguish between most favorable and less favorable, and least favorable and less favorable. There simply are no scientific rules to guide our conceptual measurement.

The criteria are very interesting because some take into account both present and future conditions. Population density is an example of one such criterion. The suggested assessment recommends placing 70 percent importance on the rating for current population within one-half mile of the proposed site, and 30 percent importance on projected 20-year population growth in the same area.

There are some technical difficulties apparent for operationalizing the siting evaluation process presented here. The ratings represent ordinal ranks that are multiplied by unequal weighting factors (i.e., present population rating times 70 percent), and linearly combined over the 14 criteria. Such linear assumptions of ordinal values violate fundamental arithmetic rules of combination (Baecher et al. 1975; Hopkins 1977). The suggested procedure also fails to offer a way to determine the overall acceptability or unacceptability of the resulting sum of impact number. However, these criticisms notwithstanding, the New York approach represents an admirable model for aiding important decisions with limited information and in the absence of firm evaluation procedures. At worst, a rating balance sheet will exist which addresses each of the criteria.

## Rhode Island

The state of Rhode Island does not have a hazardous waste siting law but has instead a formal set of rules and regulations which must be met before granting facility operating permits.[16] The rules and regulations treat land disposal facility permits with special caution since roughly 99 percent of the land has a high water table of 4 to 5 feet (Quinn 1981). General facility requirements are listed in Rule 3. These requirements compel the developer to protect ground water resources and to avoid the one-hundred-year flood plain, wetlands, recharge areas of community water systems or sole source aquifers, coastal high-hazard areas, active fault areas, and critical habitats. Other rules govern the development of site plan information and review, and design and construction requirements. Permit applications are reviewed by the Rhode Island Department of Environmental Management. Permits may be granted after environmental and site plan reviews and after public hearings by the Director of the Department of Environmental Management.

## Vermont

Vermont has no legislation designed solely to address siting hazardous waste management facilities; however, this function is included in Act 250, Vermont's land use and development law.[17] Subchapter 3 of this Vermont state law specifies that construction permits are to be granted only after an environmental review of the proposal in conjunction with an examination of the capability of the land (i.e., its physical aspects—water resources, forests, floodplains, wildlife habitats, etc.). Act 250 provides a working checklist of physical and cultural criteria pertinent to development. As part of an environmental review conducted by any of the state's nine district commissions, consideration of earthquake risk, floodlands, and groundwater resources will be required for proposed hazardous waste facility construction and operation (Whiteley 1981).

## SUMMARY

This chapter has examined the issue of finding new hazardous waste facility sites in a climate of adamant public opposition. While opposition is formidable, it has not been unconditional. Among the many siting efforts, most have failed; but a few have been successful. There may be a higher likelihood of success when a siting proposal is advocated by a reputable firm, is situated on compatible lands, is limited to locally generated hazardous wastes, and seeks to develop local support via an open negotiation process between elected officials and local residents and citizen groups.

The federal role in finding new sites has been limited to providing information concerning the need for new facilities and to developing a siting protocol that is sensitive to industry, the public interest, and government officials. Much of the required information is still outstanding. A number of EPA studies are due for completion in the next year or two. However, it is clear that EPA recognizes facility siting as a regional rather than a national problem. Consequently, much of the burden of finding new sites has been shifted to the states.

Regional approaches to finding new facility sites have lacked legislative authority and have, therefore, been ineffective in choosing new sites. The regional approach developed by NERCOM, however, has been instrumental in establishing a rational procedure to follow for proposing new facility locations and evaluating the risks and benefits related to the proposal. The regional approaches have also been helpful in defining siting criteria useful for evaluating site suitability.

The states have taken widely divergent approaches toward finding new facility sites. The Northeast states reviewed above serve to illustrate the propinquity for variation. Some states, like Vermont, rely on existing land use regulations, while other states have responded to the siting issue with more specific legislation. Some states vest review authority in siting boards, environmental bureaucracies, or some combination of the two. Some states, like New Jersey, are innovative in that they rely on comprehensive area surveys to identify candidate areas and thus channel proposals to the most "promising" areas. Other states continue to rely on advocacy processes where each proposed location is reviewed solely on its own merits with no consideration of alternative areas that may be better suited for a hazardous waste facility.

In the authors' opinion the more prudent approach, with respect to siting such potentially noxious facilities, would be to conduct areawide screening studies to identify candidate areas, and then to perform site-specific evaluations to choose the best-suited sites. Pre-screening offers a much better approach to siting hazardous waste facilities than do past practices. The siting protocol and criteria evaluation procedures afford much opportunity to use sound land use planning principles in facility location decisions.

The current situation suggests that almost every state will have to find its own new facility sites. More facility proposals are likely to arise in the near future. While many states include a provision for local override, it will probably not be widely used because of the negative political ramifications. In order to acquire local approval of site selection, emphasis will be placed on "buying off" communities through compensation and incentive techniques. We are not sanguine about the success of such efforts. There is also the potential for local rejection ranging from subtle political opposition to civil disobedience (see Chapter 8). A wide variety of factors discussed earlier in this chapter and again in Chapter 8 will influence the extent of public opposition. A key element may well be what is done at the regional scale to assure the public that their safety is of concern and that sites have not been predetermined for political reasons. This is the subject of the next chapter.

## NOTES

1. Estimates for the remaining 37 known commercial off-site TSDFs were based on information processes from the sample survey.

2. The EPA identified the following nine firms as the industry leaders based on volumes processed and gross revenues: (1) Chemical Waste Management; (2) Browning-Ferris Industries; (3) SCA Chemical Services; (4) Rollins Environmental Services; (5) IT Corporation; (6) U.S. Ecology; (7) CECOS International; (8) Conversion Systems; (9) Chem-Clear.

3. *Preliminary Highlights of Findings: National Survey of Hazardous Waste Generators and Treatment, Storage, and Disposal Facilities Regulated Under RCRA in 1981*, U.S. EPA, August 30, 1983.

4. Note that the sample did not include those facilities which failed to submit a Part A application (and are in violation of RCRA); nor did it include inactive facilities.

5. David Standley and Anthony D. Cortese, "NERCOM Issue Paper: Site Selection Process," memorandum dated August 7, 1978, in Centaur Associates, *Siting of Hazardous Waste Management Facilities and Public Opposition* (Washington, D.C.: U.S. EPA, 1979), pp. 341-351.

6. Public Law 96-573, Low-Level Radioactive Waste Policy Act of 1980.

7. Public Act No. 81-369, An Act Concerning Siting of Hazardous Waste Facilities, effective July 1, 1981.

8. Public Act No. 81-369, Section 22a-116 et seq.

9. Public Act No. 81-369, Section 22a-122(a).

10. Maine Revised Statues Annotated, Title 38, Chapter 13, Waste Management Laws: Solid Waste, Hazardous Waste, Hazardous Matter, Hazardous Waste Fund, September 1981.

11. Massachusetts General Laws Chapter 21C, Massachusetts Hazardous Waste Management Act, 1979.

12. New Hampshire House Bill 468, Chapter 567: An Act Relative to Hazardous Waste Facility Review and Waste Management, Chapter 147-A, October 1981.

13. N.J.S.A. 13: 1 E-49 et seq., Major Hazardous Waste Facilities Siting Act, adopted January 13, 1981.

14. N.Y. Environmental Conservation Law, Article 27, Title II, Industrial Siting Hazardous Waste Facilities, December, 1981.

15. ECL, Section 27-1103, Part 361.7, Siting of Industrial Hazardous Waste Facilities, 1981.

16. See State of Rhode Island and Providence Plantations Department of Environmental Management—Division of Air and Hazardous Materials—Hazardous Waste Management Facilities Operating Permit Rules and Regulations, Providence, Rhode Island, November 1980.

17. Vermont Act 250, Title Ten, Part 5, Land Use and Development, Chapter 151, 1969.

## REFERENCES

Anderson, R. and Greenberg, M. "Siting Hazardous Waste Management Facilities: Theory Versus Reality." In *Solid, Hazardous, and Radioactive Wastes*, Vol. II, edited by Majumdar, S. and Miller, E., Pittsburgh, Penn.: Pennsylvania Academy of Sciences, 1984, pp. 170-186.

Anderson, R. and Wilson, Margaret. "Assessing Land Use Suitability for Hazardous Waste Management Facilities." Proceedings of the Northeast Regional Science Association, 1981.

Baecher, Gregory B., Gros, J.C., and McCusher, K. *Balancing Apples and Oranges: Method-*

*ologies for Facility Siting Decisions*. Schloss Laxenburg, Austria: International Institute for Applied Systems Analysis, 1975.

Bellman, H.S., Sampson, C., Cormick, G.W. *Using Mediation When Siting Hazardous Waste Management Facilities — A Handbook*. Washington, D.C.: U.S. Environmental Protection Agency, SW-944, 1982.

Bennett, Bart. Chief, Office of Regulatory Affairs, New Jersey Department of Environmental Protection. Telephone interview, Fall 1981.

Booz-Allen & Hamilton, Inc. *Review of Activities of Major Firms in the Commercial Hazardous Waste Management Industry: 1981 Update*. Washington, D.C.: U.S. Environmental Protection Agency, SW-894, 1982.

Centaur Associates, Inc. *Siting of Hazardous Waste Management Facilities and Public Opposition*. Washington, D.C.: U.S. Environmental Protection Agency, SW-809, 1979.

Cornwall, G. Paper presented at "The Not-In-My-Backyard Syndrome" Symposium on Public Involvement in Siting Waste Management Facilities." York University, Toronto, Canada, May 1983.

Dee, N., Drobny, N., Baker, J., Duke, K., Fahringer, D. *Planning Methodology for Water Quality Management Environmental Evaluation System*. Columbus, Ohio: Battelle-Columbus, 1973.

Delaware River Basin Commission and New Jersey Department of Environmental Protection. *Technical Criteria for Identification and Screening of Sites for Hazardous Waste Facilities*. Prepared by Environmental Resources Management, Inc., West Trenton, New Jersey: Delaware River Basin Commission, 1979.

Haymore, Curtis. Office of Solid Waste, U.S. Environmental Protection Agency. Telephone interviews February, October 1983.

Hopkins, Lewis D. "Methods for Generating Land Suitability Maps: A Comparative Evaluation." *Journal of the American Planning Association*, Vol. 43, 1977, pp. 386–400.

Kaplan, George, Researcher, Licensing and Enforcement Division, Bureau of Oil and Hazardous Material Control, Maine Department of Environmental Protection, Augusta, Maine. Telephone interview, Fall 1981.

McMahon, R., Ernst, C., Miyares, R., Haymore, C. *Using Compensation and Incentives When Siting Hazardous Waste Management Facilities — A Handbook*. Washington, D.C.: U.S. Environmental Protection Agency, SW-942, 1982.

Morell, D. and Magorian, C. *Siting Hazardous Waste Facilities: Local Opposition and the Myth of Preemption*. Cambridge, MA: Ballinger Publishing Company, 1982.

Murphy, Roger D., Supervisor—Civil Technology Section, Bureau of Hazardous Waste Technology, Division of Solid Waste, New York State Department of Environmental Conservation. Telephone interview, January 1982.

National Governors' Association. *Summaries of State Siting Programs*. Washington, D.C.: National Governors' Association, January 1982.

New England Regional Commission. *An Introduction to Facilities for Hazardous Waste Management*. Prepared by Clark-McGlennon Associates, Boston: New England Regional Commission, 1980a.

New England Regional Commission. *Criteria for Evaluating Sites for Hazardous Management*. Prepared by Clark-McGlennon Associates, Boston: New England Regional Commission, 1980b.

New England Regional Commission. *A Decision Guide for Siting Acceptable Hazardous Waste Facilities in New England*. Prepared by Clark-McGlennon Associates, Boston: New England Regional Commission, 1980c.

New England Regional Commission. *Negotiating to Protect Your Interests: A Handbook on Siting Acceptable Hazardous Waste Facilities in New England. Prepared by Clark-McGlennon Associates, Boston: New England Regional Commission, 1980d*.

O'Hare, M., Bacow L., Sanderson, D. *Facility Siting and Public Opposition*. New York: Van Nostrand Reinhold, 1983.

Ozonoff, D. Statement before Massachusetts Hazardous Advisory Committee. Boston, Massachusetts, October 1981.

Payne, J. "Planning and Public Information: A Case History." Kentucky Symposium on Hazardous Waste Management, Policy and Methods, Louisville, Kentucky, December 8–10, 1982.

Popper, F. "Siting LULU's," *Planning*, Vol. 47, 1981, pp. 12–15.

Quinn, John. Rhode Island Department of Environmental Management, Supervisor-Solid Waste Program and Hazardous Substances. Telephone interview, Fall 1981.

Ray, Tom. Waste Management Engineer, Bureau of Solid Waste Management, Division of Public Health Services, Department of Health and Welfare, Hillsboro, New Hampshire. Telephone interview, Fall 1981.

Reynolds, D.R. and Honey, R., "Conflict in the Location of Salutary Public Facilities." In *Urbanization and Conflict in Market Societies*, edited by Kevin R. Cox, Chicago: Maaroufa Press, 1978, pp. 144–160.

Sanderson, Debbie. Massachusetts Department of Environmental Management—Solid Waste Division, Boston, Massachusetts. Telephone interview, June 1981.

Seley, J. *The Politics of Public-Facility Planning*. Lexington, MA: Lexington Books, 1983.

Steeler, J.H. and Bulanowski, G. *Abstracts of State Hazardous Waste Facility Siting Laws*. Denver, Colorado: National Conference of State Legislatures, February 1982.

Straus, Matthew A. *Hazardous Waste Management Facilities in the United States—1977*. Cincinnati, Ohio: U.S. Environmental Protection Agency, EPA/530/SW-146.3, 1977.

Swift, W.H. *Feasibility Study for Development of a System of Hazardous Waste National Disposal Sites*. Richland, Washington: Battelle Memorial Institute, 1973.

Task Force on Hazardous Waste. *Siting of Hazardous Waste, Maine Department of Environmental Protection*. Augusta, Maine: Department of Environmental Protection, 1980.

U.S. Environmental Protection Agency. *Report to Congress: Disposal of Hazardous Wastes*. Washington, D.C.: U.S. Government Printing Office, SW-115, 1974.

U.S. Environmental Protection Agency. *State Decision-Makers' Guide for Hazardous Waste Management*. Washington, D.C.: U.S. Government Printing Office, SW-612, 1977.

U.S. Environmental Protection Agency. *National Survey of Hazardous Waste Generators and Treatment, Storage and Disposal Facilities Regulated Under RCRA in 1981: Preliminary Highlights of Findings*. Washington, D.C.: U.S. Environmental Protection Agency, August 30, 1983.

Westat, Inc. *National Survey of Hazardous Waste Generators and Treatment, Storage and Disposal Facilities Regulated Under RCRA in 1981*. Washington, D.C.: U.S. Environmental Protection Agency, 1984.

Whiteley, Ann. Staff Attorney for Solid and Hazardous Waste Programs. Vermont Agency of Environmental Conservation. Telephone interview, Fall 1981.

Wood, Chris. Executive Director, Connecticut Siting Council, Hartford, Connecticut. Telephone interview, Fall 1981.

# 7

# Adding Credibility to the Siting Process at the Local Government Scale: Constraint Mapping and Location Standards as Planning Tools

The previous chapter discussed the difficulty in finding new hazardous waste management facility sites in the United States. This chapter focuses on that difficulty in small geographic regions. The objective is to present a site screening process to aid location decisions that lends credibility to a siting program. We discuss various methodological approaches to site evaluation, the use of siting criteria and location standards, and the role of different actors in the process. The technical evaluation presented relies on environmental and socio-economic impact analysis methods that are familiar to planners.

First, it is critical that the role of the technical evaluation be placed in proper perspective. Alone, it provides insufficient grounds for finalizing location decisions. It is only one step in what we all know is a highly political siting process ending in a political decision. Technical plans must comply with the legal requirements discussed in Chapters 2 and 6 concerning design operation and performance standards. Furthermore, the credibility of the technical evaluation will depend not only on its scientific competence, but also on whether people believe that it is fair, and that decisions have not been solidified before the analysis is conducted.

Constraint mapping and location standards are two technical tools familiar to planners which could be used to protect the credibility of local governments. The credibility of local governments is at stake by default since the U.S. Environmental Protection Agency concluded that a National Disposal System is presently unnecessary, and that regional solutions are more desirable. Moreover, the regional studies presented in Chapter 6 have lacked legislative support and have proved to be an ineffective vehicle for finalizing location decisions. So the ball has been bounced down to the states, to regions within states, and ultimately to the community.

The screening method presented here can be applied at the sub-state scale to identify initially suitable sites and to eliminate large areas from consideration based on potential adverse impacts. This can serve to facilitate discussion concerning siting decisions within the state political unit where the true decisionmaking power resides. It can guide industry away from clearly unacceptable sites and require government to articulate priorities explicitly. And location standards offer protection to people and property beyond other regulatory requirements.

## CONSTRAINT MAPPING

Traditional location theory was firmly grounded in microeconomic theory which took into account an extensive list of microeconomic factors. Transportation and development costs were usually stressed, and in fact, transportation costs are an important location factor for managing hazardous waste. In 1980 Booz, Allen & Hamilton et al. (1980) reported that either one flatbed truck carrying 80 drums or one tank trunk with a 6,000 gallon load could cost $30 to $40 per hour to transport, or a flat rate per mile of $1.50 to $3.00. States in the Northeast, such as Massachusetts, transport wastes for land disposal as far away as the Chemical Waste Management disposal facility in Emelle, Alabama. Furthermore, if the waste must be transported out of state, the waste management cost becomes lost income to that state. These are important economic reasons for siting new facilities in states where firms require increased capacity.

Development costs related to siting new hazardous waste facilities consist of engineering design and construction, operations, and other costs related to RCRA regulatory compliance such as financial responsibility. Engineering design and construction costs usually comprise the major capital expenditure. This cost may vary from as low as $50,000 for a transfer station or a small scale storage facility to the multi-million dollar range for a full-scale integrated TSDF. Costs may increase when a facility is proposed in a poor location in terms of critical environmental resources. Insurance premiums may become more expensive if underwriters assess a higher potential for environmental contamination or third party injury. In contrast to most other manufacturing activities, operating costs are normally low compared to capital costs because the actual operation is technology rather than labor intensive.

A prescriptive approach to facility siting should incorporate some of the microeconomic-based locational criteria considered by firms, but must be expanded to consider physical and cultural factors. Cultural factors may be derived from the social sciences and more particularly from social impact analysis. Physical factors have been firmly established in the ecology, physical geography, and environmental impact analysis literatures. Consideration of economic, environmental, and cultural factors is essential for a credible facility site evaluation approach. Local populations will not sit idly by and allow these factors to be ignored.

Social impact analysis has been used to determine the distribution of benefits and disbenefits over a given population (Ortiz 1978; Burdge et al. 1978). With respect to hazardous waste facilities, two considerations are paramount: risk of exposure and equity considerations.

The potential for impairment of public health increases as facilities are sited in close proximity to large populations. Risks are elevated in areas where the very young and elderly are present (Calabrese 1977). People from the extremes of the age pyramid either have not fully developed their immunological systems or have had them impaired as a result of the natural aging process. People with a medical history suggesting chronic ailment (e.g., respiratory and circulatory disease) are also at elevated risk. Unfortunately, while it is easy to identify age groups in a specific area, it is infeasible to identify populations with a medical history predisposed to elevated risk without extensive research.

Social impacts involving questions of equity are more complex than identifying age-risk populations. At issue for an impacted population is "some perceived discrepancy between existing environmental quality. . .and anticipated environmental quality" (Dear et al. 1978). Externalities emanating from noxious facilities may reduce the use and exchange value of property by requiring added cleaning and maintenance costs. Indirect costs to mental and physical health are "virtually incalculable" (Harvey 1975). Assigning responsibility for environmental contamination and liability for damage to health and property often entails lengthy and costly legal battles. Notwithstanding the RCRA financial responsibility requirements and the strict and several liability clauses of CERCLA, few impacted parties have obtained equitable legal redress.

Typically, it is suggested, politically powerful groups are usually successful in keeping out noxious facilities. (See Chapter 5, political hypotheses.) This results in forcing their subsequent location in "lower-income neighborhoods with low levels of participation or political acuity" (Reynolds et al. 1978). Some have referred to these as "ugly duckling" communities which usually have a surfeit of noxious industries within their borders while surrounding communities have little or none (Carey and Greenberg 1974). The lower-income populations that are impacted are also referred to as "defeated neighborhoods" (Suttles 1975), or clearly "politically impotent" (Harvey 1975). The net result amounts to an inequitable burden placed upon the politically weak community, while higher levels of environmental quality are enjoyed by the powerful, more affluent communities (Chapter 5). While social impact factors seem intuitively obvious to us, there are many who feel that they are unimportant or, at best, less important than physical factors.

Physical factors important to location decisions (reviewed in Chapter 3) have been the focal point of environmental impact analyses. The National Environmental Policy Act of 1970 (NEPA) set a precedent requiring governmental agencies to review the probable impacts and resource commitments related to "major federal actions." This scrutiny of public sector actions has led some states and local governments to require the same for private sector actions. The literature contains a good deal of information to aid environmental impact analysis related to siting disposal facilities.

Identifying an appropriate set of factors to employ as siting criteria for hazardous waste facilities is only one part of a credible siting effort. Choosing the proper evaluation technique is also important. There are four basic evaluation techniques that are reasonably suited for siting hazardous waste facilities. They are: (1) preference models; (2) cost-benefit analysis; (3) constraint mapping; and (4) matrix-mathematical models (Anderson and Wilson 1981).

## Preference Models

Preference models have been utilized to determine value tradeoffs among different choices primarily in relation to marketing consumer products. But they have also been used to determine levels of public services and tradeoffs among environmental impacts. Preference models have the basic advantage of incorporating the subjective preferences of those who make facility location decisions. This advantage may be extended to include the subjective preferences of host community residents. Acceptable tradeoffs may be determined through sampling opinions related to siting criteria, and subsequent comparing, adjusting, and bargaining among these opinions.

One noteworthy effort in this vein was reported by Fish and Romano (1980). They used a Delphi procedure to identify and rank hazardous waste facility siting factors. The authors operated on the precept that "The probability of successful siting should be increased if supportive factors are carefully developed and negative factors are recognized and addressed early in the siting process" (Fish and Romano 1980, p. 2). The Delphi participants were broadly based and included industry representatives, local government officials, state and federal regulators, and environmental and citizen activists.

Participants in the Delphi process were asked to rank 92 siting factors according to five respondent categories. The categories were (1) not a factor; (2) not important; (3) somewhat important; (4) important; and (5) critical. The 92 siting factors were organized into four groups: (1) existing local conditions and attitudes among local community leaders; (2) the siting proponent's site selection process and technical proposal; (3) economic impacts of the proposed development; and (4) local and state government involvement and technical assistance.

Fish and Romano (1980) reported that 58 of the 92 factors were determined important or critical in terms of supporting or inhibiting facility siting. The inhibiting factors identified were similar to those cited in Chapter 6. They include fear of declining property values; social stigma; proximity to existing waste sites; and, not surprisingly, the lack of credibility of regulatory agencies' enforcement standards. Supportive factors include perceived need for a new facility; the timely use of objective siting criteria; full and open public disclosure of the proposed development; attempting to choose sites with favorable natural characteristics, regardless of engineering modifications; compensation techniques; and legal authority to supercede local override powers.

The preference survey discussed above does not constitute a complete preference model because while opinions were solicited about the relative importance of different siting factors, the researchers did not construct the necessary family of indifference curves. Indeed, it may be nearly impossible to create such a series of curves given the multitude of factors involved in hazardous waste facility siting and the general absence of scientific data (Anderson and Wilson 1981). Some have argued that the preference model works best when the number of impacts evaluated is limited and when the approach is used in conjunction with a larger evaluation protocol (Keeney 1976; Paelinck 1976; Van Delft and Nijkamp 1976). Overall, any explicit articulation of people's priorities is very instructive and may help find relatively suitable sites.

## Cost-Benefit Analysis

Cost-benefit analysis should not be an important technique because the method is incapable of accurately measuring the costs, especially the long-term costs. The benefit component of the cost-benefit equation may be amenable to fairly accurate estimation. For example, by increasing TSDF capacity in an area with a deficit of capacity there will be some multiplier effect for the regional economy. New facility capacity may add to regional income through increased taxes and employment. Local economies may enjoy substantial new revenues in the form of compensation benefits offered by facility developers. A region may also benefit by having access to a nearby facility which will reduce transportation costs and perhaps deter some fraction of illegal dumping. Theoretically at least, new facilities will offer greater levels of environmental protection and avoid the unfortunate future costs for remedial actions.

The more difficult component to estimate involves the costs. There has been substantial difficulty in determining the costs related to adverse environmental impacts (Good 1971; Baecher et al. 1975). One estimate suggests that the Love Canal incident could have been avoided at a cost of $9 million by constructing a secured hazardous waste disposal facility (Conservation Foundation 1980). Instead, the EPA and state of New York have spent over $125 million to relocate families and take remedial and removal actions at the waste site. Judging from the complicated set of distributional effects outlined and examined in Chapter 5 and the difficulty of measuring the public health and environmental impacts, it is clear that substantial difficulty in measuring the costs of localized adverse impacts persists. Overall, this methodological approach is not well suited as a solitary basis for facility location decisions (see Chapter 8 for further discussion).

## Suitability Mapping

It is interesting that mapping land use and development constraints for siting "sanitary" landfills has been performed for some time by the Department of Agriculture. Soil groupings were estimated by the Department for regions, evaluated in terms of permeability and water table criteria, and a suitability rating assigned representing acceptable/unacceptable areas.

Ian McHarg (1969) refined the art of constraint mapping by developing procedures for comparing existing physical conditions to expected conditions by use of mylar overlay mapping. Given the constraints for a specific type of development, say a sanitary landfill, one can assemble mylars with the factors relevant to the constraints (e.g., slope, aquifers, floodways, wetlands, endangered species' habitats, etc.), and overlay them. The mapped region takes on various shades vis-à-vis the shaded mylars, and the researcher can interpret the shadings to evaluate the relative suitability of the land to support the landfill.

This approach works best when the number of siting criteria are limited. It becomes increasingly difficult to interpret suitability as the shaded areas become more obscure with additional overlays. Furthermore, the technique does not capture the complex relation between factors in any detail.

Others have modified the McHarg approach with varying degrees of success. Hufstader (1977) presented a semi-quantitative procedure to examine environmental impacts. Using examples from vegetative studies, Hufstader identified several factors of importance (e.g., production, type, areal distribution, species diversity) and developed criteria to measure impact designation. In the assessment phase, numbered values were assigned to different sub-geographic areas based on a rating scheme from low to high importance. These ratings were then summarized, and a composite rating was derived representing the impacts for the array of factors. The composite ratings could then be incorporated into a map to represent varying levels of impact and suitability.

A series of research efforts have been reported which combine the McHarg approach and the Hufstader rationale for regional screening. Many of these use computers to analyze impacts and produce suitability maps. Some of these models have been operationalized to determine energy facility siting (Dobson 1979); large-scale industrial location (Cleveland et al. 1979); composite landscape assessment (Fabos 1977); and to evaluate changing land use patterns (Kiefer 1973; Roberts 1979).

Hopkins (1977) cautions the researcher about the appropriate use of numerical rating schemes supporting constraint mapping efforts. Hopkins, as well as Baecher et al. (1975) point out the misleading conclusions derived from simple combinations of ratings over multiple siting or suitability factors. There is often a tendency to violate simple rules of mathematics by adding apples and oranges without proper standardization. The proper comparison of variable ratings for an array of factors requires that a commensurate scale be used, and that the intercorrelation between and among the variables be accounted for with statistical techniques. While constraint mapping is acceptable in some circumstances, it is often inappropriate when large numbers of factors are considered simultaneously.

### Matrix-Mathematical Models

A group of matrix models have been reported with respect to siting facilities and environmental impacts related to development (Lichfield 1970; Hill 1973; Bishop 1972). These models range from the quasi-comprehensive checklist approach (Greenberg et al. 1979), where factor-impact relationships are considered in singular fashion, to the larger matrix approaches (Dee et al. 1973; Leopold et al. 1971) which incorporate factor-impact relationships for a variety of factors simultaneously. Whether simultaneous or singular consideration of factors is the modus operandi of these procedures, they can help decision makers identify potential problems.

There are problems associated with matrix models. First, models that arrive at a cumulative quantitative impact score must make simplifying assumptions when they perform arithmetic operations including addition and subtraction with ordinal and nominal values (Beacher et al. 1975; Hopkins 1977). Second, few of these approaches adequately account for associations among siting factors in a statistical fashion. The result is double, triple or more counting of some criteria. Third, the chosen impact designations frequently rely on the judgment of professionals. These judgments may not be representative of societal preferences, and they may not be replicable by another set of professionals charged with identifying levels of impact.

These disadvantages associated with matrix models cannot be fully eliminated. But, it is possible to control the multiple counting problem among siting criteria partially by using mathematical procedures. Gordon (1978) used a multivariate statistical technique to identify the quantitative ecological relationship between 42 environmental variables relevant to land use decisions.

In summary, adamant public opposition may not be overcome by evidence of a thorough, consistent, and, most important, honest evaluation of facility location proposals. But anything less than such an effort may be harmful. A credible evaluation procedure should include the following: a comprehensive list of siting criteria; careful explanation of impact levels, especially when these are not completely known; a method to account for intercorrelation among the siting criteria; and some public sector participation in the process and review of results.

The preference, cost-benefit, constraint-mapping and matrix approaches are each inadequate for finalizing location decisions for hazardous waste facilities. A better approach is a hybrid version of those models discussed above. Such a hybrid approach is described in the next section.


## CASE STUDY ON THE LOWER RARITAN/
## MIDDLESEX COUNTY 208 RIVER BASIN


This section describes a method designed to screen regional areas to identify initially suitable and clearly unsuitable locations for new hazardous waste management facilities. The hypothesis is that some areas are relatively more suitable than others with regard to safety. Suitability, here, is assessed in terms of both ecological and social impacts. Subareas in the case study region are compared with respect to explicitly stated siting criteria measured on a commensurable scale. Multivariate analysis is used to account for the intercorrelation among the siting criteria variables and to reduce the large number of variables into a set of statistical factors. Those areas found to exhibit the least disadvantageous characteristics become candidate sites for the second stage of analysis, site-specific review. With respect to the second stage of analysis, location standards are presented as a planning tool to add a margin of safety between the proposed site and the environment and public health.

The technical proposal and review phase of the siting effort is then complete, and the political processes described in Chapter 6 (e.g., mediation, compensation, etc.) can function with greater confidence about risks involved with various proposed locations.

## The Study Region

The region selected for analysis is the Lower Raritan/Middlesex County 208 Area (see Figure 7-1). This region was chosen to illustrate the screening approach for two reasons. First, the Middlesex County Planning Board had conducted a "208 Program" under the Federal Water Pollution Control Act Amendments of 1972. There was a good deal of physical and cultural information available for planning purposes. These data sources were made available by the planning board.

A second reason for choosing the Middlesex 208 Area is because it is in a state where a real need exists for environmentally acceptable waste management. New Jersey was ranked as the top hazardous waste generating state in the nation, with 3.2 million metric wet tons estimated for 1980 (Pappajohn 1982) (see Chapter 1) and has the greatest number of priority abandoned hazardous waste sites (see Chapter 5).

In a state with one of the worst chemical dump problems, Middlesex County has one of the most severe problems. The county's problem stems from its past record of having accepted 50 percent of the liquid and 75 percent of the solid hazardous waste generated in the state (Neamatolla 1977). Reports have documented specific damage incidents in landfills in the county, including leachate, air, and odor problems (Geraghty and Miller 1976). It remains to be determined whether or not a county with such pronounced problems has acceptable facility sites.

## A Computerized Data Base

A geographical grid system was superimposed on the base map of the study region as shown in Figure 7-1. This grid system is comprised of 272 either full or partial cells accounting for the 350 square mile 208 Area study region. The grid cells are 2 kilometers by 2 kilometers (1.54 mi.$^2$) in area. A

## FIGURE 7-1

### Base Map and Grid System Overlay

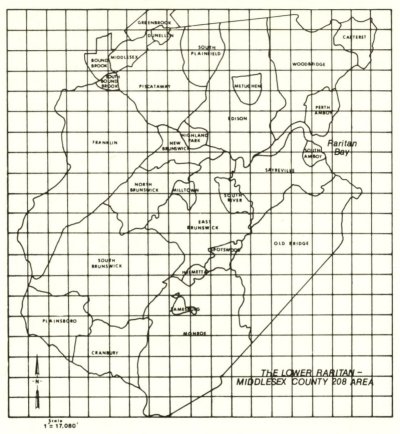

Scale
1˝= 17,080'

single cell covers about 988 acres. Some data were available at a finer grid size (one-fourth of the 988 acres) and more data would have been available if we had been willing to use a larger cell size. After a good deal of discussion with different people, the 2 kilometer by 2 kilometer cell was chosen because of the overriding importance of water resources criteria and demographic data in this urbanized region. This scale seemed to be the best for water resources data in this region. Other initial scales may be more appropriate in other areas. This section presents the criteria selected for the case study. The significance of the criteria and some of the data sources consulted to obtain them are briefly discussed.

Criteria were culled from the facility siting literature. The initial geographical data matrix consisted of 272 cells (cases) and 86 variables (see

Table 7-1). Figure 7-2 illustrates how the raw data looked for one criterion —aquifer outcrop area. Secondly, a questionnaire designed to identify the factors deemed most important to locating hazardous waste management facilities was sent to a selected sample of 115 individuals and groups with special knowledge or interest in environmental impacts or hazardous waste issues: environmental advocates, industries, government officials, and academics. These ratings were compared to the criteria selected from the literature. Then proposed U.S. Environmental Protection Agency criteria

**FIGURE 7-2**

**Spatial Distribution of Aquifer Outcrop Areas**

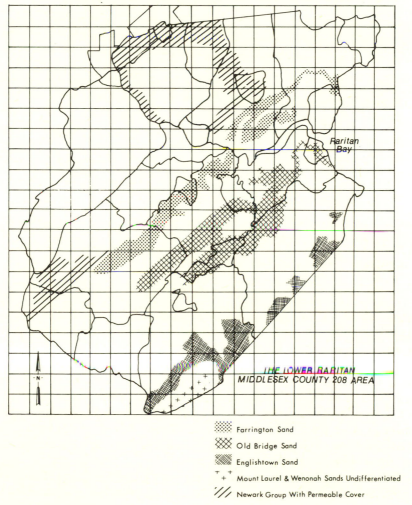

Farrington Sand

Old Bridge Sand

Englishtown Sand

Mount Laurel & Wenonah Sands Undifferentiated

Newark Group With Permeable Cover

## TABLE 7-1

## Hazardous Waste Facility Siting Criteria

*Water Supply Constraints—Group I*

1. Farrington Sand
2. Old Bridge Sand
3. Englishtown Sand
4. Mt. Laurel and Wenonah Sand
5. Newark Group—Permeable Cover
6. Diabase Sill
7. Buried Extension of Diabase Sill
8. Marshalltown Formation
9. Woodbury Clay
10. Merchantville Clay
11. Magothy Formation
12. Raritan Formation
13. Fresh Water Wetlands
14. Tidal Wetlands (1)
15. Tidal Wetlands (2)
16. Severe Septic Limitations
17. Distance to Nearest Water Pumpage Center
18. Distance to Nearest Water Pumpage Center of 2mgd +
19. Distance to Nearest Water Quality Problem Area
20. Distance to Nearest Fresh Water 2 Stream
21. Distance to Nearest Fresh Water 3 Stream
22. Distance to Nearest Tidal Water 1 Stream
23. Distance to Nearest Tidal Water 2 Stream
24. Distance to Nearest Effluent Limited Stream Segment
25. Distance to Nearest Landfill
26. Distance to Nearest Sewage Treatment Plant
27. Distance to Nearest Industrial Waste and Sewage Lagoons
28. Distance to Nearest Sewage Trunk Line
29. Distance to Nearest Product Storage Sites

*Other Physical Constraints—Group II*

30. Floodway Area
31. Flood Fringe Area
32. Flood-Prone Area
33. Cranberry Bogs
34. Class 3 Tidal Waters
35. Depth to Seasonal High Water
36. Permeability
37. Available Water per Inch of Soil
38. Hydrologic Soil Group
39. Percent Clay
40. Percent Loam
41. Percent Sand
42. Depth to Bedrock

## TABLE 7-1 (Continued)

## Hazardous Waste Facility Siting Criteria

43. Slope
44. Erodibility
45. Distance to Nearest Amphibian Habitat
46. Distance to Nearest Reptile Habitat

*Other Cultural Constraints—Group III*

| | |
|---|---|
| 47. Suburban Residential | EXISTING |
| 48. Urban Residential | ZONING |
| 49. Commercial | CONSTRAINT |
| 50. Light Industrial | |
| 51. Mixed Industrial | |
| 52. Open Space | |
| 53. Agriculture | |

| | |
|---|---|
| 54. Cultivated Farmland | EXISTING |
| 55. Park Land | LAND USE |
| 56. Agricultural and Cultivated Land | CONSTRAINTS |
| 57. Suburban | |
| 58. Urban | |
| 59. Light Industrial | |
| 60. Commercial | |
| 61. Mixed Industrial | |
| 62. Vacant | |
| 63. Mining—Sand or Gravel | |
| 64. Landfill—Solid Waste Disposal | |

| | |
|---|---|
| 65. Residential | PROPOSED |
| 66. Nonresidential | LAND USE |
| 67. Open Space Conservation | CONSTRAINTS |
| 68. Agriculture | |
| 69. Undeveloped | |
| 70. Major Institution | |
| 71. Planned Unit Development | |

| | |
|---|---|
| 72. Total Population | DEMOGRAPHIC |
| 73. Percent Population Ages 0–5 | CONSTRAINTS |
| 74. Percent Population Ages 65 Plus | |
| 75. Median Education | |
| 76. Median Income | |
| 77. Percent Population Employed | |
| 78. Percent White Population | |
| 79. Percent Black Population | |
| 80. Percent Population Below Poverty Level | |

### TABLE 7-1 (Continued)

### Hazardous Waste Facility Siting Criteria

| | |
|---|---|
| 81. Distance to Nearest Carbon Monoxide Problem Area | AIR QUALITY NON-ATTAINMENT AREA |
| 82. Distance to Nearest Particulate Problem Area | |
| 83. Distance to Nearest Navigable Channel | TRANSPORTATION CONSTRAINTS |
| 84. Distance to Nearest Rail Freight Line | |
| 85. Distance to Nearest Federal Highway | |
| 86. Distance to Nearest State Highway | |

were added. Eighty-six siting criteria were then grouped into three categories: water supply constraints; other physical constraints; and, cultural constraints. Water-related criteria are considered paramount (Table 7-2) and were therefore made a separate group.

The second group of criteria are also characteristics of the physical environment. This category largely represents criteria related to soil, topographical, and endangered species characteristics. Floodland criteria were grouped in this category because they were not considered as critical as criteria directly related to protecting potable supplies.

The third category includes socioeconomic and land use criteria used to determine distributional effects.

A fourth category of criteria was originally proposed by EPA in 1978, as discussed in Chapter 2 (Table 7-3). A minimum information base to locate

### TABLE 7-2

### Ranking of Factors Listed Most Often as Extremely Important From Siting Criteria Survey

| Rank | Extremely Important % | Siting Criteria |
|---|---|---|
| 1 | (92.3) | Proximity to public water supplies |
| 2 | (90.4) | Groundwater recharge areas |
| 3 | (90.4) | Aquifer outcrop areas |
| 4 | (82.7) | Permeability |
| 5 | (78.8) | Freshwater wetlands |
| 6 | (76.9) | Depth to water table |

## TABLE 7-3

### General Site Selection Criteria Proposed by the U.S. EPA

Facilities should not be located in close proximity to the following factors:

A. *Environmental*

1. active fault zones
2. "regulatory floodway"
3. "coastal high hazard area"
4. 500-year floodplain
5. recharge zone of sole source aquifer

B. *Ecological*

6. wetlands
7. endangered species and critical habitats

C. *Cultural*

8. 200-foot setback of active portion of facility

---

facilities (e.g., "consideration of regional, geographical, and climatic factors") is required under Section 1008(a) of RCRA. These siting factors can be categorized as environmental with one cultural (i.e., land use) requirement. These factors have widespread applicability across most of the continental United States. Although the EPA eventually dropped these site selection factors, they were used here to see if they made any difference. Some of them (e.g., endangered species, flooding) were among the 86 criteria.

### Data Sources and Criteria Measurement

The measurement for each criterion was determined using three approaches: area percentages, linear distances, and rankings based on natural breaks in the data. The criteria measurement and data sources are briefly discussed here for a few selected variables in order to illustrate our reasons for selecting specific criteria and the strengths and weaknesses of the data. A more detailed discussion can be found in Anderson (1981).

### *Area Measurement*

Aquifer outcrop areas (Figure 7-2), a water constraint siting criterion, were chosen to illustrate area percentages. An aquifer is the name used to identify rock or soil formations that contain and transmit water, and thus is a source for underground water (Leopold 1974).

Aquifer outcrop areas are the primary recharge areas for groundwater supplies in the study region. There are five aquifer units in the study region, of which three are of major importance and the remaining two are of local importance (see Table 7-4). Four of the five aquifer units—the Farrington, Old Bridge, Englishtown, and Mt. Laurel and Wenonah Sands—have been proposed as sole source aquifers (pursuant to Section 13–24(e) of the Safe Drinking Water Act) to EPA by the Lower Raritan/Middlesex County 208 program. The Newark Group, while not considered a sole source aquifer, is nonetheless a major water resource for the northwestern sector of the 208 area.

The major potential impact from siting hazardous waste management facilities on or in close proximity to aquifer outcrop areas is that hazardous substances may migrate into the aquifer and contaminate water supplies. The most obvious impact from aquifer contamination is partial or total loss of the water supply available from the aquifer. Groundwater contamination, as measured in Chapter 3, is the single largest environmental impact related to hazardous waste facilities. Reducing any portion of current groundwater supplies through hazardous constituent contamination will impact remaining aquifer water resources by increasing demand on their supplies. Another impact, but of far less importance, is the loss of recharge area due to locating a facility with impermeable cover in an outcrop area.

The aquifer outcrop area data were obtained from a map provided by the Middlesex County 208 program at a scale of 1 inch = 4,000 feet. To delineate the aquifers, this map used information from Henry C. Barksdale's report on the groundwater supplies of Middlesex County.

The percentage of each cell occupied by any of the following five aquifer units was included as Group I siting criteria:

a. percent Farrington Sands
b. percent Old Bridge Sands
c. percent Englishtown Sands
d. percent Mt. Laurel and Wenonah Sands
e. percent Newark Group Impermeable Cover.

Thus, for all 272 cells in the study region an area percentage was determined for each of the five formations mentioned above.

The strength of these data is that they provide physical measurements for the significant aquifers in the study region. In addition, qualitative information is available which describes the lithography, thickness, and yield of the aquifer. This allows a prioritization of aquifers in terms of water supply protection.

There are two weaknesses in the data. The first, and most important, is that the velocity and direction of groundwater flow in these aquifers is not

**TABLE 7-4**

**Aquifer Units and Their Groundwater Potential in the Study Region**

| Aquifer | Thickness (feet) | Water Yield[a] gpd/mi² | Importance[b] as Aquifer | Lithologic Information |
|---|---|---|---|---|
| Englishtown Sands | 100 | 750,000 | Local | White, yellow, or gray quartz sand, some clay lenses |
| Farring-ton | 30-150 | 500-2,000 | Major | Gray to yellow, fine to medium-grained sand. Contains some clay layers |
| Mount Laurel | 40-80 | 750,000 | Local | Slightly glauconitic sands with local beds of sandy clay |
| Newark Group | 5,000 | 500,000 | Major | Red shale inter-bedded with silt-stone and sandstone |
| Old Bridge Sands | 20-110 | 200-1,000 | Major | White to yellow, fine to coarse-grained sand |

Notes: [a]New Jersey Department of Environmental Protection, *Land-Oriented Data System*, Bulletin 74, August 1974.
[b]Geraghty and Miller Inc., Lower Raritan/Middlesex County 208 Water Quality Management Program Task 8 Groundwater Analysis, November 1976.

known. This is especially the case with regard to the Newark group, which is thought to have a multitude of cracks and fissures. The second weakness is that the data allowed us to focus only on significant aquifers at the expense of the smaller aquifers with lower groundwater yields.

## Linear Distance Measurement

Air quality nonattainment areas illustrate data source and measurement for linear distance. Carbon monoxide and particulates, two of six criteria pollutants included under the National Ambient Air Quality Standards (NAAQS) program authorized pursuant to the Clean Air Act and Amendments (1970, 1977), are relevant to the screening approach. The NAAQS are defined in terms of the primary and secondary standards for protection of human health and public welfare.

Air quality constraints are important primarily at facilities with incineration. The following commercial incineration systems are currently or potentially capable of handling a wide variety of chemical wastes:

a. liquid injection incineration
b. multiple hearth incineration
c. rotary kiln incineration
d. catalytic combustion
e. molten salt pyrolysis/combustion
f. fluidized bed incineration
g. wet air oxidation.

The chemical wastes thermally treated range from solvents and sludges to aqueous organics, organic chemical vapors and gases, and rubber wastes. Presently there are no available air quality data in the study region for the vast spectrum of organic and inorganic elements that may be emitted as a result of incinerating these wastes.

Available data on standard air quality parameters in the study region are also rather limited. In the study region there are localized nonattainment areas with respect to carbon monoxide (CO) and particulates. These pollutants have been associated with adverse impacts on human health. For the purpose of this analysis, facilities utilizing incineration should not be located in close proximity to densely populated areas or areas with above average numbers of the population at the extremes of the age pyramid. The assumption here is that areas already burdened with excess concentrations of CO and particulates should not accept additional, and perhaps more hazardous, air pollutant loads, unless concomitant reductions were made from other sources.

Air quality data were obtained from the New Jersey Department of Environmental Protection's *Proposed New Jersey State Implementation Plan for the Attainment and Maintenance of Air Quality Standards*. This source differentiated between CO and particulate levels for each of the communities in the study region. The linear distance from each cell centroid to the nearest nonattainment areas for the following parameters were included as Group III siting criteria:

   a. carbon monoxide nonattainment area
   b. particulate nonattainment area.

The strong part of the monitoring program, and consequently the strength of the data, was the operation of 10 monitoring stations to detect particulate concentrations. The gases were only sporadically monitored for and, according to the data source, only the carbon monoxide data are reasonably reliable. Other data would have been preferred. The assumption underlying the measurements is that hazardous waste sites, especially incineration sites, should be kept as far away from non-attainment areas as is possible. Given that insufficient meteorological data were available to calculate pollutant plumes, it had to be assumed that simple linear distance would translate into protection. This assumption obviously can be questioned as it can for the other criteria that were measured linearly.

### Measurement Based on Natural Breaks

The number of people living in each grid cell varied considerably. Therefore, frequency distributions were used to determine natural breaks in the data, and thus categorize each cell with respect to demographic factors.

As seen in Chapter 3, there are numerous unanswered questions concerning the impact of hazardous waste facilities and public health and safety. Demographic factors are significant for reasons of elevated exposure risks and equity. Elevated exposure is of particular importance to groups at both extremes of the age pyramid. These age cohorts represent the most obvious, but not exhaustive list of hypersusceptible populations.

Demographic data are helpful for estimating distributional effects as was discussed at length in Chapter 5. Questions of equity arise from the potentially highly localized distributional effects of hazardous waste sites. For example, should new sites be located in neighborhoods where residents are below median income and are ethnically diverse? The spatial distribution of the populations serves as an indicator of potential risk due not only to hazardous waste but also to other factors such as noise impacts from trucks.

Demographic data obtained from the Bureau of the Census were gathered by census tract, using tract maps prepared at a scale of 1 inch: 6,000 feet by the Middlesex County Planning Board. Certain assumptions were necessary to allocate tracts to cells and to make the grid system compatible to other data sets in the study. One assumption was that since a single census tract could cover more than one cell, the portion of land area of the tract was used as the percentage multiplier to allocate population size to the cell. For example, if 50 percent of census tract 1 was located in cell A, then the population allocation to Cell A would be 50 percent of census tract 1. This assumption requires a uniform distribution of population to be accurate, a questionable assumption.

The following variables were obtained for each of the 272 cells in the study region and included as Group III siting criteria:

a. total population
b. percent population ages 0–5
c. percent population age 65 and over
d. median income of families and unrelated individuals
e. median education of persons 25 years and older
f. percent white population
g. percent black population
h. total employed population
i. percent population below the poverty level.

### Criteria Evaluation: Estimating Impact Levels

This section describes how the data were converted into a commensurable scale. The ranking method for area data was based on the assumption that as the percentage of land area in a cell occupied by a resource that we want to protect (e.g., an aquifer) increases, the suitability of that cell as a facility location decreases. Conversely, as the percentage of land area occupied by a resource decreases, the suitability for facility location increases. This rationale was translated into a ranking scheme (Table 7-5).

The percentage of land area in each cell was converted to a rank of 1 to 4. The EPA criteria data, as well as the other three groups of siting constraints, were converted into these ranks. The extreme ranks, 1 and 4, represent the most and least suitable ratings, respectively. It is assumed that if an aquifer occupies 5 percent or less of a cell (i.e., less than or equal to 49.5 acres), then aquifers probably do not impose a constraint. A rank of 4 indicates a severe disadvantage. The assumption here is that if greater than two-thirds of the cell is occupied by the aquifer formation, it would be difficult to locate a facility of at least 200 acres with a buffer zone without poten-

**TABLE 7-5**

**Criterion Ranking for Site Suitability Analysis
for Old Bridge Aquifer**

| Percentage Land Area | Ranking | Assumption |
|---|---|---|
| 0–5 | 1 | Probably no adverse impacts on the aquifer formation (Most Suitable) |
| 6–15 | 2 | Probably no adverse impacts, but facility should be located away from aquifer (Some Caution) |
| 16–66 | 3 | Treatment and disposal facility potentially allowable with extreme caution and reasonable mitigation plans in engineering design (Caution) |
| 67–100 | 4 | Disposal facilities should not be located, and any treatment facility requiring surface impoundments should also not be located (Least Suitable) |

Source: R. F. Anderson and M. R. Greenberg. "Hazardous Waste Facility Siting: A Role for Planners." *Journal of the American Planning Association,* Vol. 48, 1982, pp. 204–218.

tially causing considerable adverse impacts to the aquifer. Hypothetically, it is possible to locate the facility in such a cell without causing adverse impacts, but the risk of accidental contamination and the added engineering costs for design safeguards make this an unsuitable site.

Ranks 2 and 3 are not as clear-cut as the extreme ranks. They call for an exercise of judgment because there are no precise guidelines. A rank of 2 indicates that some caution should be taken to avoid portions of a cell occupied by a moderate presence of an aquifer. A facility of 200 or more acres can probably be placed in a cell that has between 6 percent (roughly 60 acres) to 15 percent (roughly 148 acres) occupied by an aquifer without potentially adversely impacting the aquifer. A rank of 3 indicates that enough of a cell is occupied by an aquifer (16 to 66 percent or roughly 158 to 652 acres) such that a good deal of caution should be taken when considering location of facilities in the cell.

Ideally, a set of distance estimates grounded in scientific research would have specified acceptable distances. In the absence of any estimates, one falls back to the assumption that the farther away the better. Should distances fall away in a linear or a non-linear fashion? In the absence of answers to this question, the simplest assumption—linearity—was applied (see Table 7-6 and Figure 7-3). For example, it is assumed that as distance increases from a critical habitat (i.e., reptile habitats), potential impacts decrease; and the converse is also assumed. A rank of 4 indicates that a cell (or any part of a cell) is no farther than 1.86 miles from a reptile habitat (in the cell or the adjacent cell). Figure 7-3 illustrates that the affected area (Area A) is confined to the group of cells adjacent to cell number 142, where the reptile habitat is located. A rank of 3 (caution) was assigned to cells in the next group of adjacent group and a rank of 1 (most suitable) was assigned to cells located 4.32 miles or more from the reptile habitat (Area D).

## TABLE 7-6

### Criterion Ranking for Site Suitability Analysis
### for Reptile Habitats

| Distance from Cell Centroid to Reptile Habitat | Ranking | Assumption |
|---|---|---|
| 4.32 miles | 1 | Probably no adverse impacts on reptile habitats outside a 4.32-mile diameter reach from the habitat (Most Suitable) |
| 3.09 to 4.31 miles | 2 | Probably no adverse impacts, but some caution should be taken to identify and avoid habitats and ecological systems directly related to habitats (Some Caution) |
| 1.86 to 3.08 miles | 3 | Extreme caution should be taken to mitigate impacts on habitats via engineering control designs (Caution) |
| Under 1.86 miles | 4 | This diameter encompasses cells adjacent to habitats and delineates the unsuitable area (Least Suitable) |

## FIGURE 7-3

### Schematic Illustration of Impact Areas Surrounding Reptile Habitats

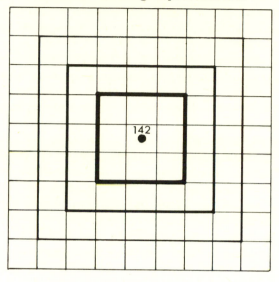

| Area | Distance From Habitat (in miles) | Rank |
|------|----------------------------------|------|
| ▬ A | ≥ 0 ≤ 1.86 | 4 LEAST SUITABLE |
| ▬ B | > 1.86 ≤ 3.08 | 3 CAUTION |
| ─ C | > 3.08 ≤ 4.31 | 2 SOME CAUTION |
| ─ D | ≥ 4.32 | 1 MOST SUITABLE |

● REPTILE HABITAT

The general assumption was also made that cells with a rank of 4 for any siting parameter are least desirable locations. Cells with a rank of 3 are probably the next worst locations for facilities, and only treatment facilities with no surface impoundments should be located in these cells. Cells with ranks of 1 and 2 are probably suitable for most types of facilities, including integrated facilities utilizing surface impoundments and lined disposal pits with leachate collection and treatment systems.

The same ranking scheme was applied to the demographic variables. However, for these siting variables the ranking was determined by the frequency distribution of each variable over the 272 cells. When possible, and where normal distributions were observed, the ranks corresponded to quartiles. Other variables with skewed distributions were attributed ranks according to judgments made on the basis of size of cluster and numerical distance between clusters.

Next, factor analysis, a statistical technique designed to determine mathematical clusters of variables (in this case siting criteria) that covary in space, was used to lessen the problem of multiple counting of criteria that covary. The results are multiple criteria factors and criteria that did not covary with other criteria.

Composite suitability of each cell was judged in two stages. A composite rating was derived for each of the 272 cells, first for the EPA criteria and secondly for the water supply constraints. These two sets were analyzed because the criteria were deemed to be so important that cells with poor ratings on these two sets of criteria should be ruled out. The rating procedure was as follows. If any of the multiple criteria factors or singular criterion had two or more rankings of 4 (most unsuitable), the composite ranking would equal 5, or least suitable. Cells with rankings of 1 (most favorable) or 2 were given the best composite rating, and so on. The final activity of the first stage of analysis was to identify the relative suitability of each cell vis-à-vis the composite ratings derived from the EPA and water supply data sets.

The second stage of analysis focused on the remaining criteria: other physical constraints and cultural constraints. The data were treated in the same way. The result from both stages is the identification of the overall relative suitability for each cell as a host for a new hazardous waste management facility.

Selected case study results are presented as an illustration.

### Site Suitability Screening Results

#### EPA Criteria

Part of the first stage of screening focused on the proposed EPA siting criteria and the water resources criteria applied to the study region. The first result of factor analyzing the EPA siting criteria was a set of maps which included three multiple criteria factors and six singular criterion.

Each of the 272 cells in the study was rated from 1 to 5, where 1 indicates the most suitable cells for facility location (Table 7-7). Thirty-nine percent of the region was divided between 12 percent with extensive disadvantages

**TABLE 7-7**

**Frequency of Composite Ratings for the EPA Criteria**

| Rank | | Approximate Percent of Region | Actual Number of Cells |
|------|---|---|---|
| Most Suitable | 1 | 34.9 | 95 |
| Some Caution | 2 | 17.3 | 47 |
| Caution | 3 | 8.5 | 23 |
| Substantial Caution | 4 | 27.6 | 75 |
| Least Suitable | 5 | 11.7 | 32 |
| Total | | 100.0 | 272 |

and about 27 percent with one serious disadvantage. This 39 percent of the region would present considerable environmental problems for locating integrated facilities, disposal facilities, or any facility utilizing surface impoundments. While it is not impossible to locate these types of facilities in the cells with ratings of 4 and 5, it is recommended that they be avoided.

The 61 percent of the study region with no serious disadvantages might be considered candidate sites for facility locations. Overall, using the EPA siting criteria to screen the study region reveals that—based on this limited set of factors—a majority of the study region's land area could be a candidate site for new hazardous waste management facilities.

The initial EPA criteria, when applied to a region via the screening procedure used here, offer a baseline of comparison to a wider array of siting criteria. The EPA criteria alone do not constitute a fully acceptable set of criteria, and decisions to choose candidate sites would be premature based on these criteria alone. The most important siting criteria are related to water supply, only some of which are present in the EPA criteria.

## Water Supply Criteria: Group I Variables

Companies, government officials, environmental advocates, and academics all identified water supply constraints as the most important siting criteria in the Lower Raritan Middlesex County 208 area. These are listed in Table 7-8 as 23 variables. Also listed in the table are the measurement assumptions used to rank the siting variables.

**TABLE 7-8**

**Water Supply Constraint Variables and
Associated Ranking Procedures**

| | | Ranking Procedure | |
| Water Supply Constraint | Area 1-4 | Linear Distance 1-4 | Natural Breaks in the Data 1-5 |
|---|---|---|---|
| 1. Farrington Sand | x | | |
| 2. Old Bridge Sand | x | | |
| 3. Englishtown Sand | x | | |
| 4. Newark Group Formation | x | | |
| 5. Diabase Sill Formation | x | | |
| 6. Extension of Diabase Sill Formation | x | | |
| 7. Marshalltown Formation | x | | |
| 8. Woodbury Clay Formation | x | | |
| 9. Merchantville Clay Formation | x | | |
| 10. Magothy Formation | x | | |
| 11. Raritan Formation | x | | |
| 12. Tidal Wetlands 1 | x | | |
| 13. Tidal Wetlands 2 | x | | |
| 14. Fresh Water Wetlands | x | | |
| 15. Distance to Nearest Water Pumpage Center | | x | |
| 16. Distance to Nearest Water Pumpage Center 2mgd + | | | x |
| 17. Severe Septic Limitations | x | | |
| 18. Distance to Nearest Water Quality Problem Area | | | x |
| 19. Distance to Fresh Water- 2 Streams | | x | |
| 20. Distance to Fresh Water- 3 Streams | | x | |
| 21. Distance to Tidal Water-1 | | x | |
| 22. Distance to Tidal Water-2 | | x | |
| 23. Distance to Effluent Limited Segments | | x | |

The analysis resulted in the identification of five multiple criteria statistical factors and six singular criteria.

Composite suitability ratings were derived for each cell based on the multiple and singular criteria. Compared to the EPA criteria, the water supply criteria rule out a much larger area (see Table 7-9). Thirty-five percent of the study region exhibited no serious disadvantages. The remaining 65 percent of the study region exhibited serious siting disadvantages.

The water supply criteria, like the EPA siting criteria, do not represent a fully comprehensive set of criteria for locational decision making. However, the water supply criteria were determined to be the most important siting factors for the study region. It is clear that application of the water supply criteria offers the potential for a greater level of public health and environmental resource protection. There were 95 cells determined as suitable via the EPA criteria; and only 10 cells were suitable via the water supply criteria. Therefore, with regard to the initially most suitable areas for locating a hazardous waste facility, the water supply criteria are clearly the most stringent. In other regions, the 8 proposed EPA criteria might be more important.

The first stage of analysis resulted in the derivation of composite ratings for the EPA and Water Supply criteria. A comparison of these relative suitable ratings allows the identification of a subset of cells in the study region which do not exhibit potentially obvious major environmental disadvantages with regard to facility siting. Sixty-six cells (24 percent of the study region) were identified as having composite ratings ranging from caution, to some caution, to most suitable for both sets of criteria. It is these cells (see

**TABLE 7-9**

**Frequency of Composite Ratings for the Water Supply Constraint Criteria**

| Rank | | Percentage of Region | Actual Number of Cells |
|---|---|---|---|
| Most Suitable | 1 | 3.68 | 10 |
| Some Caution | 2 | 11.03 | 30 |
| Caution | 3 | 20.22 | 55 |
| Substantial Caution | 4 | 32.72 | 89 |
| Least Suitable | 5 | 32.35 | 88 |

Figure 7-4) which exhibit the more suitable attributes for hosting a new facility. The second stage of analysis is focused on these cells. Interestingly, it should be noted that as a test the second stage of analysis was also conducted on all 272 cells, and the results from both efforts were strikingly similar. So the initial elimination of all but 66 cells by applying the EPA and water supply criteria made little difference in this area, although it might in others.

*Other Physical Siting Criteria*

Physical and other ecological characteristics of the study region were evaluated to identify the relative suitability of the 66 cells. The Other Physical Criteria (Table 7-10) consisted of non-water supply factors: floodlands, soil group characteristics, erosion, slope, permeability and critical species habitats. The assigned initial ranks were based on natural breaks in the data. Six of the variables were removed from consideration because they exhibited very little variation, an extremely low frequency of occurrence, or a very remote possibility of adverse impact (the six variables are numbers 1, 2, 3, 4, 5 and 6—Table 7-10).

The remaining 11 variables were analyzed, and two multiple criteria and four singular criteria resulted.

The composite ratings based on these criteria yielded no cells that are most suitable (Table 7-11). However, 26 cells (39 percent of the 66 cells) rated as warranting some caution, and thus should not be eliminated from further consideration. The remaining 61 percent of the cells present some relative siting disadvantages on these criteria.

*Cultural Siting Criteria*

These criteria were grouped into four subsets for analysis. They are (1) existing land use; (2) air quality constraints; (3) transportation constraints; (4) demographic constraints. As in the previous analyses, the results from analyzing these criteria were used to determine composite suitability ratings for each of the 66 cells.

The land use variables were aggregated into three groups based on assumptions about compatibility with hazardous waste facilities. Some land uses are incompatible with one another and should be segregated. Hazardous waste facilities and residential-commercial facilities should not be mixed. Similarly, waste facilities located in rural areas near parks and prime agricultural lands are not compatible with those uses. On the other hand,

## FIGURE 7-4

## Spatial Distribution of 66 Cells Selected For
## Second Level Macro Screening Analysis

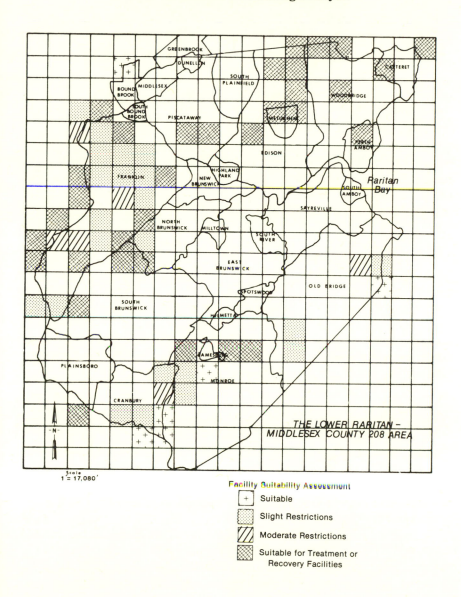

Facility Suitability Assessment

| + | Suitable |
|---|----------|
|  | Slight Restrictions |
| ///  | Moderate Restrictions |
|  | Suitable for Treatment or Recovery Facilities |

**TABLE 7-10**

**Descriptive Statistics for Group II Siting Criteria
Variables and 66 Cells**

| Siting Variable | Arith-metic Mean | Arith-metic Standard Deviation | Median | Range |
|---|---|---|---|---|
| 1. Floodway Area (%) | 1.8 | 4.7 | <1 | 0.00–25.00 |
| 2. Flood Fringe Area (%) | <1 | <1 | <1 | 0.00–37.00 |
| 3. Flood-Prone Area (%) | 1.2 | 2.7 | <1 | 0.00–11.90 |
| 4. Cranberry Bogs (%) | 0.0 | 0.0 | 0.0 | 0.0 |
| 5. Distance (mi.) to Nearest Tidal Water-3 Bodies | 13.80 | 6.22 | 15.44 | 0.57–23.77 |
| 6. Distance to Amphibian Habitats (mi.) | 7.90 | 3.48 | 8.45 | 0.71–13.97 |
| 7. Distance to Reptile Habitats (mi.) | 8.25 | 2.83 | 8.02 | 3.13–16.67 |
| 8. Percent Clay | 17.10 | 5.60 | 15.50 | 0.00–35.00 |
| 9. Percent Loam | 47.30 | 14.40 | 45.50 | 0.00–60.00 |
| 10. Percent Sand | 34.10 | 15.40 | 35.00 | 0.00–95.00 |
| 11. Depth to Bedrock (ft.)[a] | 5.94 | 3.13 | 5.93 | 0.00–10.00 |
| 12. Depth to Seasonal High Water (ft.)[b] | 3.32 | 1.48 | 3.74 | 0.00–5.00 |
| 13. Permeability (inches/hr.) | 0.61 | 0.59 | 0.55 | 0.00–3.10 |
| 14. Available Water (inches/inch soil) | 0.15 | 0.03 | 0.15 | 0.00–0.22 |
| 15. Slope (%) | 2.66 | 1.70 | 2.50 | 0.00–9.00 |
| 16. Erodibility (K factor)[c] | 0.28 | 0.11 | 0.28 | 0.00–0.43 |
| 17. Hydrologic Soil Group[d] | 1.86 | 0.96 | 1.72 | 1.00–4.00 |

Notes: [a]Depth to bedrock measurements do not go beyond 10 feet as per the soil reports. A measurement of 10 feet indicates that the true depth is equal to or greater than 10 feet.
[b]A measurement of 5 feet for depth to seasonal high water indicates that the true depth is equal to or greater than 5 feet.
[c]Erodibility is measured as a "K" factor where a low number indicates limited erosion potential and vice versa for a high number.
[d]Hydrologic soil group measurements are given in classes 1 to 4. The mean class is 1.86, closer to class 2 than to class 1. Class 4 soil groups can absorb the most amount of rainfall, while class 1 soil groups absorb the least amount of rainfall.

**TABLE 7-11**

**Frequency of Composite Ratings for the Other
Physical Constraint Criteria**

| Rank | Percent of 66 Selected Cells | Actual Number of Cells |
|------|------------------------------|------------------------|
| 1 Most Suitable | 0.0 | 0 |
| 2 Some Caution | 6.0 | 4 |
| 3 Caution | 33.0 | 22 |
| 4 Substantial Caution | 44.0 | 29 |
| 5 Least Suitable | 17.0 | 11 |

some land uses attract new hazardous waste facilities because of their compatible industrial activities. Indeed, such a mix would be advantageous in terms of agglomeration economies and a generally reduced threat of transportation-related toxic substance spills. These three groups are listed in Table 7-12.

As explained earlier, the air quality constraints included measurements of distance to nearest carbon monoxide nonattainment area and particulate nonattainment area. The transportation category was comprised of four variables which potentially have a direct influence on the production function and safe transportation of hazardous waste generating and management firms. The variables are proximity to freight railroads, federal highways, state highways, and navigable channels.

One set of demographic criteria consisted of the population at risk criteria: (1) total population, (2) population age 0–5 years, and (3) population age 65 and over. As stated earlier in the chapter, the major concern is to identify cells with relatively large total populations and large populations at the extremes of the age pyramid.

The four separate analyses resulted in three multiple criteria compatibility and exclusion factors, and two singular criteria for each of the 66 cells. Composite ratings were determined based on these results (see Table 7-13).

In conclusion, the spatial distribution of the composite suitability ratings based on cultural criteria indicates that few cells are without obvious siting limitations. It should be noted that some of the composite ratings may be more easily modified than others. For instance, while equal weights are given to populations at risk and the transportation factor, it appears that the former should be more limiting than the latter. However, this then

### TABLE 7-12

### Land Use Variables Comprising the Exclusion
### and Attraction Factors

| Existing Land Use Siting Variable | Rural Exclusion Factor | Urban Exclusion Factor | Compatible Land Use Factor |
|---|---|---|---|
| 1. Parkland | E | | |
| 2. Agriculture | E | | |
| 3. Suburban | | E | |
| 4. Urban | | E | |
| 5. Light Industry | | | C |
| 6. Commercial | | E | |
| 7. Mixed Industry | | | C |
| 8. Vacant | | | C |
| 9. Mining—Sand and Gravel | | | C |
| 10. Landfill | | | C |
| Total Number of Land Uses | 2 | 3 | 5 |

becomes a question for the political arena which is historically the floor of debate for such trade-offs.

It was not surprising that after the second part of constraint mapping that no cells were devoid of some siting limitations. But 26 cells (less than 16 percent) had no more than one major caution, so that there are some areas that should undergo further study.

## DISTRIBUTIONAL EFFECTS OF PROPOSED SITES
## IN CENTRAL NEW JERSEY AND MINNESOTA:
## DEBATABLE CRITERIA

One area for further investigation is distributional effects. In Chapter 5, we presented a case study of distributional effects of abandoned sites in New Jersey. Thirty-one towns and cities in New Jersey with the worst abandoned sites tended to have populations that were relatively poor, and con-

**TABLE 7-13**

**Frequency of Composite Ratings for the Cultural
Constraint Criteria**

| Rank | Percent of 66 Selected Cells | Actual Number of Cells |
|------|------------------------------|------------------------|
| 1 Most Suitable | 7.6 | 5 |
| 2 Some Caution | 19.7 | 13 |
| 3 Caution | 15.2 | 10 |
| 4 Substantial Caution | 34.8 | 23 |
| 5 Least Suitable | 22.7 | 15 |
| Total | 100.0 | 66 |

tained a greater proportion of younger, older, and black residents than the state as a whole and neighboring communities. One of our fears is that distributional effects will occur in future siting efforts unless distributional variables are specifically taken into account. It should be noted that some scientists and engineers have argued against our proposal because they feel that the combination of environmental and demographic constraints is already so long that the addition of social and economic impacts would probably eliminate any possible site. We believe that distributional impacts are important because failure to take them into account could lead to serious political repercussions and acts of civil disobedience. They should be spotted during the screening process with an eye toward negotiation, compensation and other measures that will clearly show that the hazardous waste management industry is not deliberately picking on powerless people.

It is difficult to test for distributional effects because so few sites have been proposed. The state of Minnesota and central New Jersey are exceptions. In the first case, the Minnesota Waste Management Board (1981) has done a very careful screening analysis of many criteria including hydrological, other physical, land use compatibility, emergency services, historical sites, and distance from waste sources. It did not take distributional effects into account. In the second case, the authors evaluated socioeconomic criteria for the 66 selected cells reported above to estimate potential distributional effects, especially for the least disadvantageous cells identified as hypothetical distributional sites. The Minnesota study is briefly discussed first.

By late 1982, Minnesota had suggested disposal sites in 5 towns and processing sites in 34 towns. A statistical analysis was made comparing the Minnesota waste sites to the state of Minnesota as a whole. The proposed disposal sites are located in 5 towns with very few residents (range 384 to 2,952 in 1980). The populations of the communities, three of which are in the Twin Cities area, were relatively old and poor. Except for the lack of minorities in these 5 towns, the towns fit the profile that conventional wisdom holds of powerless communities: sparsely populated areas of relatively powerless, elderly people.

The 34 communities proposed for processing sites are clearly different from the 10 proposed for Superfund and 5 proposed for disposal. Many are in the Twin Cities area, but many others are scattered throughout the state, including Rochester and Duluth. Compared to the state as a whole, the 34 have populations that were statistically significantly ($p < .01$) younger and more affluent.

Potential distributional effects in the Lower Raritan/Middlesex County 208 Water Basin case study region in central New Jersey were examined with socioeconomic and ethnic status variables (see Table 7-1, variables 75–80).

We conclude that not only do all sub-areas in the study region have some siting disadvantages, but even the best areas would incur some distributional effects. Seventeen of 26 cells that were identified as the most suitable have relatively high levels of blacks and persons below the poverty level. For planning purposes, an advocacy apparatus should be built into the process to help these relatively powerless populations adequately represent their interests. Primary among these interests might be problems of residential dislocation and loss of recreational space and other open space amenities. This advocacy apparatus should be set in motion well before locational decisions are solidified. This is why we strongly believe that distributional effects should be considered during the constraint mapping phase.

## USING LOCATION STANDARDS TO ADD
## CREDIBILITY TO FACILITY SITING DECISIONS

A major virtue of constraint mapping is that it is flexible enough to allow measurements to be varied and tested. Assumptions should be explicitly articulated and as such, open to close public and professional scrutiny and discussion. The use and effects of facility location standards are quite different from both the scope of siting criteria and the way they are evaluated. Rather than stating a siting criteria as follows: hazardous waste facilities *should* not be located near the 100-year floodplain; a location standard is more likely to assert: facilities *shall* not be located in the 100-year floodplain. Location standards are usually written such that facilities are prohibited from certain critical areas. The major purpose served by location standards is that they either restrict facilities from environmentally sensitive areas and areas of potential public exposure, or they regulate facility design and operation in such areas to reduce local impacts.

Regulatory requirements specified as location standards were introduced in Chapter 2. There it was noted that Part 264 of the regulations (Subpart B) states that facilities could not be located within 200 feet of a fault experiencing displacement in Holocene time; and that facilities could be located in the 100-year floodplain only if owners or operators could satisfactorily demonstrate washout prevention. These location standards are supplemented by other provisions: surface impoundments are prohibited from locating in the 100-year floodplain, and design standards reduce the probability that landfills and land treatment units will discharge wastes into the environment. Location characteristics are considered when reviewing new facility permit applications. From a planner's perspective, it is noteworthy that these standards ignore established land use planning techniques such as buffer zones.

Section 3009 of RCRA allows state hazardous waste programs to go beyond the minimum acceptable regulatory strategy prescribed under RCRA. Over two-thirds of the states are pursuing EPA authorization to conduct their own programs. This means that roughly a third of the states will adopt federal RCRA location standards and/or rely on other environmental laws to protect resources. Some states will have greater levels of protection than others.

The states have varied in their approaches to establishing buffer zones for new facilities. Connecticut requires a 400-foot separation distance between land based facilities (e.g., landfills, surface impoundments, waste piles) and other land uses; and 150 feet between non-land based facilities (incinerators) and all other uses. These distance requirements may be reduced by as much as 50 percent if facility owners or operators demonstrate that a facility will not cause public safety and health impacts. Michigan, New Jersey, and Oklahoma have each established a 200-foot separation distance from the active portion of a land disposal facility and the property boundary. Other states do not specify minimum separation distances, but they do consider the mix of land uses and their present and future characteristics in the area surrounding the proposed site. Many of these location standards are useful vehicles for avoiding both sudden and non-sudden accidental releases of hazardous substances.

Sudden release events at hazardous waste facilities have most frequently occurred in the form of fires and explosions. They are usually associated with storage and treatment facilities but less frequently with landfills.

Stored or treated ignitable and reactive wastes have a high potential for the sudden event primarily because of faulty design or operation of facilities. Buffer zones can prevent injury, death, and property destruction.

The chronic release event usually is associated with storage, treatment, or disposal facilities where liquid hazardous wastes (or other hazardous wastes in landfills) leak or leach into surface and groundwater resources. Such contaminant migration may lead to chronic, irreversible damage to human health and environmental resources.

The use of buffer zones is well established in local zoning ordinances; buffer zones are usually directed at controlling the effects of noise and traffic and segregating certain land use activities. Safe separation distances between waste facilities and human and environmental receptors have not been established. Similar to the situation regarding siting criteria, there are no clear scientific rules to guide the development of location standards. Some states have begun to deal with this problem through administrative and advisory mechanisms available in their hazardous waste programs. We illustrate the issues surrounding two location standards addressing sudden and chronic releases, which were recommended by the Massachusetts Hazardous Waste Advisory Committee, and promulgated as state regulation in the fall of 1983 (Anderson 1983).

The first example involves the storage of ignitable or reactive wastes and the potential for explosion and fire. No scientific or engineering guides exist to determine an adequate safe separation distance, i.e., buffer zone. Two regulations directly addressing the fire event exist. The U.S. EPA through RCRA requires storage areas comprised of portable containers holding ignitable or reactive hazardous wastes to be situated at least 50 feet from the property boundary. The National Fire Prevention Association (1981) (NFPA) has devised a schedule of buffer zone distances based on the size of storage tanks and containers and their volume. Essentially, the NFPA schedule increases buffer zones as size and volume increase. The NFPA and EPA rationales are based on providing adequate space for firefighting equipment to enter the area. These provisions may not be adequate for many types of hazardous wastes. Both provisions also suffer from the lack of consideration for explosions.

Limited research on safe separation distances from hazardous substance spills, fires and explosions are available to aid decision makers. The U.S. Department of Transportation (1980), and the U.S. Department of Housing and Urban Development (1975) developed guides which provide essential baseline information for establishing buffer zones.

The buffer zone encompassing a spill, fire or explosion event consists of two zones of impact. The first is called the isolation zone. This is the immediate area (see Figure 7-5) surrounding the event. The isolation zone

## FIGURE 7-5

### Impact Zones Related to Fire and Explosion at Storage or Treatment Facilities Handling Ignitable or Reactive Wastes

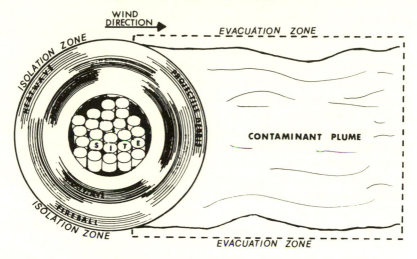

roughly delineates the primary area enveloped by the fireball, shockwave, and scattered debris. This area should have no people or sensitive resources. The U.S. DOT emergency guide lists the range of distances appropriate for different substances. For example, acrylonitrile has a 550-foot distance, while titanium tetrachloride has a 30-foot distance. Clearly, some substances require a larger buffer than other substances. Engineering design is an intervening factor which can serve to reduce the larger buffer zone considerably.

The second zone is called the evacuation zone. This area takes the shape of a polygon, sometimes a corridor, wherein the contaminated air plume migrates. The evacuation zone may vary from 100 feet to a 20-mile area. The extent of this zone is estimated based on assumptions concerning the particular waste type, volume, concentration and atmospheric conditions. It is infeasible to incorporate this substance-event-specific area into a firm buffer zone. Similar to areas surrounding nuclear power plants and defense weapons, pre-existing land uses become captive to this phase of the hazardous substance release event. The Massachusetts approach focused on the isolation zone since the evacuation zone could not be appropriately addressed as a location standard. It can, however, be addressed in emergency preparedness plans.

The regulatory options available to control the isolation area fall into three categories. One is prohibition of activity within 50 feet of the property boundary, as stated by the EPA. Since 50 feet is not a large enough buffer for every substance the distance can be raised to 150 or 300 feet. The advantage of this approach is that public health and safety are protected by the attenuation of explosive impact over distance. The disadvantages are that costly additional capital outlays for increased acreage are required to accommodate the buffer zone; and the use of well-established engineering controls such as fire doors and concrete and earth berms which can substantially reduce the diameter of the isolation zone are ignored.

A second approach to writing a location standard for the isolation zone is to set a small distance standard (e.g., 50 feet) and to allow engineering design and operational controls to substitute for land acquisition. The advantage of this approach is that it allows flexibility. The disadvantage of this approach is that it relies, in the end, on voluntary compliance with and government enforcement of design and operation standards. The historical record of industry compliance and government enforcement does not make one optimistic about this approach.

A third option involves a case-by-case evaluation using a standard set of criteria. A firm buffer zone distance requirement is not stated. Instead, each proposal for a new facility would consider the type, volume and concentration of the ignitable and reactive wastes; their potential for explosion; ambient atmospheric conditions; engineering controls; and surrounding land uses. The state permitting agency would then set a specific distance requirement based on evaluation of these criteria. The advantage of this procedure is its flexibility in setting regulations which allow choices among less costly approaches to achieve compliance. The disadvantage as stated before is the problem of compliance.

The Massachusetts Hazardous Waste Advisory Committee considered the above three approaches. It chose a hybrid of the three approaches: a 300-foot buffer zone was accepted as a result of the research of the DOT and HUD reports, information volunteered by insurance underwriters, and the consensual opinion of the committee members. Option 3 was adopted, with a 300-foot buffer which can be increased or decreased on a case-by-case basis by the state and promulgated as part of the Phase II interim authorization regulations.

A second illustration of mitigation through location standards involves the chronic release of contaminants into groundwater. Three strategies were considered in determining an adequate buffer zone. First, the owner of a facility could be required to purchase property surrounding the facility along the natural underground water flow path. Second, the owner could be required to purchase the water rights within this area, but not the actual property itself. The advantage of the first two strategies is that ownership will presumably lead to protection of the water. However, owners may not be interested in protecting the value of the water.

The third strategy requires a setback of the active portion of the landfill from the property boundary. It is based on a time-travel evaluation of how far and how fast a contaminant plume might travel underground. The landfill is required to have monitoring wells at the downgradient perimeter. If contaminants are discovered, there must be enough land area available for remedial action equipment to retard the migration within a reasonable period of time. This use of the buffer zone requires an individual standard be established for each landfill, taking into account specific groundwater flow and subsurface geography of the surrounding area. This third option was adopted.

This strategy is illustrated in Figure 7-6. At least a 1,000-foot buffer zone would surround the lateral portions of a landfill. The downgradient buffer zone would then be determined. Some existing wells might preclude siting, or the time-travel zone might indicate that there is enough time and space to control contaminant migration adequately before it enters the existing well. Existing wells on the lateral, downgradient portion may also preclude siting because the area from which the groundwater is drawn (the cone of influence) might overlap the contaminated flow path. Due to the complexities of groundwater flow as described in Chapter 3, there is no better alternative than to conduct site-specific, case-by-case evaluations.

Buffer zones may not always be feasible. Chronic emissions from incinerators may require buffer zones as large as or even larger than evacuation zones. Another problem is the storage of volatile wastes which escape from containers and tanks when routinely opened (and sometimes when they are assumed to be closed). The problem is that there is virtually no reliable information concerning an isolation zone, or time-travel zone for volatile wastes. Notwithstanding these problems, buffer zones should be used to protect the public against many sudden releases and some chronic emissions from hazardous waste management facilities. At the present time, buffer zones are notably underutilized.

## SUMMARY

The major objective of this chapter was to present two familiar planning tools that would bring badly needed credibility to the hazardous waste facility siting process at the sub-state scale. Other than the use of multivariate methods to overcome the problem of multiple counting of criteria, we deliberately refrained from using complicated indexes and weighting schemes so that the results would be transparent. In fact, several more com-

## FIGURE 7-6

### Buffer Zone to Protect Underground
### Drinking Water Sources

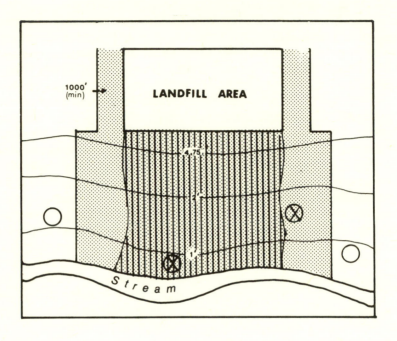

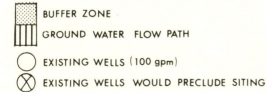
BUFFER ZONE
GROUND WATER FLOW PATH
EXISTING WELLS (100 gpm)
EXISTING WELLS WOULD PRECLUDE SITING

plex approaches were tried but quickly abandoned because it became clear that an approach that relied too heavily on statistics and pollutant modeling would sacrifice more in reduced public participation than it might gain in precise results. This type of analysis, which is not required by RCRA or the roughly equivalent state laws, can be extremely helpful in narrowing down the debate normally associated with public opposition to new facility siting. By evaluating like groups of siting criteria, in an iterative fashion, we found that three to four percent of the 350-square mile study region in central New Jersey should receive more careful scrutiny.

We also presented a discussion of the use of location standards as a method for protecting the public from facilities. Location standards have the potential of adding a margin of safety around new sites that is over and above safety standards inherent in the engineering design standards for specific types of facilities.

Obviously, constraint mapping and location standards are not the only methods that planners can apply to hazardous waste management. But we think that they are two of the most important technical methods. There are technical limitations to their use that have been detailed in this chapter. Moreover, many people to whom we have spoken are against both tools for political reasons. Those who oppose constraint mapping argue that areas that are not eliminated through screening will bring great pressure to bear on decision makers to exclude them for other reasons. These other reasons may be criteria not included in the constraint mapping and imperfect delineation by the analysts because of inadequate data and poor methods. Or these reasons may include the political strength of the area. We have experienced this political pressure, so we concur that those who conduct the constraint mapping will feel the pressure. Alternatives to constraint mapping are chaotic processes leading to an inefficient search for sites and incomplete, case-by-case evaluations of proposals with a few criteria. It is highly unlikely that sites can be found that even are close to the least disadvantageous sites unless constraint mapping occurs at the state and/or regional scales. In short, we strongly advocate that planners accept the political fallout that will occur with constraint mapping in order to strive for a technically credible site selection process.

Those who oppose buffer zones for political reasons do so on the grounds that large buffer zones will be interpreted by the public as an admission that the technology is not safe. This argument is not without logic, but it should not carry in the face of hindsight which could show that lives could have been saved and lawsuits avoided had a larger buffer zone been required.

Overall, in light of the many shortcomings of hazardous waste management in the United States that have so far been presented in this book and will be continued in the next chapter, we strongly recommend constraint mapping and location standards to state and local planners.

### REFERENCES

Anderson, R. F. "Geographic Options for Establishing Safe Separation Distances Between Hazardous Waste Facilities and Human and Environmental Receptors." Paper presented at the 1983 New England — St. Lawrence Valley Conference of the Association of American Geographers, Burlington, Vermont, November 4, 1983.

Anderson, R. F. and Greenberg M. R. "Hazardous Waste Facility Siting: A Role for Planners." *Journal of the American Planning Association*, Vol 48, 1982, pp. 204–218.

Anderson, R. F., A Macro-Screening Process for Siting Hazardous Waste Management Facilities: A Case Study on the Lower Raritan/Middlesex County 208 Area, Doctoral Dissertation, Rutgers Univerity, New Brunswick, New Jersey, May 1981.

Anderson, R. F. and Wilson M., "Assessing Land Use Suitability For Hazardous Waste Management Facilities." *Northeast Regional Science Review*, Vol. II, Amherst, Massachusetts, University of Massachusetts, 1981, pp. 90–106.

Baecher, Gregory B., Gros, J. C., and McCusher, K., *Balancing Apples and Oranges: Methodologies for Facility Siting Decisions*. Schloss Laxenburg, Austria: International Institute for Applied Systems Analysis, 1975.

Barksdale, Henry C. *Special Report #8, The Groundwater Supplies of Middlesex County*. State of New Jersey, State Water Policy Commission, 1943.

Berry B. *Geography of Market Centers and Retail Distribution*. Englewood Cliffs, New Jersey: Prentice-Hall, 1967.

Bishop A. B., "Approach to Evaluating Environmental, Social and Economic Factors." *Water Resources Bulletin*, Vol. 8, 1972, p. 4.

Booz-Allen & Hamilton, Inc. and Putnam, Hayes & Bartlett, Inc. *Hazardous Waste Generation and Commerical Hazardous Waste Management Capacity — An Assessment*. Washington, D.C.: U.S. EPA, SW-894, 1980.

Burchell, Robert W., and Listokin, David. *The Environmental Impact Handbook*. New Brunswick, New Jersey: The Center for Urban Policy Research, 1975.

Burdge, Rabel J., et al. "Social Components of Environmental Impact Statements." In Jain, Ravinder K., and Hutchings, Bruce, editors, *Environmental Impact Analysis*. Chicago: University of Illinois Press, 1978.

Calabrese, Edward J. *Pollutants & High Risk Groups: The Biological Basis of Increased Human Susceptibility to Environmental and Occupational Pollutants*. New York: John Wiley & Sons, Inc., 1977.

Carey, George W., and Greenberg, Michael R. "Toward a Geographical Theory of Hypocritical Decision-Making." In *Human Ecology*, Vol. 2, 1974, pp. 243–257.

Cleveland, James A., Grover, Richard B., Petrillo, Joseph L., and Ladd, Elizabeth. "Using Computers for Site Selection." *Environmental Science and Technology*, Vol. 13, 1979, pp. 792–797.

Conservation Foundation Letter. Hazardous Waste Control Efforts: A Frightful Mess. Conservation Foundation, April 1980.

Dear, Michael J., and Long, Jonathan. "Community Strategies in Locational Conflicts." In Cox, Kevin R., editor, *Urbanization and Conflict in Market Societies*. Chicago: Maaroufa Press, 1978, p. 116.

Dee, N., Drobny, N., Baker, J., Duke, K., Fahringer, D. *Planning Methodology for Water Quality Management Environmental Evaluation System*. Columbus, Ohio: Battelle-Columbus, 1973.

Dobson, Jerome E. "A Regional Screening Procedure for Land Use Suitability Analysis." *Geographical Review*, Vol. 69, 1979, pp. 224–234.

Dombrowski, Daniel R. Earthquakes in New Jersey. New Jersey Department of Environmental Protection—Bureau of Geology and Topography, 1973.

Fabos, Julius Guy, and Caswell, Stephanie J. *Composite Landscape Assessment: Assessment Procedures for Special Resources, Hazards, and Development Suitability; Part II of the Metropolitan Landscape Planning Model (METLAND)*. Massachusetts Agricultural Experiment Station, University of Massachusetts at Amherst, Research Bulletin 637, January 1977.

Fish A.R. and Romano S.A.A Systematic Approach to Siting Waste Management Facilities. Third Annual Conference of Applied Research and Practice on Municipal and Industrial Waste, Madison, Wisconsin, September 10–12, 1980.

Geraghty and Miller, Inc. *Middlesex County 208 Area-Wide Waste Treatment Management Planning Task 8 — Groundwater Analysis*. Middlesex County, New Jersey: Middlesex County Planning Board, 1976.

Good D. A. *Cost-Benefit And Cost Effectiveness Analysis: Their Application To Urban Public Services and Facilities*. Philadelphia, Pennsylvania: Regional Science Research Institute, July 1971.

Gordon, S. I. "Performing Land Capability Evaluation by Use of Numerical Taxonomy: Land Use and Environmental Decision-Making Made Hard?" *Environment and Planning*, Vol. 10, 1978, pp. 915–921.

Greenberg, Michael R.; Belnay, Glen; Cesanek, William; Neuman, Nancy; and Shepherd, George. *A Primer on Industrial Environmental Impact*. New Brunswick, New Jersey: The Center for Urban Policy Research, 1979.

Harper D. New Jersey Geological Survey, Trenton, New Jersey. Contacted November 1979.

Harvey, David. "Residential Location and Public Facilities." In Gale, Stephen, and Moore, Eric G., editors, *The Manipulated City*. Chicago: Maaroufa Press, 1975, p. 275.

Hill, M. *Planning for Multiple Objectives*. Philadelphia, Pennsylvania: Regional Science Research Institute, Monograph No. 5, 1973.

Hopkins, Lewis D. "Methods for Generating Land Suitability Maps: A Comparative Evaluation." *Journal of the American Planning Association*, Vol. 43, 1977, pp. 386–400.

Hufstader R. W. "Generalized Criteria And Environmental Impact Analysis." *Journal of Environmental Systems*, Vol. 7, 1977–78, pp. 115–119.

Isard, Walter. *Location and Space-Economy*. Cambridge, Massachusetts: The M.I.T. Press, 1956.

Keeney, R. I. Preference Models of Environmental Impact. International Institute for Applied Systems Analysis, Laxenburg, Austria, RM–76–4, January 1976.

Kiefer, Ralph W., and Robbins, Michael L. *Computer-Based Land Use Suitability Maps*. In *Journal of the Surveying and Mapping Division ASCE*, pp. 39–62, September 1973.

Leopold L., Clark F., Hanshaw B. and Balsley J. *A Procedure For Evaluating Environmental Impact*. Washington, D.C., U.S. Geological Survey, Circular 645, 1971.

Lichfield N. "Evaluation Methodology of Urban and Regional Plans: A Review." *Regional Studies*, Vol. 4, 1970, pp. 151–165.

McHarg, Ian. *Design with Nature*, New York: Natural History Press, 1969.

Minnesota Waste Management Board. Basis for Selection on October 8, 1981 of Proposed Candidate Areas for Hazardous Waste Land Disposal Facilities, and accompanying maps. Mimeo, 1981.

National Fire Prevention Association. Flammable and Combustible Liquids Code, NFPA-30. Quincy, Massachusetts, 1981.

Neamatolla, Mounir. *Middlesex County — A Program for the Safe and Economical Disposal of Hazardous Wastes*. Middlesex County, New Jersey: Solid Waste Management Bureau, 1977.

New Jersey Department of Environmental Protection. "Authorized Chemical Waste Processing Facilities." Trenton, New Jersey: Solid Waste Administration, 1979.

———. *Proposed New Jersey State Implementation Plan for the Attainment and Maintenance of Air Quality Standards*. Prepared by the Division of Environmental Quality, Bureau of Air Pollution Control, submitted to the U.S.E.P.A. under Section 107 of the 1977 Amended Clean Air Act, delivered December 29, 1978.

Ortiz, Luis E. "Social Impact Assessment: A Framework for Research." In Jain, Ravinder K., and Hutchings, Bruce, editors, *Environmental Impact Analysis — Emerging Issues in Planning*. Urbana: University of Illinois Press, 1978.

Paelinck, J.H.P. "Qualitative Multiple Criteria Analysis, Environmental Protection and Multiregional Development." Papers of the Regional Science Association, Vol. 36, 1976.

Pappajohn E. Hazardous Waste Generation Estimates. U.S. Environmental Protection Agency, Memorandum, September 1982.

Reynolds, David R., and Honey, Rex. "Conflict in the Location of Salutary Public Facilities." In Cox, Kevin R., editor, *Urbanization and Conflict in Market Societies*. Chicago: Maaroufa Press, 1978, p. 144.

Roberts, M. C., Randolph, J. C., and Chiesa, J. R. "A Land Suitability Model for the Evaluation of Land Use Change." *Environmental Management*, Vol. 3, 1979, pp. 339–352.

Rushton, Gerard. *Optimal Location of Facilities*. Wentworth, New Hampshire: Compress, Inc., Preface, 1979.

Smith, Robert H. T., Taaffe, Edward J., and King, Leslie J., editors. *Readings in Economic Geography: The Location of Economic Activity*. Chicago: Rand McNally, 1968, p. 33.

Subcommittee on Oversight and Investigations, *Waste Disposal Site Survey* (Washington, D.C.: Committee on Interstate and Foreign Commerce, House of Representatives, 96th Congress), October 1979.

Suttles, Gerald D. "Potentials in Community Differentiation." In Gale, Stephen, and Moore, Eric G., editors, *The Manipulated City*. Chicago: Maaroufa Press, 1975, p. 43.

Sykes, L. Lamont Geophysical Laboratory. Contacted via telephone, November 1979.

U.S. Department of Housing and Urban Development. *Safety Considerations in Siting Housing Projects*. Prepared by Arthur D. Little Inc., Washington, D.C.: U.S. GPO, 1975.

U.S. Department of Transportation. *Hazardous Materials: 1980 Emergency Response Guidebook*, DOT-P 5800.2. Research and Special Programs Administration, 1980.

Van Delft A. and Nijkamp P. "A Multi-Objective Decision Model For Regional Development, Environmental Quality Control and Industrial Land Use." Papers of the Regional Science Association, Vol. 36, 1976.

# 8

# Changes Needed to Gain Credibility

There was no explicit hazardous waste management policy in the United States in 1975. The result of decades of neglect has been the creation of a credibility gap that has converted an eminently manageable problem into an environmental problem of monstrous proportions in the eyes of the public. Today there are laws, but the policy remains in conflict. Some view CERCLA and RCRA as having imposed costly technology that will penalize American industry. Others view CERCLA and RCRA as having rightfully imposed restrictions on hazardous waste disposal, but charge that the laws do not go far enough and that implementation and enforcement of the laws has not been vigorous.

In fact though not in symbol, landfilling is accepted as the normal method of hazardous waste management, albeit the new generation of landfills will be better than their predecessors. In addition, the policy does not regulate all hazardous wastes, does not go far enough to encourage non-landfilling options, and provides no assurance that there will continue to be a federal role in the cleanup of abandoned sites.

In order to close the credibility gap hazardous waste management policy in the United States should be based on the following four principles that are presently lacking:

1. Vigorous cleanup of abandoned sites to erase these eyesores which undermine the credibility of government and especially industry.
2. Pursuit of technical, economic and regulatory incentives to eliminate land disposal as an option for most types of waste as soon as possible.
3. No exemptions from RCRA that allow hazardous waste to be casually handled by small industrial generators and reusers.
4. Participation of federal, state and local governments, industry, and citizens in managing hazardous waste, with federal government leadership in overseeing most management areas and state leadership in siting new facilities.

The unsatisfactory present policy is the result of three conditions:

1. Economic efficiency and regulatory reform—It is feared that strong government intervention would jolt the economy and blunt innovation. We will argue that present federal economic efficiency policies will cost much more in the long run than alternatives and will unfairly penalize people who reside near sites.
2. Technological inertia—More than 80 percent of hazardous waste has been landfilled and very little was subject to government oversight. It will be argued that innovation need not be blunted and would be encouraged by policy changes.
3. Public opinion—American environmental management efforts are characterized by strong public support for legislation and lofty goals, but insufficient support to challenge the established interests and dramatically change their inexpensive disposal methods. We will argue that public opinion toward hazardous waste management will become more cynical and more radical unless the present policy is shifted in favor of a rational program implemented by credible actors.

The first part of the chapter presents the arguments for changing these three conditions and touches on some of the needed changes. The second focuses specifically on needed policy changes in the context of abandoned, existing, and proposed sites.

## PRESENT CONDITIONS: ECONOMIC EFFICIENCY ARGUMENT

There are two main reasons why economic efficiency has become such an important criterion. The history of environmental and consumer protection legislation is one impetus. Legislation passed during the 1970s included complex regulations, enforcement procedures, efforts to involve the public, and aggressive attainment schedules. In the rush to promulgate politically popular remedies for pollution, relatively little attention was paid to the economic impact of anti-pollution goals, for instance, zero discharge on the competitiveness of American industry, the economies of regions, and government spending.

Putting aside the economic benefits of better health and less property damage for the moment, the costs of environmental protection during the 1970s were high. *U.S. News and World Report* (1983) estimates them to have been $450 billion. Some regions and industries were particularly hard-pressed, such as the Ohio River steel industry. The projected economic price tag for protecting the environment in the 1980s is $690 billion (*U.S. News and World Report* 1983). This amount is high even in a trillion dollar economy. And it certainly exceeded what had been spent before 1970.

Primarily in response to the costs of the water and air pollution programs (estimated at over $600 billion during 1980–1989), the federal government seemingly has become afraid to create new programs and has deferred or dropped some goals. For example, OSHA's proposed noise standards were deferred, EPA's fuel additive testing program and DOE's appliance efficiency standards program were cancelled, auto safety and emission standards were relaxed, and air quality standards were relaxed in Ohio (Christman 1981). The federal government, notably EPA, will have to assume some new responsibilities (e.g., the health and environmental impacts of biotechnology) because of public demand and because the line agencies are better equipped than the courts, the congress, and the executive branches to conduct scientific analyses of complex technologies (O'Brien and Marchand 1982). But it is unlikely that the federal government will jump at the chance to tackle new problems that will create new programs.

Hazardous waste management has been responsible for only a tiny part of the regulatory cost, but it could become very expensive. The OTA (1983) estimated that industry and the government spend $4–5 billion (in 1981 dollars) to meet the requirements of CERCLA and RCRA, and will spend $12 billion in the near future. Chemical manufacturers expect to spend $10 billion in the next five years to improve treatment and another $2 billion per year in operating costs (Chemical Manufacturers Association 1982). Estimates for cleaning up abandoned sites range from $10 to $40 billion (Hart 1979, Rishel et al. 1982) compared to the $1.6 billion available under CERCLA by 1985. Every issue of *EPA Update* lists agreements between EPA and industry whereby industry will contribute to the cleanup of specific waste sites. And EPA has sued and will continue to sue to recover cleanup money. But it is wishful thinking to believe that present Superfund dollars, negotiated settlements, and court cases will cover what is needed for cleanup of abandoned sites. OTA (1983) estimates that switching from landfilling to more expensive methods would increase costs 50 to 100 percent in the short-term. Clearly, the short-term costs of better treatment of new hazardous wastes and the legacy of past practices will be felt economically and politically.

Politics is a second reason for including economic efficiency as a decisionmaking criterion. Conservatives feel that efficiency-based decisions would show the public that the economic benefits of regulation are overstated. Proponents of greater regulation believe that such analyses would show the opposite. Both sides are gambling on the outcome of economic studies to justify ideological positions.

Whatever the outcome, the results of supposedly objective economic studies of costs and benefits should lessen the onus on elected officials for tough decisions. The last two presidents of the United States have issued executive orders requiring all federal agencies to perform cost-benefit analyses on all regulations (Miller 1980, Deland 1981a). Briefly, cost-benefit analysis expresses all the major benefits and costs of an action in dollars. If the benefits are greater than the costs, then the proposed action is considered efficient.

Cost-benefit analysis is presently not fully instructive for formulating hazardous waste policy. The disadvantages as well as the advantages of the method have been widely described (*Conservation Foundation Letter* 1980a, Epstein 1982, Lave 1981, Swartzman et al. 1983). As applied to hazardous waste management they include the following: there are too many unknowns; many costs and benefits cannot be quantified; second and higher order consequences and long-term consequences are difficult to assess; sensitivity analysis is difficult to do; and values of disparate things like the cost of a life and the value of a vista are hard to compute or compare. Cynics contend that cost-benefit analysis is used to justify decisions already made by powerful special interests. Kelman (1981) argued that economists are committed to efficiency, not to environmental protection and basically do not really care about environmental protection.

We can find no evidence that formal cost-benefit analysis was behind the present EPA hazardous waste policy; but the absence of a credible scientific and engineering baseline and analysis, so often seen in cost-benefit studies, is apparent. OTA (1983) points out that EPA policy seeks the lowest-cost alternative that is technologically feasible, reliable and protects public health and the environment. This approach seems fine until it is recognized that with the important exceptions of PCBs and principal organic hazards constituents (POHCs), there are no performance standards requiring that particular wastes receive specific levels of treatment or destruction, nor is there an enforceable definition for safe abandoned and existing landfills. But short-term economic costs are relatively easy to calculate, so ad hoc decisions favoring the most inexpensive, short-term storage or disposal solution can easily dominate.

As a general policy, the Conservation Foundation (1983) argued that the steadily mounting costs of dealing belatedly with problems like occupational exposure, hazardous waste and decaying infrastructure are dragging down the American economy. Costle (1980), a former EPA administrator, has noted that proper disposal of the waste that ended up in Love Canal and along the roads in North Carolina would have cost between 1/10 and 1/100 of the final removal and remedial cost. The OTA (1983) estimates that the continued use of landfills for many forms of waste could in the long run result in cleanup and compensation costs 50 to 100 times the cost of using methods that would destroy, neutralize or reuse the waste. Moreover these estimates do not include potential economic ramifications on the economy of communities, lawsuits, and the psychological effects on people living near hazardous waste sites.

One of the most frustrating aspects of the present EPA hazardous waste policy is that we have heard people defend it as a way of attempting to correct what they perceive as errors in other environmental regulations. For example, it is widely known that a good deal of the high costs of the water and air pollution programs have come from trying to remove the last 5 to 7 percent of pollutants. This can cost as much as removing the first 90 to 95 percent. Landfilling is not analogous to primary and secondary water pollution treatment nor to the analogous air pollution equipment. The water and air pollution equipment eliminates 90 percent or more of the potential waste before it can get into rivers or the air. The only waste permanently rendered harmless or even clearly controlled in landfills is that which degrades before it escapes from the landfill. When choosing between landfilling and other hazardous waste management techniques, the choice is not between eliminating 90 or 99 percent of the emissions. For many forms of hazardous waste the choice is between putting it into the ground, patching up problems as they arise, and hoping that the patches work; as opposed to destroying, neutralizing, recycling, or not creating the waste. We do not think that the argument against spending large sums of money to clean up the last 5 to 10 percent of potential pollutants is relevant to the hazardous waste case when the choice is between landfilling on the one hand and incineration, recycling and process changes on the other hand. The incremental pollution argument becomes pertinent when choosing between methods that permanently eliminate nearly all of the wastes as the threat, but leave different types and amounts of residuals.

Furthermore, there are equity issues in the use of landfills that are not as likely to occur with alternative hazardous waste techniques. The most equitable economic policy is to shift the cost for managing hazardous waste back to the industries manufacturing and selling the products that create the waste and to the people using the products. This would allow the marketplace to determine the true cost of the product. Landfilling is a hidden subsidy to the consumers of products which will be paid by future generations and by people who live near landfills. We are not opposed to the use of economic efficiency as a criterion. But we are opposed to its being used without first determining the minimum acceptable solution. Basically, in our opinion, there is too much of a risk that the free lunch we are trying to get by using landfills is going to cost us a pound of economic flesh in the future.

While we are opposed to the use of formal cost-benefit methods at this time, we are in favor of applying quantitative methods to decisionmaking about hazardous waste management issues such as, what can be burned at each kind of incinerator, and what sites are the least disadvantageous for each type of hazardous waste facility. Setting forth all of the decision-making variables in a risk assessment framework should help make decisionmaking variables explicit, even if some of the variables can only be set forth as ranks or as nominal categories. In addition, it should help avoid ultraconservative engineering designs or underdesigned facilities.

Briefly, the risk assessment process normally has two major parts. The first part seeks scientific evidence about causes and effects. Sources of possible hazard are located, pathways linking sources to people and the environment are identified, and probable risks are calculated by analyzing and forecasting the interaction of hazards with the population at risk. Science is perceived as a paradigm of acquiring sound knowledge. However, as suggested in Chapter 3, scientific studies of risk are usually severely constrained by data limitations and by a lack of understanding of underlying physical, biological, chemical, economic and social processes (Lowrance 1976, 1981; Whyte and Burton 1980; Kates 1977, 1978).

The second part of the risk assessment process follows and involves transmitting results to decisionmakers. Elected officials, agency administrators and other decisionmakers superimpose the uncertainties of cultural and moral values and institutions on the uncertainties of scientific measurement, modelling, and testing. Whatever the limitations, the results of formal risk assessment should be knowledge about the trade-offs between different actions.

It is clear from the Mitre hazard ranking model (Chapter 4) and other publications (Long and Schweitzer 1982; Energy Resources, Inc., 1979; Schwing and Albers 1980; and Taylor and Klingshirn 1981) that risk assessment is going to be increasingly used in hazardous waste management. We concur with its use so long as its users recognize that there are no magic formulas that can be summed to weigh the advantages and disadvantages of different approaches at every site.

## PRESENT CONDITIONS: STIFLING TECHNOLOGY ARGUMENT

A second major factor contributing to the sorry state of hazardous waste management in the United States is technological inertia. These days it is often said that regulations stifle innovation, which, in turn, reduces productivity. The evidence for this claim is not strong. The Senate Committee on Commerce, Science and Transportation (Environmental Science and Technology 1980a) reported that 8–12 percent of the slowdown in the growth of productivity in the 1970s may be due to government regulation. The Committee noted that design standards, which are typical of environmental regulations, slow down productivity more than do performance standards.

With regard to innovation in the hazardous waste industry, Pojasek (1980) argues that with the exception of solidification technology, there have been few innovations in treatment technologies in the past 30 years. He traces the absence of innovation to the failure to recognize the impact of indiscriminant dumping of hazardous wastes. In other words, there was no popularly perceived need for innovative techniques. We believe that with the exception of a few wastes noted in Chapter 2, there remains insufficient incentive in RCRA and CERCLA to trigger innovations that would prevent damage and be economically efficient in the long run. Far from stifling innovation, EPA policy does not even contain regulatory or adequate financial incentives that will force the adoption of incineration and other technologies already widely used in other nations and in parts of the United States.

An important opportunity to put science and technology in a positive light is being missed. With strong political support, science and technology could contribute to better management of hazardous waste. Broadly speaking, a net of information and technology should be cast around hazardous substances so that they can no longer be discarded without consideration for their impacts. More specifically, there are five key areas to which science and technology must be encouraged to contribute:

1. Determining the relative hazardousness of different chemicals;
2. Following hazardous substances from their creation to their ultimate reuse, destruction or disposal;
3. Monitoring the spread of hazardous substances in the environment;
4. Designing techniques that will limit the release of hazardous waste into the environment;
5. Searching for the least disadvantageous new sites.

Each of these areas will be briefly discussed.

## Hazardousness of Chemicals

In Chapter 3 it was shown that the hazardousness of most chemicals was not known and that our knowledge of the dangers implied by hazardous wastes was even less complete than it was for pure chemicals. Due to the pressures of time and the limits of budgets and imagination, and despite the high priority this subject has in the minds of scientists and the National Science Foundation (*EPA Journal* 1980a, National Science Foundation 1980), we do not foresee the lifting of this scientific smog in the near future.

We are not sanguine about science providing quantitative measures of hazardousness for the many chemicals and mixtures that end up in landfills.

OTA (1983) has suggested and we concur that for purposes of hazardous waste management chemicals be grouped into broad categories of hazardousness (e.g., high, medium, low). Groups already exist for some criteria such as reactive and ignitable, corrosive, and toxic (see Chapter 1 for a discussion of RCRA definitions). The grouping approach has four important advantages:

1. Categorical groupings can accommodate criteria that were not included in the U.S. EPA hazardousness criteria.
2. Groupings of hazardous waste can be keyed to specific performance standards and to specific types of sites where management of these wastes is permitted.
3. Groupings can be done more quickly than can dose-response models which, in addition, are not directly keyed to hazardous waste management practices.
4. Grouping of chemicals places hazardous management practices on an honest scientific footing in the eyes of the public because it acknowledges the very incomplete state of our knowledge.

Like the Mitre hazard ranking model (Chapter 4), grouping of chemicals by degree of hazardousness is imperfect and there will be mistakes. But grouping is badly needed to establish a baseline for making decisions about how to control hazardous wastes.

### Keeping Track of Hazardous Substances

The hazardous waste manifest system is one of the most widely acclaimed sections of RCRA (see Chapter 2 for a detailed presentation), and well it should be. We view the manifest system as the first step in placing a net of information around hazardous substances, not just hazardous wastes.

The early U.S. manifest system experience was not comforting. State estimates of their hazardous waste generation differ substantially from the state estimates made by the federal government (tabulated in Chapter 1). John Lehman of the U.S. EPA (Miller 1981b) explained these differences by noting that due to the absence of a federal form, states and local governments issued their own manifests. Furthermore, as noted earlier in the book and later in this chapter, some wastes which most people consider hazardous are not defined as hazardous under RCRA and some generators are exempted.

The American manifest system experience is better than Western

Europe's. Dickson (1983) describes the embarrassing odyssey of 41 barrels of dioxin-contaminated waste from the 1976 Seveso, Italy, factory explosion to a slaughterhouse on the outskirts of Paris. A commission of the European Economic Community had proposed a manifest system in 1978. Dickson (1983) believes that this incident will lead to an EEC manifest system.

If honest and complete manifest data can be obtained, they can be valuable for planning and regulatory actions. Without a good manifest system, the public cannot be honestly assured that hazardous waste is being controlled. A good manifest system will provide a data base for innovative approaches such as operating waste exchanges (U.S. EPA 1977) and for determining if interesting proposals for privatization of the regulation of hazardous materials (Petty 1982, Ubell 1982) can succeed for all or some part of the waste stream.

It should be expected that there will be public pressure to extend the manifest system approach beyond wastes to include hazardous substances. The overwhelming majority of industries can be expected to object vociferously. State "right-to-know" laws are the initial political battleground.

## Monitoring the Spread of Wastes Released into the Environment

A good manifest system will keep track of the wastes until they reach a treatment site. On-site monitoring is a crucial element of any program to assure the public that wastes are not threatening their health and the environment. For example, environmental monitoring is needed to determine if remedial measures at abandoned sites are working. Initial remedial actions have proven to be less than completely efficacious in the vast majority of cases (U.S. EPA 1981). Monitoring must be carefully done and widely reported to lessen the chance of the same problems at other sites.

Monitoring equipment has dramatically improved during the last decade, so much so that large segments of the public have been shocked out of their blissful ignorance into a state of fear by concentrations of chemicals that were not detectable five years ago. Monitoring will continue to improve, especially if a regulatory spur is given. Hopefully, with sufficient demand, the price of monitoring will decrease.

We can expect the refinement of gas chromatography and mass spectrometry to more precise and lower levels of detection. Biological tests will be improved so that waste mixtures can be more quickly characterized than is currently possible. In comparison to chemical monitoring and biological monitoring systems, personal monitors are not technically advanced nor in wide use, except for some occupational environments (e.g., radiation monitors). But with government interest in their development, it would not be surprising to find them worn by people who work at hazardous waste sites like radiation badges are worn at nuclear sites. Lastly, new techniques using ultraviolet and infrared light, and lasers need testing (Patel 1978). If perfected, they can be helpful in detecting abandoned sites.

A wider variety of more accurate monitoring equipment is necessary, but this alone is insufficient. Some of the deficiencies recognized by the National Research Council (1977) in its evaluation of environmental monitoring programs also characterize monitoring for hazardous waste, especially at some abandoned and existing sites. The most important are inadequate application of scientific principles in the design of monitoring programs, especially of those monitoring groundwater (e.g., location of samplers, frequency of sampling); in the evaluation of samples for statistical significance; and in quality assurance.

**Treatment Technology**

The goal of technology applied to hazardous waste management should be to offer economically and politically acceptable alternatives to landfilling. The best option is not to create the waste. This can be accomplished by finding substitutes that will not create hazardous wastes and by creating closed process systems that transfer industrial wastes inside the facility for recycling. If hazardous substances must be moved, the goal should be to separate hazardous from non-hazardous wastes at the source, concentrate the hazardous waste, and move it to another site where it can be reused. If hazardous wastes must be moved and cannot be reused, they should be detoxified, stabilized or destroyed.

Land disposal should only be used for wastes in the least hazardous group. Land disposal that includes biological degradation and emplacement in carefully selected geological formations or in the oceans should be thoroughly analyzed as alternatives to conventional landfilling. The best science must be brought to bear on each of the major options and suboptions. A few of the most important will be mentioned. It is crucial that we learn the effects of different classes of substances on liners that range from compacted clay to hot sprayed asphalt and to synthetic polyethylene, vinyl chloride and butyl rubber. Similarly, the utility of interception trenches, leachate capturing systems and other hardware for land disposal must be tested, not assumed to work. In the case of treatment, there is a good deal of research on processes that would chemically transform and then solidify wastes before disposal or use. Indeed, Pojasek (1980) cites solidification technology as the only major innovative technology in the hazardous waste industry during the last three decades. The products of these methods must be tested under severe environmental conditions before they are allowed to be used or to be dumped in the oceans, salt mines or landfills.

Incineration, treatment and other technologies already exist for most types of hazardous waste (Kiang and Metry 1982, Pojasek 1979–1981). But new and potentially better options than small-scale, land based incinerators are being tested and designed. For example, cement kilns may be a way of destroying certain organic wastes (Environmental Science and Technology 1981). But cement kilns suffer from all of the political disadvantages of land-based incineration. EPA's mobile incinerator (*EPA Journal* 1982a) offers the advantage of eliminating the movement of the waste, but the disadvantage of land-based incineration. At-sea incineration on artificial islands, rigs, or on ships may eliminate the need for scrubbers and may lessen broadly based public opposition compared to land-based sites (Halebsky 1978, *New Jersey Hazardous Waste News* 1981). Choice of at-sea incineration areas should be carefully considered. Texans and Louisianins have voiced strong opposition to proposals for incinerating organic wastes in the Gulf since prevailing winds would likely transmit airborne hazardous constituents. Also the possibility of transportation accidents at the land-sea transfer point is probably high, and accidents at sea could wreak havoc on the aquatic environment. Different incineration techniques are appropriate for different wastes; but it is clear that incineration could replace landfilling as the model technology. The U.S. EPA (*EPA Journal* 1982c) estimated that 60 percent of hazardous waste could be incinerated compared to the 6 percent actually incinerated in 1982. The Netherlands, a nation with a high water table, has banned landfills. We have to believe that areas of the United States that are dependent on groundwater, like Florida, would be wise to consider this policy.

**Screening for New Sites**

In Chapter 7 we showed that it is possible to use statistical methods and computers to evaluate large numbers of criteria at fine geographical scales. While every area will have some advantages and disadvantages for different types of facilities, some areas should be eliminated from consideration at an early stage because other sites are clearly less disadvantageous. The least disadvantageous areas defined in an ecological study like the one in Chapter 7 do not necessarily contain acceptable sites because field studies might show that some of the data were inaccurate, and other criteria that cannot be evaluated in an initial screening study could rule out an area. But screening studies provide clues about where to look and not look for sites.

It should be noted that a health and environmental-based screening approach rather than an economic-based method was deliberately chosen. Economic-based siting methods such as linear or mixed linear and integer programming (Greenberg 1978) work best when the initial sites are not severely restricted as they are in the case of large-scale hazardous waste management facilities. An economic-based approach might be valuable for a specific type of hazardous waste facility for which environmental and health considerations do not rule out all but a few locations, such as oil reclamation.

Group techniques (e.g., Delphi) may also be used to choose initial areas, criteria for the screening of sites, and weights for these criteria. These methods are also an avenue to get public participation of the highest caliber.

Summarizing, "chemophobia" and "technophobia" are widespread reactions to the rapid development of science that few people comprehend and that has not always turned out as we had expected or at least hoped. It is vital that a determined and creative application of science and technology be marshalled to counteract the externalities created by an uncontrolled science and technology. The suggestions offered in this section would help.

We feel so strongly about the need to create a positive image for science and technology in the management of hazardous waste that we make the following suggestion with little trepidation, but with the knowledge that some people who have heard it have been incredulous. The United States has many technological showpieces. The Kennedy Space Center and the Hoover Dam are exemplary. Even some steel mills, petroleum refineries and electricity generating stations encourage citizen visits. Yet all of these cope with hazards and each has had to overcome disasters that have killed people. Can you think of a better way of demonstrating that industry and government are serious about hazardous waste management than by building a national center for hazardous waste management? It would be a fully integrated facility which actually deals with wastes, tests experimental techniques, and serves as a center of research. Such a facility should be constructed in a state with many priority abandoned and functioning sites, and a large waste stream such as New Jersey or Michigan.

## PRESENT CONDITIONS: LACK OF PUBLIC SUPPORT
## FOR STRONG ACTION ARGUMENT

The third condition contributing to our present unsatisfactory management of hazardous waste is tied to public opinion. In one of the most revealing comments about the making of environmental policies in the United States, John Quarles (1976, p. 242), the first Deputy Administrator of the U.S. EPA, said that:

The most important lesson from our environmental experience is that government will not act to face hard national problems until the people demand that it do so.

In the late 1960s the public became acutely aware that the environment and perhaps public health were threatened by pollution. The public has demanded action, so much so that environmental protection seems to have become a continuing public concern, like unemployment, inflation, health care and crime (Council on Environmental Quality 1980, Resources for the Future 1978 and 1980, Environmental Science and Technology 1983, and *Amicus* 1981). In the words of pollster Louis Harris (*Washington Post* November 3, 1981), a healthful environment "happens to be one of the sacred cows of the American people," and the "desire on the part of the American people to battle pollution is one of the most overwhelming and clearest we have ever recorded in our 25 years of surveying public opinion in this country." It is commonly heard that this support has prevented the gutting of the Clean Air and Clean Water acts at a time when the administration is not enamored of environmental protection and at a time when the public's opinion of other regulations is low (Resources for the Future 1980, Council on Environmental Quality 1980).

Hazardous wastes appear to be the number one public health and environmental issue. In a 1980 survey (Resources for the Future 1980), Americans were more concerned with the disposal of hazardous waste than they were with cleaning up waterways, the presence of toxic substances in the environment, the purity of drinking water, air quality, a noisy environment, and with the problems of the poor. Only the cost of living and energy shortages were of greater concern than industrial chemical wastes. A RFF national poll (1980) and a New Jersey poll by the Eagleton Institute (1982) show that about two-thirds of the public is very concerned about hazardous waste; less than 5 percent of the people were unconcerned. Thus, support for dealing with hazardous waste is not limited to affluent and young people, it is broad based.

Public opinion is particularly important in the siting issue, a fact recognized by the EPA in the early 1970s when it commissioned research to determine public attitudes towards a national system of disposal sites (Lackey et al. 1973). Less than a decade later, as discussed in detail in Chapter 6, it has become extremely difficult to site a new facility in the United States because of public opposition. The 1980 RFF survey asked the public's reaction to living near the following types of facilities: a 10-story office building; large factory; coal-fired power plant; nuclear power plant; and hazardous waste disposal site (a new facility). The cumulative percentage of people willing to accept a new hazardous waste disposal facility 4–5 miles from their place of residence was 20 percent; at 10 miles only 28 percent; and only about half would accept one at a distance of 50 miles! Only for nuclear power stations was the negative statement as strong. People were far more willing to live near a high-rise building, a factory, and even a coal-fired power station than a brand new, state-of-the-art hazardous waste facility.

The March 1982 Eagleton Institute survey of 603 New Jersey residents is even more discouraging. Less than half of the sample residents would be willing to have a disposal site in their county. The persons who lived in one of the 31 dumpsite towns (towns with at least 4 abandoned sites and/or 1 of the worst sites) were even more unwilling to host a new site. Offering tax incentives made almost no difference. Less than 6 percent of those living in the 31 New Jersey dumpsite towns would change their opinion even if tax incentives were offered. The percentage for the remaining communities is not much better: 12 percent. Virtually no homeowners were willing to have a new site in the same county.

One interesting additional observation from these surveys is that these strongly negative reactions were not paralleled by a firm grasp of the problems at sites. When asked about events at Love Canal, only a small minority of those questioned by RFF (1980) knew what had happened. Far more people accurately answered factual questions about the Three Mile Island incident and about other environmental threats than about the Love Canal problem. There is every reason to believe that the basis for the public's opinion of hazardous waste sites is not a rational, carefully reasoned consideration of the costs-and-benefits of treating waste at a state-of-the-art facility versus dumping it somewhere. Basic values and strong emotions to protect themselves and their property apparently dominate.

The "not-in-my-backyard syndrome" for hazardous waste management facilities reflects the nature of personal decisionmaking among people with limited information at the public's mistrust of those handling hazardous waste. People react differently to risks that a statistician would say were equally serious. Smoking and driving while intoxicated, for example, may be far more dangerous than living adjacent to a hazardous waste facility or a nuclear power facility. But careful weighing of risk by the public is distorted by an array of considerations that are emotional or at least as much emotionally-based as they are factually-based. Scanning an array of considerations thought to influence people's evaluation of risk (Lowrance 1976), it is not hard to understand why the public does not want to live near hazardous waste sites. Briefly, the risks are involuntary and not likely to be related to employment. They are not clearly known, but the effects may be latent, may be irreversible, and are of a dreaded nature. Moreover, there are technological alternatives to hazardous waste sites, especially to landfills, and the sites have a long history of being misused.

If these considerations are regarded as one strike against hazardous waste facilities, the second strike is the recent explosion of negative information about chemicals. At the same time that we are running out of space for disposal sites in urban areas, advances in detection equipment have allowed us to find chemical pollution in places that would not have been possible in 1970. We have also begun to appreciate the interconnectivity of different parts of the environment and the capacity of science to generate information on new risks faster than ever before. These developments have led to what many have called "chemophobia," a fear that does not seem to be neutralized by chemical industry advertising.

The third strike against hazardous waste sites is that they have been so poorly managed so far. The public has little confidence in guarantees that new facilities will not become the next generation of Love Canals. Because of this legacy and the fact that the public has rarely been consulted in the construction of new facilities, even though the public seldom has the expertise to judge the adequacy of a design, a very wide credibility gap exists in the eyes of the public.

We expect some people to become more radical in efforts to convince the general public that those who control hazardous waste are incompetent and untrustworthy people who are willing to sacrifice people to save a few dollars. Thousands, perhaps millions, of Americans are already committed to opposing nuclear power. We expect the militance, characteristic of nuclear power protests, to occur at hazardous waste sites with an already cynical public becoming more frustrated with industry and government. Two examples of what may become commonplace have already occurred. Residents of Wilsonville, Illinois who had earlier toted guns and later fought in court, dug a trench across the only road to a hazardous waste landfill, supposedly to repair a culvert (Centaur Associates 1981).

The second example is more extreme. One of the initial 115 worst cases in the U.S. was illegally dumped, PCB contaminated soil in North Carolina. Soil was removed from 210 miles of highways and trucked to the Warren County landfill. More than 100 people were arrested trying to prevent the disposal of the material. Whatever the scientific reasons, on the surface, the choice of Warren County appeared to be a classic example of dumping on the powerless. Warren County had no urban population in 1970. The proportion of families with incomes less than $3,000 in 1970 was the second highest in North Carolina. And Warren County had the greatest percentage of blacks in the state (about 60 percent).

The media are not the cause of mismanagement of hazardous waste in the U.S., but they are quite capable of reporting mismanagement in the most dramatic of tones and scenes. A recent widely acclaimed film "In Our Water" is exemplary. It describes the arduous efforts of Frank Kaler of

Jamesburg, New Jersey to document contamination of his water supply by a landfill that was not supposed to be receiving hazardous waste, and to get a new water supply. Called a "fine, forceful documentary" by the *New York Times*, in our opinion the 60-minute film is a blunt story of corporate greed and government ineptitude. In the words of Frank Kaler (Ball 1982)

> I used to tell my kids when we went to the parade "Take off your hat, this is your flag, your country." Today I teach my kids that they can buy their share of American justice if they have enough money, that the laws are made by the rich and powerful to protect the rich and powerful, and the richest and the most powerful in this country today are the industrialists. They run this country.

Government officials are not portrayed as corrupt in this film, they are portrayed as bunglers who lose important photographic evidence and who do not really care about the people.

While not as dramatic as the filming of Frank Kaler, the media have had a field day with hazardous waste management in the last several years. There were the stories of duplicity and complicity between EPA officials and industry over Superfund, followed by resignations of the highest ranking Superfund officials. Industry's equivalent of these embarrassments were the attempts to ship hazardous waste to third-world nations for disposal. Stories about failures of so-called state-of-the-art technologies have been widely publicized. For example, there was a serious accident, which included fatalities, at a site in New Jersey which was supposed to incinerate PCBs. There were found to be leaks at disposal sites which were not supposed to leak for more than a century. These are only some of the recent examples of why the media do not even have to resort to "carcinogenic name dropping" (Hrudey, 1982) to sell mismanagement of hazardous waste as a story. One rarely finds news stories that credit industry and government attempts to manage hazardous waste properly. The credibility gap is not helped by this unbalanced presentation of hazardous waste management.

We may be wrong about the increasing likelihood of a political movement condoning, if not organizing, militant protests at hazardous waste sites. But frankly, the legacy and present management of hazardous waste sites in the U.S. play into the hands of radical political elements in the U.S. If we are right, hazardous waste sites could become the focal point for ideological conflict about the direction of the American political system because, like nuclear power, the country is stuck with the problem of hazardous waste sites. There are no simple and cheap fixes, nor is there the option of abandoning the hazardous waste management effort as there was with the Vietnam War. If militance becomes commonplace around existing and proposed sites, local officials, like planners, will face a scared, resentful and irate citizenry.

It is hard to be sanguine about changing the public's opinion on hazardous waste sites. Major policy changes would have to be made to make a dent in the wall of mistrust. Among these policy changes are dropping opposition to right-to-know laws, providing monitoring data at frequent intervals at all sites, providing a reasonable victim compensation fund, making real progress toward non-land disposal options, and enlisting citizen participation in the siting process. In short, it is hard to conceive of the public changing its opinion without straightforward demonstrations in deeds, not words, by federal and state governments and industries that hazardous waste is a high priority. The public should not be left to decide whether a "Waste Alert" (*EPA Journal* 1979) has been sounded or whether in the words of Brown (1980), EPA and industry are involved in a "garbagegate" to save money.

## NEEDED POLICY CHANGES

The first part of this chapter focused on misconceptions inherent in present hazardous waste management policies. Policy recommendations were included as part of that presentation insofar as they lent strength to or clarified the arguments. The second half of the chapter focuses on policy recommendations, some of which appeared earlier. Given the focus of this book on hazardous waste sites, they are presented in the context of abandoned, existing, and proposed sites.

### Needed Policy Changes: Abandoned Sites

An astute observer labelled CERCLA as disaster relief, not environmental legislation (Sanjour 1979). Yet prominent people, including Rita Lavelle, former administrator of Superfund (Hileman 1982, pp. 72A–75A), and more recently, William Ruckelshaus, EPA administrator (*Sun*, 1983), have been quoted as saying that Superfund might not be renewed or renewed with little increase in funding. We are not surprised by these statements for two reasons. One is that there is a general federal policy of reducing non-military spending and shifting responsibility for other programs to state governments. Shifting responsibility for the funding and cleanup of abandoned sites to the states is consistent with this policy.

Second, it is not surprising that forsaking abandoned sites would be proposed because they are orphans of our society with no economic value. Existing chemical waste sites generate some jobs and taxes, and more important in the short run, they are necessary to maintain regional economies. New waste sites would also bring some jobs and taxes, and presumably will be less damaging than their predecessors. Likewise, nuclear power plants, liquified natural gas plants, prisons, airports, sewage treatment plants, and abandoned factories that can be reused may not be viewed with fondness by local residents (Popper 1983), but they bring some benefits to communities and support regional economics.

Abandoned hazardous waste sites seem to have no redeeming value. It can be argued that the tens of billions of dollars needed to clean up or, at least, to control abandoned sites should not be spent because the sites no longer serve a useful function as repositories for the continued stream of unwanted by-products.

Superfund provides only a small fraction of the money that is estimated to be needed to clean up abandoned sites. Nevertheless, we believe that federal abandonment of Superfund would be a mistake that probably would cripple hazardous waste management in the United States at all levels. Abandonment will surely be viewed by the public as a lack of caring by American government.

Furthermore, we believe that industry should insist upon the cleanup of abandoned sites and should support its commitment with financial and technical support far beyond what is required under CERCLA. The reason industry should do this is to buttress its own low credibility. Abandoned hazardous waste sites serve as a reminder of industry's past failures to include protection of public health and the environment in its decision-making matrix.

Overall, management of abandoned sites may have nothing to do with existing or proposed sites, except in the eyes of the public. We doubt that the credibility of the hazardous waste management industry and the EPA's hazardous waste management efforts could survive abandonment of the program.

Nor do we believe that the program should be shifted totally to the states. While we do not have a complete survey of state programs, there appear to be very great differences among the states. Some states are more capable than others, but even the most capable states need some federal assistance in the form of funding, technology, and enforcement. New Jersey, for example, has an eight-year plan to clean up 132 abandoned sites, including all on the Superfund priority list (Griffin 1983). The almost 200 million dollars will come from New Jersey's Spill Fund (which industry unsuccessfully tried to void as duplicating Superfund), the state's Hazardous Waste Site Bond issue, and from the federal Superfund. In fact, New Jersey sued the federal government to free Superfund monies (*Star Ledger* 1981). As part of its cleanup, New Jersey intends to develop cleanup criteria, in other words, to define how clean is clean. This is a step we wish EPA would take.

New Jersey's abandoned waste cleanup program is among the best, but it needs assistance. It cannot fund the program by itself, nor can it deal with illegal trucking of wastes across state lines to circumvent the manifest system. Despite the high rating of New Jersey's program, some of its efforts to clean up abandoned sites have been severely criticized.

Most other states are far more dependent on federal technical and financial assistance than is New Jersey. Almost every state has economic resource constraints similar to those of the federal government. And some states have proposition-13 restrictions whereby their ability to raise revenues via property tax is constrained. Even during the 1970s, a period of great concern with the environment, the budgets of environmental and natural resources departments of state governments dropped from 3 to 2 percent (*Conservation Foundation Letter* 1981). The federal government must be prepared to assume responsibility for states that cannot provide their 10 percent share to fund the cleanup of abandoned sites (Environmental Science and Technology, 1983; OTA, 1983). It must set an example for the states by providing technical, legal, and regulatory support for methods that end land disposal and storage of hazardous waste. In its own best long-term interest, industry should insist upon strong federal and state programs.

Victim compensation is another area that should not be left to the states. Numerous writers have pointed out that environmental lawsuits using torts are difficult to win because of the long latency of many of the diseases and the problem of confounding, contributing causes (CEQ 1980, *Newsweek* 1982, *Conservation Foundation Letter* 1980b). CERCLA allows for recovery of damages to a tree, but not for an individual's loss of income, out-of-pocket medical costs, and such difficult to measure impacts as pain and suffering (*Conservation Foundation Letter* 1980b). To date, few of the states have their own compensation legislation. In the authors' opinion the monies in these states are far below what is likely to be needed (*New Jersey Hazardous Waste News* 1982).

A team of 12 lawyers hired by the U.S. EPA analyzed alternative ways of providing compensation. Grad (Deland 1982b), the reporter for the panel, described the task as presenting "the legal system with a task which is unprecedented in its scientific and medical complexity and in its potential for major health and economic impact." The team recommended a two-tiered plan, one part of which is no-fault and would probably be funded by a mechanism like Superfund. The second tier would require the claimant to make a case. Since the two-tiered plan has been called potentially the most expensive environmental program for industry, it is essential that a reasonable program be agreed upon. The federal government, not the states, must lead in the development of a compensation program.

Finally, the federal government should take the lead in liability mechanisms, and it must seek consistency between CERCLA and RCRA. First, the CERCLA insurance requirements are greater than those under RCRA. Second, OTA (1983) points out that the CERCLA and RCRA insurance regulations leave a 5-year gap in coverage. RCRA's apply until closure; CERCLA's liability trust fund does not accept full responsibility until five years after a facility is closed.

Although less dramatic than federal abandonment of the cleanup program, an action that would undermine the credibility of the hazardous waste management program in the United States is to quickly redevelop abandoned hazardous waste sites. The senior author remembers the laughter in "Tootsie" when a play called "Return to Love Canal" was mentioned. We did not laugh when it was reported that the Love Canal Area Revitalization Agency was planning residential redevelopment in the area surrounding the site (*Planning* 1983). After purchasing over 400 residences and tearing down over 200 homes, it is hard to believe that the public could be convinced that redevelopment of a site that is identified with hell on earth is anything but foolhardy. We suggest that the site, already a tourist attraction, be redeveloped as a monument in the same way that selected bombed-out cathedrals have been left in Germany as reminders of the Second World War.

More generally, we recommend the California statute as a model for land use surrounding abandoned sites (State of California, 1982). It creates a "border zone" of 2,000 feet around hazardous waste sites. Many types of development, including subdivisions, residences, hospitals, schools, and day care centers are excluded from this zone without a special variance. The state has the burden of proving that a site has the potential to create a hazard. But once proven, applicants for a variance have the burden of proving that their activity is commensurate with a hazardous waste site.

### Needed Policy Changes: Creating an Industry to Manage Existing and Proposed Sites Credibly

There is a strong consensus that private industry, not government, should operate hazardous waste management facilities. One reason is ideological: It is said that government should be excluded from activities that may turn a profit. Another reason is that in the United States private industry is more likely than government to attract the needed workforce. Third, many people are suspicious of government attempts both to operate and control risky activities. Industries are seen as being more responsive to public opinion and government regulation than are government bureaucracies.

A reliable hazardous waste management industry must be created. Prior to 1970, almost all hazardous waste was handled on-site or at dumpsites. In

1975, approximately 95 firms operating 110 facilities constituted the industry (Snell Foster 1976, Leshendok 1976). Their revenues were about $100 million. Several of the firms were large and reputable; others were neither of the above. Unfortunately, some of the firms on the list also appeared on the Superfund list of priority abandoned sites. Major hazardous waste firms have expanded their capacity despite the economic recession. In 1981, they increased their income by more than 20 percent and added new facilities (Environmental Science and Technology 1982).

Important actions by the federal government and to a lesser extent the states are needed to build a reliable hazardous waste management industry. Some of these have already been discussed in this chapter and so will only be briefly described.

### Expected Performance of Hazardous Waste Managers

Clear and unwavering guidance must be given to industry, the military, and other generators about what performance is expected so that appropriate technologies can be designed. Reiterating, we strongly believe that landfilling should be phased out for all but a few chemicals that are weak hazards and will degrade relatively quickly. One cannot be sanguine about the landfilling of PCBs, other heavy organic substances like pesticides, herbicides, other halogenated substances, many volatile light organic chemicals, toxic inorganic substances like cyanide and arsenic, and wastes that attack liners. The federal government does prescribe performance standards, and it does regulate some, but not all of these substances. It, not the states, must control all of these very hazardous substances because industry has demonstrated its willingness to transport waste across state boundaries to save dollars.

A large segment of the waste stream is intermediate in hazardousness between those substances that should be controlled by the federal government and those that need little control. The federal government should write performance standards for this intermediate group. But selection of specific management techniques for this group of chemicals should be left to the states or to interstate compacts. This approach allows for differences in regional economic bases. For example, a state like New Jersey with large pharmaceutical, paint, organic chemical, and petroleum refining industries is in a better position to forge ahead with waste exchanges than a rural state with limited exchange options. If the most hazardous wastes are not allowed in landfills, then a Catch-22 situation would be avoided wherein existing disposal sites are closed down and new facilities are not opened leading to insufficient capacity in some regions. As the hazardous waste management industry grows, and reuse and substitution increase, landfilling should be phased out for this second class of hazardous wastes.

Part of the policy of creating a viable industry based on high technology is to put pressure on landfills. Landfilling must be squeezed tighter than it is under RCRA. With respect to existing sites, this means carefully choosing those sites to remain operating that will cause the least damage and at the same time provide sufficient capacity. It also means requiring the retrofitting of existing sites that do not meet RCRA requirements for new sites. Retrofitting will be strongly opposed by some interests, but it is illogical to allow a grandfather clause for existing disposal sites because, unlike most grandfathers, land disposal sites are likely to become more troublesome, not more mellow with age. With respect to new sites, the regulations described in Chapter 2 must be implemented and enforced, and a disposal fee must be set that truly reflects the long-term costs of controlling wastes in landfills. Such a fee must be devoid of hidden subsidies to be paid by future taxpayers and nearby residents. If existing and new land disposal facilities were so treated, we believe that the match between what is landfilled and what should be landfilled would be much better than it presently is.

Despite the carefully written rules governing facility permits (see Chapter 2), consistency in the formulation and application of policy is a critical change needed at the federal level to build a stable, private market for hazardous waste management. EPA's Spring 1982, short-lived policy of allowing generators to dispose of bulk wastes in landfills containing no more than 25 percent liquids in volume was a blow to the hazardous waste industry and was seen as a knuckling-under to chemical industry legal actions and political pressures (Deland 1982, *Sun* 1982, Piasecki 1983). During a period when EPA's credibility was shaken, this policy change was a serious blow to those who would have the public believe that written policies and rules were more than paper accumulating dust on shelves.

Exemptions are a major threat to public health and the environment and a serious inconsistency. The small generator exemption may seem like a logical way of reducing red tape, the boiler exemption a way of using chloroform, carbon tetrachloride and benzene wastes as fuels; and the military may seem impregnable to civilian oversight. But frankly, it makes little sense to insist on 99.99 percent destruction of a supposedly dangerous waste, while exemptions allow the same waste to be handled with no care or less care. Nor does it make sense for EPA to have water and air regulations that make it difficult to develop hazardous waste plans. The effect on the hazardous waste industry of pretreating industrial wastes before discharge to public sewers, sludge disposal, and ocean dumping of sludge and other wastes needs review insofar as they should be part of a holistic EPA waste management policy.

## *Joint Planning of the Industry by Government and Industry*

The second needed action is careful government and private planning of the hazardous waste management industry. This requires strengthening the manifest system, carefully screening every applicant into the hazardous waste management industry as is suggested in Chapter 2, and discouraging criminals.

Unless the manifest system is given enforcement teeth, it will not be feasible to control hazardous wastes. Unscrupulous haulers and generators will turn to illegal dumping and stockpiling as marginal facilities are closed. And it will be unrealistic to try to plan hazardous waste facilities and waste exchanges or to try innovative techniques. Presently, the manifest system can be evaded by not reporting and by forging signatures. The civil and criminal penalties discussed in Chapter 2 will be needed to encourage compliance.

Part of the government responsibility is to scrutinize carefully all proposed entrants into the hazardous waste management industry market. Perhaps the financial responsibilities set forth in RCRA (see Chapter 2) will suffice to exclude the unqualified, but we doubt it. As we have learned from the nuclear power industry's technical and management failures and from the bankruptcy declared by asbestos manufacturers, financial involvement does not guarantee performance, and bad performance does not mean full acceptance of responsibility. There is a need to assure technical and management qualifications as well as financial capability. The bonding and liability under RCRA are a necessary but insufficient guarantee that waste can be properly managed by those that are bonded. The last thing that this industry needs is an unqualified entrant seeking some quick dollars, ready to cut costs to keep profits up, and to abandon the site and declare bankruptcy. Without government screening of applicants, it is not hard to foresee the errors of a few destroying the combined efforts of the hazardous waste management industry. Entrants have to be strong enough to deal with economic setbacks. Doubtless, there will be fluctuations in the economy that will cause capacity to be underutilized sometimes and overtaxed on other occasions.

Economic stress will not be the only pressure. Whoever manages the waste will be living in a fishbowl. Any operational problems will be magnified. Citizens and governments will expect immediate responses to questions. Accidents will happen, so private operators and transporters will have to deal with them. In short, the market ethic must be constrained in the case of hazardous waste management. If it becomes dominant, there will be disasters which will drive trustworthy industries out of the business to avoid tarnishing their reputations.

Part of the plan to build a reputable hazardous waste industry is joint federal-state and private industry efforts to eliminate criminal activity. Such joint programs will probably be needed more in the future than today because dumpers are more likely to have to cross state boundaries if states like New Jersey, California, and Massachusetts make it difficult for dumpers to find local dump sites (Environmental Science and Technology 1980b, 1981; *EPA Journal* 1980b, 1981a). Furthermore, sabotage for political ends by people who oppose industry, and who oppose government and industry siting efforts has to be considered in these plans.

## Government and Industry Incentives

Federal incentives for cooperation with the above policies is the third needed action. Federal research budgets have been slashed in recent years (*EPA Update* 1983, Hileman 1983). Without debating the general merits of this policy, it is a serious error in the hazardous waste field. There are several large, private hazardous waste management companies. But there are no IBMs, Xeroxes and AT&Ts to lead the industry. Unless the federal government provides technical assistance and/or industry strongly supports such an effort, each industry will be left to find unique solutions, probably on its own site. These solutions may be satisfactory and some may be marketed, but from the national perspective, they will not be the best from the perspective of either the economy or health and environmental protection.

OTA (1983) discusses many options for federal incentives in some detail including tax credits, low-interest loans, federal procurement policies, help in obtaining tax-exempt bonds, rapid amortization of equipment, streamlining permitting processes for innovative techniques, and other forms of administrative assistance. At a minimum, the federal and state governments should examine mechanisms for providing rewards to industries that reduce their use of hazardous materials, develop recycling technologies, and use non-landfilling solutions.

It may seem Pollyannaish to advocate incentives at a time when the federal environmental budget has been drastically shrinking and the federal government is trying to give programs back to the states. But in the long run, incentives may save future generations from spending thousands of dollars per ton to clean up landfilled waste and may help keep some American-based industry from moving to nations with less protective policies. Realistically there has to be a carrot along with a stick in formulating hazardous waste policies.

*Collaborating to Find New Sites*

The fourth but certainly not the least difficult part of creating a viable hazardous waste management industry is finding new waste sites (Miller 1981a). The federal government could control the siting process; but there seems to be little interest in such a policy. The fourth needed action is a siting policy that is open to local governments and to the public.

The siting process was described in great detail in Chapters 6 and 7 and does not need recapitulation. Here we will review the parts of the process that relate to an open siting process.

Before doing that, however, the federal role in the siting process should be set forth, if only to show that we do not expect the entire burden for hazardous waste management to fall on the federal government. Federal land may be suitable for waste sites, and depending upon the location, waste sites on federal land could substantially reduce public opposition. Otherwise, the federal role in siting should be indirect. Through use of the manifest system and its enforcement, through directly regulating the most hazardous wastes and providing performance standards for the middle category of wastes, and through squeezing the landfilling industry, EPA would effectively determine the capacity needed in the industry. Furthermore, the federal government will undoubtedly find itself in the middle of interstate disputes over the equity of dumping state A's hazardous waste in state B.

We begin by assuming that elected officials will seek as much public input as possible to buttress what are politically dangerous decisions. So we will not bother to consider whether public participation is the equivalent of opening a Pandora's box or rubbing an Aladdin's lamp (Ducsik 1981). As we see it, public participation is required for an effective and workable hazardous waste policy.

One place where the public must be involved is in the siting process. We argue that by using the method presented in Chapter 7, and by participating in up-front screening of areas, the public will be better protected than it will by allowing industry to propose less acceptable sites. Citizen participation can be incorporated into a constraint mapping effort which involves choosing and weighting criteria.

We doubt that many states will follow the example set forth in Chapter 7 of looking for the least disadvantageous sites (see Minnesota, 1981, for a clear exception). The constraint mapping procedure demands large amounts of high quality data, and we have witnessed public outcry from communities that contained the most acceptable initial areas. It is politically safer to appoint a siting board and allow its members to make case-by-case judgments than it is for the state to stick out its political neck by identifying the areas that are the least disadvantageous. When a contaminated aquifer is found beneath a site which supposedly had a natural barrier, the state that acted on a case-by-case basis can avoid the blame by arguing that the private industry is fully responsible because it did not find the crack in the impermeable layer. But the state that performed constraint mapping will find it difficult to avoid some of the blame because its data and scientists picked the area as not among the worst which, in turn, steered the industry to the area.

Whether criteria are mapped or not mapped, siting boards are likely to have members representing the public. For example, Michigan has a 9-member board with power to override any local zoning laws. Recognizing the practical limits of state power, 2 of the 9 members of the Michigan siting board are appointed on an ad hoc basis by the local government and 2 by the county government. Five affirmative votes are needed to pass an action. So the local people are one vote away from a negative decision.

Many states have the power to take whatever lands they need for hazardous waste sites. But elected officials will and should press for negotiations between state and local governments and citizens in order to avoid as much as possible the charge that states are usurping local autonomy. Some states will undermine the power of their siting boards by granting veto power to local governments or by excluding specific areas, such as areas with large numbers of people.

Open negotiations between industry and the public living near the proposed site are a positive step in siting. In recent years, professional mediators have become active in resolving issues arising from siting decisions (Straus 1979). Mediators might be intermediaries.

Here are some items that industry could offer to local governments and citizens living near proposed sites. First, with respect to local governments, no matter how carefully they are screened, some industries will go out of business. Therefore, operations should be audited on an annual basis by consultants hired by the local government, but financed by the industry and/or state government. Local fire and policy departments should be trained in accident response and equipment should be purchased for the community (*EPA Journal* 1982b, Smith, 1981). Periodic drills should be held based on emergency response plans. Another helpful step would be to purchase and set aside a buffer zone next to the facility, or use large lot zoning, TDR, PUD and other methods to control population density near the site (Nero 1977, Morell and Magorian 1982). Lastly, control of traffic entering the site is a desirable step.

With respect to people living near proposed sites, economic incentives are talked about, but we have doubts about their success. The New Jersey survey reported earlier in this chapter does not suggest that they will work. But research on nuclear power plants suggests that economic incentives may attract people to communities (Greenberg and Krueckeberg 1982). There are many forms of economic incentives of which the following are meant to be exemplary, not exhaustive: direct payments to property owners near the plant; direct payment to property owners whose property does not appreciate as much as property in the community as a whole; lower property tax rates paid for by diversion of a portion of the tipping fee; building of community facilities such as schools, roads, and playgrounds; and free use of the site by the local public for their hazardous waste; and a discount for local industry. Some firms (e.g., Recycling Industries, Braintree, Massachusetts) have successfully developed non-profit services to collect household hazardous wastes from nearby communities. The state of Florida has authorized (with appropriations) a statewide program to purge household hazardous wastes over a three-year period via private industry collection and management. Government partnership with industry in this way may lead to vast benefits for Florida, a state which contains an incredibly diverse and extensive aquifer which serves as the potable source for nearly the entire state population.

Frankly, unless the credibility gap is somehow miraculously closed, hazardous waste management will occur almost exclusively in existing industrial properties, on oceangoing ships, and on a few sites that are controlled by the federal and state governments and are not near settlements. These results may be satisfactory in most cases, but they would not be the best from the point of view of minimizing cost and of protecting either the public or the environment.

## SUMMARY

The litany of shortcomings of hazardous waste management practices in the United States is long. Despite this legacy, it seems quite possible that strong leaders could turn the situation around. The solutions will be relatively expensive in the short run and will be opposed by many industries and people who want to reduce the role of government. But hazardous waste management is figuratively as well as literally more volatile than environmental problems that have been struggled with by the government during the 1970s. The health, environmental, economic, and political risks are much greater than the threats from the regulated water and air pollutants; and policies must reflect this volatility, not efforts to limit costs in the short run.

Four major policies should be the cornerstones of the American hazardous waste program:

1. Vigorous cleanup of abandoned sites to erase the eyesores which undermine the credibility of government and especially industry.

2. Pursuit of technical, economic, and regulatory incentives to eliminate land disposal as an option for most forms of waste as soon as possible.
3. No exemptions from RCRA that allow hazardous waste to be casually handled by small industrial generators and reusers.
4. Participation of federal, state, and local governments; industry; and citizens in managing hazardous waste with federal government leadership in overseeing most management areas and state leadership in siting of new facilities.

The vigorous cleanup of abandoned sites means, first of all, that CERCLA (Superfund) must be renewed. Since the estimates of the cost of cleanup are not reliable (because of insufficient data about each site and because there is no definition of what constitutes a clean site), the renewed CERCLA must emphasize mechanisms for funding cleanup of abandoned sites. EPA must pursue legal remedies that will allow it to recover money from parties responsible for abandoned sites. The federal government and the states, but primarily the federal government, must provide sufficient funds to clean up all sites that have or can cause health, environmental, economic, and social damage, not just those sites whose cleanup can be funded through funds recovered through litigation. There appears to be great variation among the states in willingness to identify sites for cleanup and to provide state funds for cleanup. When CERCLA is reconsidered by the Congress, it must go on record as not allowing recalcitrant states to abandon the cleanup of abandoned sites. Industry should strongly support, not oppose, such efforts. It would be to their long-run benefit to improve their credibility. This is because the public is intolerant of industry and government blaming each other for the problem. An open declaration by industry to fund cleanup beyond levels required under CERCLA would provide a major morale boost to hazardous waste management in the United States.

Planners cannot realistically advise local governments about land use in the areas surrounding tens of thousands of abandoned and existing hazardous waste sites without clear definitions of what is a safe site. Research is badly needed to get working definitions of safe sites, For example, one definition of a safe site could be based on post-cleanup utility. One type of site would be one at which the waste is controlled but remains a threat, so that adjacent land uses must be severely restricted and an alternative water supply has to be sought. A second type would be one at which all large concentrations remain, so that the site would have to be fenced off. Industrial and commerical land uses appropriate to the area would not be permitted on the site, but would be permitted adjacent to the site. A third type of safe site would be one that has literally been sanitized, and therefore no constraints should be placed on land use on or adjacent to the site.

The pursuit of incentives to eliminate land disposal and the reduction in the number of generators exempt from the provisions of RCRA are both part of a larger policy to develop a credible hazardous waste industry. The record of the 1970s shows that carrots and sticks are needed to achieve environmental goals.

Many sticks are needed. A reliable hazardous waste industry cannot be built if illegal dumping continues to be a thriving business. Since dumpers do not respect political boundaries, the federal government must assume the major role in curtailing illegal dumping. Second, the federal government must control entrants into the field of hazardous waste management. RCRA's economic-based liability and closure provisions are insufficient. Technical and administrative experience must be factored into decision-making about who can manage hazardous waste, even though tests for such experience will be difficult to implement. Third, the number of exemptions to RCRA's provisions should be reduced. This step will protect public health and the environment and will increase the supply of waste to be properly managed. Fourth, we have little faith in published estimates of the number of generators or the amounts and types of hazardous waste generated in the United States. Trying to plan without reasonable working estimates of the supply of waste will keep some good, but conservative, firms out of the hazardous waste management industry. Therefore, refined estimates of hazardous waste management potential at the regional scale must be obtained.

A last stick is needed in order to change the role of the land disposal industry to reflect its real cost to society. This means bringing existing sites up to an acceptable level by requiring retrofitting; by increasing monitoring requirements at existing sites; by setting post-closure monitoring requirements at levels that reflect the types of waste at the site rather than arbitrarily fixing them at 30 years; and by measuring the real, potential, long-term costs of land disposal (e.g. water pollution and finding new water supplies, accident response and planning, fair victim compensation, diminished land value, and distributional effects).

The federal government should provide some carrots to industry, state and local governments, and the public. For example, the government could do the following:

1. Sponsor research and pilot projects that seek alternatives to land disposal;
2. Establish a national, high-technology center for hazardous waste management;
3. Lead in the development of a typology of hazardous wastes to be used to promulgate performance standards for treatment, reuse, and disposal of all extremely and moderately hazardous wastes;

4. Oversee the control of the most dangerous hazardous wastes at sites that must be approved by the federal and appropriate state governments;
5. Provide performance standards for the states to manage moderately hazardous wastes;
6. Take the lead in defining fair levels of victim compensation and industry liability.

The above recommendations are a major part of a holistic hazardous waste management strategy. Basically, the federal government should lead those areas that can be most effectively managed by a level of government that has the fewest budgetary constraints; the level that can formulate policies that prevent one area from gaining an unfair advantage over another or an unfair burden of waste management; and the level of government that should have access to the best science and technology. In a diverse nation like the United States, the state and local governments, no matter how hard they work, cannot match the federal government's access to the economic, political, and scientific/technical resources needed to manage hazardous wastes.

The 1970s proved that an explicit federal role in land use control was not politically acceptable. To try to have the federal government control siting, other than to provide federal lands to the states, is to potentially undermine a critical aspect of the federal hazardous waste management program. Therefore, the states and local governments should control the siting process. In doing so, they should involve the public at every step, conduct constraint mapping studies, measure public attitudes toward incentives for accepting sites, involve the neighboring public and industry in direct negotiations, and control land use surrounding sites. Lastly, the state governments, through university programs and through its own auspices, must take leadership in educating media representatives and the public about hazardous waste management. Education must be done on a continuing basis, not solely in response to crises.

The authors of this book believe that the changes recommended here would better protect public health and the environment, lead to innovations in an industry which has been stagnant for many years, be economically superior to present policies in the long run and provide credibility in the eyes of the public that does not want to live near hazardous waste sites and is increasingly ready to use force to manifest its opposition.

## REFERENCES

*Amicus Journal.* "The Public Mind." Vol. 2, 1981, pp. 7–8.

Ball, J. "Critics Acclaim New Film on N.J. Pollution." *New Jersey Hazardous Waste News,* vol. 2, 1982, pp. 2–3.

Brown, M. *Laying Waste: The Poisoning of America by Toxic Chemicals.* New York: Pantheon Books, 1979.

Centaur Associates. *Siting of Hazardous Waste Management Facilities and Public Opposition.* Washington, D.C.: U.S. Environmental Protection Agency, 1979.

Chemical Manufacturing Associates. *The Chemical Balance: Benefiting People, Minimizing Risk.* Washington, D.C.: The Association, 1982.

Christman, R. "Reagan and the Environment." *Environmental Science and Technology,* vol. 15, 1981, p. 127.

*Conservation Foundation Letter.* "Cost-Benefit Analysis: A Tricky Game." December 1980a.

*Conservation Foundation Letter.* "Many Victims of Pollution are Shortchanged." January 1980b.

*Conservation Foundation Letter.* "Budget Cuts Raise Ominous Questions." May 1981.

*Conservation Foundation Letter.* "Clean-Up and Fix-Up Costs Rise Relentlessly." March 1983.

Costle, D. "The Next Decade." *EPA Journal,* 1980, vol. 10, pp. 2–5.

Council of Environmental Quality. *Eleventh Annual Report of the Council on Environmental Quality, 1980.* Washington, D.C.: U.S. Government Printing Office, 1980, pp. 223–230, 412–417.

Deland, M. *Environmental Science and Technology.* Vol. 15, 1981, p. 625.

————. *Environmental Science and Technology.* Vol. 16, 1982, p. 225A.

————. "A Compensation Fund for Hazardous Waste Injuries." *Environmental Science and Technology,* vol. 16, 1982b, p. 553A.

Dickson, D. "The Embarrassing Odyssey of Seveso's Dioxin." *Science,* vol. 220, 1983, pp. 1362–1363.

Ducsik, D. "Citizen Participation in Power Plant Siting, Aladdin's Lamp or Pandora's Box?" *APA Journal,* vol. 47, 1981, pp. 154–166.

Eagleton Institute. Rutgers University Poll, New Brunswick, New Jersey: The Institute, 1982.

Energy Resources Co., Inc. *Economic Impact Analysis of Hazardous Waste Management Regulations on Selected Generating Industries.* Springfield, Va.: National Technical Information Service, 1979.

*Environmental Science and Technology.* Vol. 14, 1980a, p. 1275.

*Environmental Science and Technology.* Vol. 14, 1980b, p. 1276.

*Environmental Science and Technology.* Vol. 15, 1981, p. 728.

*Environmental Science and Technology.* Vol. 16, 1982, p. 371A.

*Environmental Science and Technology.* Vol. 17, 1983, pp. 65A–66A.

*EPA Journal.* "Waste Alert." Vol. 5, no. 2, 1979, pp. 1–40.

*EPA Journal.* "The New Decade." Vol. 6, no. 1, 1980a, pp. 26–33.

*EPA Journal.* "Cleaning Up in New Jersey." Vol. 6, no. 6, 1980b, pp. 10–11.

*EPA Journal.* "FBI to Aid in Hazardous Waste Investigation." Vol. 7, no. 7, 1981, pp. 21–22.

*EPA Journal.* "Moveable Burner." Vol. 8, no. 4, 1982a, pp. 20–21.

*EPA Journal.* "Training Local Health Officials." Vol. 8, no. 4, 1982b, p. 23.

*EPA Journal.* "EPA Paves Way for PCB Burning." Vol. 8, no. 1, 1982c, pp. 20–23.

*EPA Update.* "EPA Budget Proposal for 1984 Slightly Below Current Spending." Vol. 1, no. 3, 1983, p. 1.

Epstein, S. "Cost-Benefit Analysis." *Amicus Journal*, vol. 3, 1982, pp. 41–47.

Greenberg, M. *Applied Linear Programming*. New York: Academic Press, 1978.

Greenberg, M. and Krueckeberg, D. *Population Trends Around Forty-Nine Operational Nuclear Power Sites in the United States, 1960–1980*. Report to Brookhaven National Laboratory for the Nuclear Regulatory Commission, 1982.

Griffin, M. "New Jersey Plan Will Clean Dumps in Four Years." *New Jersey Hazardous Waste News*, Vol. 3, 1983, pp. 1 and 4.

Halebsky, M. *A Study of the Economics and Environmental Viability of a U.S. Flag Toxic Chemical Incineration Ship*. 3 vols., Springfield, Va.: National Technical Information Service, 1978.

Hart, F.C., Inc. *Preliminary Assessment of Cleanup Costs for National Hazardous Waste Problems*. Washington, D.C.: U.S. Environmental Protection Agency, 1979.

Hileman, B. "Enforcement by EPA." *Environmental Science and Technology*, vol. 17, 1982, pp. 72A–75A.

———. "Funding Proposals for EPA." *Environmental Science and Technology*, vol. 17, 1983, pp. 121A–123A.

Hrudey, S. "Fear of Hazardous Wastes: A Self-Fulfilling Prophecy?" *Environmental Science and Technology*, vol. 16, 1982, p. 537.

ICF, Inc. *Liability Coverage: Requirements for Owners or Operators of Hazardous Waste Treatment, Storage, and Disposal Facilities*. Springfield, Va.: National Technical Information Service, 1982.

Kates, R., ed. *Managing Technological Hazard: Research Needs and Opportunities*. Boulder, Colorado: Institute of Behavioral Science, University of Colorado, 1977.

———. *Risk Assessment of Environmental Hazard*. New York: John Wiley and Sons, 1978.

Kelman, S. *What Price Incentives? Economists and the Environment*. Boston: Auburn House Publishing Co., 1981.

Kiang, Y., and Metry, A. *Hazardous Waste Processing Technology*. Ann Arbor, Michigan: Arbor Science Publishers, 1982.

Lackey, L., Jacobs, T., and Stewart, S. *Public Attitudes Toward Hazardous Waste Disposal Facilities*. Springfield, Va.: National Technical Information Service, 1973.

Lave, L. *The Strategy of Social Regulation*. Washington, D.C.: The Brookings Institution, 1981.

Leshendok, T. *Hazardous Waste Management Facilities in the United States*. Springfield, Va.: National Technical Information Service, 1976.

Long, F. and Schweitzer, G., eds. *Risk Assessment at Hazardous Waste Sites*. Washington, D.C.: American Chemical Society Symposium Series 204, 1982.

Lowrance, W. *Of Acceptable Risk*. Los Altos, Cal.: Wm. Kaufmann, Inc., 1976.

———. "Probing Societal Risks." *Chemical and Engineering News*, vol. 59, 1981, pp. 13–20.

Miller, S. "Cost-Benefit Analysis." *Environmental Science and Technology*, vol. 14, 1980, pp. 1415–1417.

———. "Destroying Hazardous Waste." *Environmental Science and Technology*, vol. 15, 1981a, pp. 1268–1269.

———. "Hazardous Waste Management." *Environmental Science and Technology*, vol. 15, 1981b, pp. 1413–1416.

Minnesota Waste Management Board. "Basis for Selection on October 8, 1981 of Proposed Candidate Areas for Hazardous Waste Land Disposal Facilities." Mimeograph, 1981.

Morell, D. and Magorian, C. *Siting Hazardous Waste Facilities*. Cambridge, Mass.: Ballinger Pub. Co., 1982.

Nagle, E. "RCRA Liability Insurance Rules: Evolution and Unresolved Issues." *The Environmental Forum*, 1982, pp. 16–20.

National Materials Advisory Board, National Research Council. *Management of Hazardous*

*Industrial Wastes: Research and Development Needs*. Washington, D.C.: National Academy Press, 1983.

National Research Council, Committee on National Statistics, Environmental Studies Board, Numerical Advisory Board. *Environmental Monitoring*. Vol. IV, Washington, D.C.: National Academy of Sciences, 1977.

National Science Foundation. *The Five-Year Outlook: Problems, Opportunities and Constraints in Science and Technology*. Vol. 1, Washington, D.C.: Superintendent of Documents, 1980.

Nero, A., Schroeder, C., Yen, W. *Control of Population Densities Surrounding Nuclear Power Plants*. Berkeley, California: Lawrence Berkeley Laboratory, 1977.

*New Jersey Hazardous Waste News*. "Toxic Island Planned for N.J. Coastal Site." Vol. 1, 1981, pp. 1 and 4.

*New Jersey Hazardous Waste News*. "Recent Landfill Law Compensates Victims." Vol. 2, 1982, pp. 3–4.

*Newsweek*. "Toxic Torts: A Quagmire." March 1, 1982, pp. 53–54.

O'Brien, D., and Marchand, D. *The Politics of Technology Assessment*. Lexington, Mass.: D.C. Health, 1982.

Office of Technology Assessment. *Technologies and Management Strategies for Hazardous Waste Control*. Washington, D.C.: Superintendent of Documents, 1983.

Patel, C. "Laser Detection of Pollution." *Science*, vol. 202, 1978, pp. 157–173.

Petty, R. "Proposed Amendment to the Resource Conservation and Recovery Act of 1977." Working issue paper, mimeograph, 1982.

Piasecki, B. "Struggling to be Born." *Amicus Journal*, vol. 4, 1983, pp. 9–11.

*Planning*. "News." Vol. 49, June 1983, pp. 4–5.

Pojasek, R. "Developing Solutions to Hazardous Waste Problems." *Environmental Science and Technology*, vol. 14, 1980, pp. 924–929.

———. *Toxic and Hazardous Waste Disposal*. 6 vols., Ann Arbor, Michigan: Ann Arbor Science, 1979–1981.

Popper, F. "LULUs." *Resources*, no. 73, 1983, pp. 2–4.

Quarles, J. *Cleaning Up America*. Boston, Ma.: Houghton Mifflin and Co., 1976.

Resources for the Future. "The Public Speaks Again: A New Environmental Survey." *Resources*, no. 60, 1978, pp. 1–6.

———. "Public Opinion on Environmental Issues." *Resources*, Jan.–Feb. and March–April, 1980.

Rishel, H., Boston, T., and Schmidt, C. *Costs of Remedial Response Actions at Uncontrolled Hazardous Waste Sites*. Springfield, Va.: National Technical Information Service, 1982.

Sanjour, W. Testimony before a subcommittee of the Senate Committee on Governmental Affairs, August 1, 1979.

Schwing, R., and Albers, W., Jr., eds. *Societal Risk Assessment, How Safe Is Safe Enough?* New York: Plenum, 1980.

Smith, A., Jr. *Managing Hazardous Substances Accidents*. New York: McGraw-Hill, 1981.

Snell Foster, Inc. *Potential for Capacity Creation in the Hazardous Waste Management Service Industry*. Springfield, Va.: National Technical Information Service, 1976.

*Star Ledger*. September 19, 1981, p. 5.

State of California. *Health and Safety Code*. Sacramento, California: The State, 1982.

Straus, D. "Environmental Mediation." *Environmental Science and Technology*, vol. 13, 1979, pp. 661–665.

Sun, M. "EPA Relaxes Hazardous Waste Rules." *Science*, vol. 216, 1982, pp. 275–276.

———. "Ruckelshaus Promises EPA Cleanup." *Science*, vol. 220, 1983, p. 801.

Swartzman, D., Liroff, R., and Croke, K. *Cost-Benefit Analysis and Environmental Regula-*

*tions: Environmental Politics, Ethics, and Methods*. Washington, D.C.: Conservation Foundation, 1983.

Taylor, G., and Klingshirn, J. *Socioeconomic Analysis of Hazardous Waste Management Alternatives: Methodology and Demonstration*. Springfield, Va.: National Technical Information Service, 1981.

Ubell, E. "A Proposal for the Legal/Political Privatization of Regulation of Hazardous Materials." Mimeograph, New York, 1982.

United States Environmental Protection Agency, Office of Water and Waste Management. *Remedial Actions at Hazardous Waste Sites: Survey and Case Studies*. Washington, D.C.: The Agency, 1981.

———. *Waste Clearinghouses and Exchanges: A Summary, New Ways for Identifying and Transferring Reusable Industrial Process Wastes*. Springfield, Va.: National Technical Information Service, 1977.

*U.S. News and World Report*. "Cleaner Air and Water, Can We Afford 690 Billion Dollars?" February 28, 1983, pp. 27-32.

*Washington Post*. "It's a Depression at EPA." November 3, 1981.

Whyte, A., and Burton, I. *Environmental Risk Assessment*. New York: John Wiley and Sons, Inc., 1980.

# Index

abandoned sites, Chapter 4 *passim* (106–29); damage caused by, Chapter 3 *passim* (84–105), 117–23, 127; distributional effects of, 88, 222–24; dumpsites as, 84; New Jersey and, Chapter 5 *passim* (130–63), 252–53; numbers of, 106–13; policy changes needed for, 251–54

Agriculture, U.S. Department of, 196

air quality, 27, 28, 91–92, 208–209, 218, 221, 247

Alabama: hazardous waste generation in, 14, 17

Alaska, 52, 123

Ambient Air Quality Standards, Nation (NAAQS), 208

American Samoa, 144

amount of hazardous wastes, 4, 5–9, 10, 12, 27–28, 188n2; abandoned sites and, 106–13; challenges to determining, 6–9, 12–13, 27 14-industry study and, 5–6; manifest data as a source of determining, 24, 25; SIC codes and, 7–9, 13. *See also* distribution of hazardous wastes; inventories

Anderson, R. F., 205

annual reports, 49, 53

Apple Real Estate Agency, 149

aquifer outcrop areas, 205–206, 208

area criteria measurements, 205–208

Arizona, 17, 52

Arizona, University of, 90

Arkansas: hazardous waste generation in, 17

Arthur D. Little, Inc.: waste inventory report of, 20–24

Baram, M., 36

Barksdale, Henry C., 206

Battelle, 177

Bealer, R., 100–101

Bellman, H. S., 175

Belnay, Glen, 152

Betz, Converse and Murdoch, 151

Biological Effects of Ionizing Radiation, Committee on (National Academy of Sciences), 96

Booz-Allen & Hamilton, Inc. et al.: report of, 9, 13, 170–72, 173, 192

Bordentown, New Jersey, 168–69

border zone. *See* buffer zone

Bridgeport, New Jersey, 167

Brown, Michael, 85, 98, 99, 130, 251

buffer zones, 225, 226–29, 231, 254, 260

Bulanowski, G., 179

Bureau of the Census, U.S., 10, 209–10

California: hazardous waste generation in, 16; location standards and, 52; regional inventories in, 24–25; sites in, 124, 254; small generator exemption in, 43

Canada, 100

cancer, 95–96, 98, 136–37, 138–39, 142, 160, 161

Cantlon, J., 98

Carey, Hugh, 98

Census, U.S. Bureau of the, 10, 209–10

*Census of Manufactures*, 8

Centaur Associates, 101, 166, 168

CERCLA (Comprehensive Environment Response, Compensation, and Liability Act), 31, 68–79, 79–80; cleanup costs and, 55, 252; definition of hazardous wastes in, 68, 69, 70; enactment of, 39; incentives and, 241; liability clauses of, 56, 193, 253–54; new sites and, 164, 174; public opinion about, 235, 250, 251; regulatory costs and, 237; renewal of, 262; state inventory funds of, 68; Title I, 69, 70–76; Title II, 69, 76–

269